The Ag
1770–1870

The Age of Change 1770–1870

Documents in Social History

J. T. WARD

Adam and Charles Black · London

First published 1975
A. & C. Black Ltd
4, 5, & 6 Soho Square
London W1V 6AD

ISBN 0 7136 1576 1

Filmset and Printed in Great Britain by
BAS Printers Limited, Wallop, Hampshire

Contents

Acknowledgements

I am grateful to many people who generously helped me in the preparation of this book. Mr. J. F. Burnett of Magdalene College Cambridge first suggested the subject to me. Some of my colleagues in the University of Strathclyde—Professor S. G. E. Lythe, Dr. John Butt, Mr. B. F. Duckham, Dr. W. H. Fraser, Mr. J. R. Hume and Dr. J. H. Treble—lent me material, as did Mr. Frank Beckwith of Leeds, the late Colonel G. W. Ferrand, OBE, of Oving, and the late Mr. G. G. Hopkinson of Brighouse. I am equally indebted to Colonel R. J. P. Warde-Aldam, TD, for allowing me to use the Frickley Hall MSS, to Miss G. M. Phillips of Mingle End (for her collection) and to the following editors and publishers for permission to quote from their works:

Messrs. Cassell, for *Home Letters written by Lord Beaconsfield*, ed. Augustine Birrell (1928)

The Clarendon Press, Oxford, for James Woodforde's *Diary of a Country Parson*, ed. John Beresford (1921–31)

Anchor Books, for Alexis de Tocqueville, *Journeys to England and Ireland*, ed. J. P. Mayer (1968)

To many members of the staff of my tolerant publishers, and to Misses Lynda Kelly, Marion Merrifield and Catherine Summerhill, my efficient typists, I must express my sincere gratitude.

Introduction

The century from 1770 was a period of enormous and widespread change, social, political and economic. The Britain of Squire Western, Coke of Holkham and 'Farmer George' III, of Palladian mansions and boozy bucolic squires, of immemorial tradition and custom, 'orders' and 'ranks' and pyramidical notions of a (largely immobile) society was already changing in the 1770s. The rural water-powered cotton spinning mill was starting to change the old picture of domestic textile manufacture. Beyond and sometimes underneath classically-landscaped parks entrepreneurially-minded aristocrats proved and won their own coal and ironstone. Industry began its trek from Southern traditional habitats to Northern English and Western Scottish locations. Arthur Young—himself an unsuccessful farmer but a splendid agricultural writer—was disseminating information about the agricultural changes which made British farming a model for the world. Adam Smith was challenging a decrepit mercantilist system of State interference and presenting to a receptive generation the messages of liberal economics, local and international divisions of labour and general *laisser-faire*.

Across the Atlantic a colonial rebellion ended the first British Empire and provoked long doubts over the wisdom, expediency, morality or general utility of expensively maintaining and protecting 'ungrateful' and often unremunerative dependencies; across the Channel there were already rumblings of that traumatic revolution of intellectuals, bourgeoisie and *sans-culottes* which was to overturn the proud French Monarchy and the established order of Europe. Yet these changes were taking place against a background of an ancient social pattern. Britain was still regional and local in loyalty: London was an aberration in a nation of intense county feelings, where the administrative unit was the parish. Most people's horizons were bounded by the orders and morals and patronage administered from the hall and the rectory, and their lives were determined by the timeless passing of the seasons, followed by Christian or pagan celebrations. They were bound to the land—not, indeed, as Continental serfs of a full-blooded feudal system—but by nature and necessity. Except among such groups as the Scottish colliers, few were legally tied. But for most country folk an annual trip to a county fair was the great adventure.

The blandishments of the recruiting sergeant in the village tavern or the unsavoury activities of the naval press-gang inevitably took some unsuspecting yokels further away—often to early deaths in insanitary men o' war or barracks in tropical climes. But at home the social order seemed permanent and secure. Britons remained superstitious; the age of warlocks and witches had not entirely departed, and people could still recall the protests against the change in the calendar in 1752, over the 'eleven lost days.' Even riots were conservatively-minded. Participants demanded old 'meal' prices, the retention of old labour-intensive industrial techniques, the maintenance of 'Church and King' against new-fangled dissent. A loyal, illiterate, hard-working, to some extent deferential, heavily-drinking and heartily-eating race—that race affectionately but grotesquely portrayed by its cartoonists—faced a great age of change.

A century later Britain was urbanised and industrialised. Two Reform Acts—a Whiggish gesture to the middle classes in 1832 and a Tory 'leap in the dark' to bring urban working men 'within the pale of the constitution' in 1867—had moved the nation towards democracy. Britain remained proud and confident, but her pride and confidence rested on new bases. The City of London financed, organised and insured the world's enterprises. British financiers had planned many of the world's railways, British engineers had built their lines, locomotives and rolling stock, and British navvies had sometimes constructed them. Lancashire cottons had clothed the world. From smoky, slum-strewn, slag-heaped industrial conurbations the kingdom sent forth textiles and coal and iron to the world—generally in the world's greatest merchant fleet. But change was again approaching.

The mid-century Liberal political dominance and industrial leadership were both ending. An age of elementary education, social investigation, 'unskilled' trade unionism, steel-making, jingoistic Imperial pride, plutocracy, hedonism and 'emancipation' was dawning. The secure certainties—religious, political, moral and social—which had sustained so many Victorians were starting to be questioned. Even the economic theories and 'laws' of classical political economy—the central ethic of so much of the nineteenth-century social dynamic—was being eroded. By 1885 G. J. Goschen was mourning in the *Nineteenth Century* magazine that

'We live in a period of universal scepticism as to the economic doctrines of the past. The belief in the all-sufficiency of private enterprise has been broken down. The regard for private rights is weakened . . . The old watchwords have lost their conclusive authority.'

Simultaneously, some British industries were starting to face unwonted competition from foreign rivals, and agriculture, after golden years in the third quarter of the century, was about to face widespread ruin caused by cheap prairie corn and refrigerated Antipodean meat. But between about 1770 and 1870—dates much more appropriate and meaningful than the orthodox, century-dominated opening and terminal years, in many ways—Britain underwent a series of revolutions. While Britain's changes were less immediately dramatic than the Continental convulsions which so regularly upset ancient dynasties and antique societies (and were certainly less bloody) they were, in the long run, more important. The first industrial revolution created the first industrial society. And the first industrial society, for all its apparent continuities with past forms of social organisation, actually effected and involved widespread social changes. The purpose of this book is to examine some of the changes, attitudes, policies and philosophies experienced, embraced, adopted and adumbrated by contemporaries during Britain's period of seminal change.

I

In the Britain which experienced this age of regular change old and new institutions and ideas for long co-existed. The notion of 'rank' within a particular 'interest' group for long persisted into an age when (often vaguely-defined and never satisfactorily analysed) 'class' feelings were developing. To talk of 'working class' or 'middle class' movements or attitudes in Britain is to use convenient shorthand rather than meaningful absolute definitions. Society remained hierarchic. Count Alexis de Tocqueville observed that

'The French wish not to have superiors. The English wish to have inferiors. The Frenchman constantly raises his eyes above him with anxiety. The Englishman lowers his beneath him with satisfaction.'

Yet the upper echelons of this society scarcely constituted a class in themselves. A minute titled group, buttressed by primogeniture and entail, owned vast landed estates. But it was never an exclusive, remote body. Its eldest sons continued to dominate much of British life, while younger sons entered the professions and commerce. It did not disdain to 'soil' its hands or lineages by involvement in entrepreneurial ventures or marriage into 'commercial' families. And it generally quickly accepted into county society the newly-arrived family from the ranks of industry or trade. Old and new wealth thus constantly intermingled.

Daniel Defoe had noted the regular transformation of merchants into squires in 1726. 'Trade is so far here from being inconsistent with a gentleman', he wrote in his *Complete English Tradesman*, 'that, in short, trade in England makes gentlemen, and has peopled this nation with gentlemen.' Landownership had always been the accolade and ambition of the successful businessman, and the habit of the merchants was perpetuated by such industrial revolution dynasties as the Arkwrights, Marshalls, Crawshays, Fieldens, Hudsons, Peels, Bairds and Cunliffe-Listers. It was all very natural, right and proper. 'To found a family, and to convert his wealth into land,' Samuel Taylor Coleridge approvingly noted in his essay on *Church and State* in 1830, 'are twin thoughts, births of the same moment, in the mind of the opulent merchant, when he thinks of reposing from his labours.'

The age of change, however, was also an age of contrasts. While some successful textile manufacturers sought the 'gentility' of manors and quarterings and invented genealogies in the crop of the early Victorian social registers—against which W. M. Thackeray railed—others condemned the 'land monopoly' and sought to establish the supremacy of a self-made entrepreneurial class over a largely hereditary traditional group.

The old rich, with all their failings—*ad hoc* administration of justice, open nepotism, conspicuous consumption and personal eccentricities—had at least been part of the fabric of their society. The Duke of Dorset could hold his own with the best of eighteenth-century cricketers; Sir Tatton Sykes could (and regularly did) better the achievements of the peasantry whom he ordered at Sledmere; a long line of noblemen shared the risks and discomforts of military and naval life. And if, at its worst, the great estate was a demesne of toiling peasants, grasping (and sometimes dishonest) agents, disputatious farmers and absentee, careless and rashly-spending proprietors, there was another side. Great and small landed estates were often places in which mutual obligations were honoured, where loyal service was rewarded by generous patronage and protection; at the best, there was a sense of a mutually-obligated community. Some early industrial communities—Styal, Turton, New Lanark and Catrine—perhaps maintained something of this squirearchic paternalism. It was a feature of old Britain which especially attracted foreign observers. The Swiss traveller Henry Meister noted in his *Letters written during a Residence in England* (1799) some differences between revolutionary France and traditionalist England:

'There is as great an inequality of ranks and fortune in England as in France; but in the former the consequence and importance of a man as a member of society is far more respectable. Individuals of the lower classes are better cloathed, better fed, and better lodged than elsewhere;

and often, as far as I could learn, with no better means than the same classes enjoy with us.'

An intense feeling of family and local loyalties long survived in rural areas. 'The English love their old castles and country seats with a patriotic love,' the American historian W. H. Prescott commented in 1850, with excusable exaggeration. 'They are fond of country sports. Every man shoots or hunts.' And love of the land affected more than agriculture, important and productive though that was. In 1767 Lord Kinnoul told Thomas Graham of Balgowan that 'the laying out of the ground in a natural way was carried to greater perfection in England than in any part of Europe.'

Snobbish and deferential many Britons might be; and in the shires the Dukes of Omnium and their kind still exercised Whiggish power from a score of Gatherum Castles. Such perpetuation of 'feudalism' and 'lordolatory' incensed radicals and cynics. But Ralph Waldo Emerson saw a balancing virtue. England's stability (so proudly demonstrated during successive Continental revolutions) was 'the security of the modern world,' for

'The conservative, money-making, lord-loving English are yet liberty loving; and so freedom is safe, for they have more personal force than any other people.'

This innate stability allowed Britain to sustain her role against revolutionary and Napoleonic France as (in Wordsworth's words) 'a bulwark to the cause of man.' And when in 1848, as thrones toppled all over Europe, Londoners of all ranks enrolled as special constables to defend the capital from threatening Chartists, Lady Palmerston considered that this

'example of union and loyalty and a determination to stand by our constitution . . . would have a great effect everywhere, in England, in Ireland and in Europe.'

II

Despite British steadiness, one factor of society which horrified many foreign visitors was the stark contrast between rich and poor. The American Edwards Lester found much to admire, in his book *The Glory and Shame of England* (1841), but observed that he had 'seen more magnificence than he ever wished to see in his own country, and more wretchedness than he ever supposed could exist.' The Italian Ugo Foscolo considered that in England 'poverty was a disgrace which no merit could wipe off.' Britons' penchant for making money with single-minded determination and their concomitant lack of sympathy for the poor shocked many observers from abroad. De Tocqueville thought that people 'still seemed convinced that extreme inequality of wealth was the natural order of things.' Emerson tartly commented that 'an Englishman who has lost his fortune is said to have died of a broken heart.'

Not only foreigners were horrified by the attitudes of the *nouveaux riches* towards their employees and dependents. Thomas Carlyle fulminated against national greed. Richard Oastler and the Northern Tory-Radicals campaigned against the long working hours of children in the mills and factories. The Radical agitator Samuel Bamford wrote in 1842 that Britain had 'exhibited the spectacle of a small community combatting the world and buying or beating it all round.' But

'The times which have been, never will return; we cannot recall that which has departed, and is still going; we cannot, any more than we can still the ocean, prevent our manufactures from being set up in other nations. We have read them too profound a lesson for that.'

His remedy was simple:

'During fifty years, the English nation has been engaged in a gluttonous scramble for wealth, and now the time is coming when there must be a disgorging from the highest to the lowest.'

Such sentiments were natural in the desperate slump conditions of the summer of 1842; but within a decade Britain was to enter its boom period as the world's workshop. More continuous was the bleakness of much of the new industry. 'A man may assemble five hundred workmen one week and dismiss them the next,' observed Sir Walter Scott, with characteristic Tory horror, in 1820,

'without having any further connection with them than to receive a week's work for a week's wages, nor any further solicitude about their future fate than if they were so many old shuttles.'

In the long run a major consequence of steam-powered large-scale urban production was the emergence of 'class' feelings. But the pace of social change varied with the speed of technological change. Richard Cobden made the point in a letter to Joseph Parkes in 1857; he had always believed that

'the social and political state of [Birmingham] was far more healthy than that of Manchester; and it arose from the fact that the industry of the hardware district was carried on by small manufacturers, employing a few men and boys each, sometimes only an apprentice or two; whilst the great capitalists in Manchester formed an aristocracy, individual members of which wielded an influence over sometimes two thousand persons. The former state of society was more natural and healthy in a moral and political sense. There was a freer intercourse between all classes than in the Lancashire town, where a great and impassable gulf separated the workman from his employer. The great capitalist class formed an excellent basis for the Anti-Corn-Law movement, for they had inexhaustible purses, which they opened freely in a contest where not only their pecuniary interest but their pride as "an order" was at stake. But he very much doubted whether such a state of society was favourable to a democratic political movement . . .'

'Here I saw, or thought I saw, a degenerate race,' wrote the Leeds Tory surgeon C. T. Thackrah in 1832, after seeing Manchester cotton operatives leaving the mills. 'It is essentially a place of business,' commented the liberal writer William Cooke Taylor of the cotton capital in 1842, 'where pleasure is unknown as a pursuit, and amusements scarcely rank as secondary considerations.' When Léon Faucher visited Manchester in 1844 he observed that

'The centres of industrialism are seats of corruption, in which the population enjoy an atmosphere neither more salubrious nor moral, than in those large towns, which are formed by political institutions, or by the demands of commerce.'

But Manchester was almost unique in its social and geographic divisions.

However bad conditions were in the mills and mines, life was worse for the slum-dwelling unskilled, unemployed or machine-displaced hand workers. Their odious living conditions were dramatically revealed by Henry Mayhew's mid-century investigations in London. Hippolyte Taine was revolted by the human derelicts of the filthy alleys off Oxford Street and 'the streets on London Bridge where families, huddled together with drooping heads, shivered through the night.' The aim of social reformers, Tory Evangelical and radical Benthamite alike was, however hesitantly, to ameliorate the conditions revealed by Blue Books and private investigations. The age of King Cotton and King Coal, of the penny post and popular agitations, of trade unions and co-operatives, remained a dirty age. *Punch* regularly complained, in 1858, blaming the noxious Thames for many metropolitan troubles:

Filthy river, filthy river,
Foul from London to the Nore,
What art thou but one vast gutter,
One tremendous common shore?

The children of the poor still toiled in mills and mines. The children of the affluent might be tormented by servants and teachers. This was palpably no time to be a child. Foreigners were shocked by the extent of prostitution. In the Haymarket and the Strand Hippolyte Taine found that

'Every hundred steps one jostles twenty harlots; some of them ask for a glass of gin; others say, "Sir, it is to pay my lodging." This is not debauchery which flaunts itself but destitution—and such destitution! The deplorable procession in the shade of the monumental streets is sickening; it seems to me a march of the dead. That is a plague-spot, the real plague-spot of English society.'

Wide reform was needed.

III

The physical contours of Britain were changing rapidly. The long series of agrarian changes had created the tidy, enclosed countryside of hedged and drained farms so admired by visitors. Coal and other mines scarred some areas. The canal network traversed large mileages. And from the 1820s thousands of 'navigators' tore, burrowed and built their way across the land to create the railway system. Social changes rapidly followed. Ancient rural immobility was eroded; Dr. Thomas Arnold rejoiced at the passing of 'feudality'. The roads and roadside communities declined, while new railway towns developed. Coal, manufactures, food, milk, newspapers, commuters, holidaymakers, the mail, soldiers, livestock, fertilisers—all could be carried more quickly and cheaply than ever before, across a nation in which regionalism was starting to decline.

The leadership given by the Monarchy varied considerably. 'Prinny' (George IV) was described by Leigh Hunt as

'a libertine over head and ears in debt and disgrace, a despiser of domestic ties, the companion of gamblers and demireps, a man who has just closed half a century without one single claim on the gratitude of his country or the respect of posterity.'

In the changed conditions of 1837 the first Victorians did not feel easy about the future. 'A very young Queen coming to the throne of this mighty empire . . . gives token of unpropitious times to come,' gloomily forecast William Dyott. In fact, Britain was on the verge of a new golden age, under a Queen whose life-style matched that of many of her subjects, influenced by a religious revival.

British religion was a mystery to some foreign visitors. Family prayers, solemnly performed in bourgeois households awed them. Taine disliked the fact that the master 'on Sunday evening . . . was [the] spiritual guide [and] chaplain' to family, servants and visitors alike. 'If an American is an infidel,' commented Hawthorne in 1855, 'he knows it, but an Englishman is often so without suspecting it—being kept from that knowledge by family prayers'. Yet religion played an important role in Victorian life—in education, in social reform and in politics. What a Kingsley-type Christian Socialist cared for was summed up in Thomas Hughes's *Tom Brown's Schooldays*. As Tom left for the Rugby School of Flashman and Dr. Arnold, Squire Brown declared that

'I don't care a straw for Greek particles . . . If only he'll turn out a brave, helpful, truth-telling Englishman, and a gentleman and a Christian, that's all we want.'

If this was scarcely a nation-wide aspiration, at least it represented a widespread feeling among many Victorian parents.

IV

This book is a collection of extracts from contemporary writings illustrating the changing attitudes, policies and achievements of Britons between about 1770 and 1870. The first section introduces some general attitudes and comments. In the second part contemporaries comment on life in the countryside. The changes in transport are examined in the third section, and urban life in the fourth. Social policies are described in the fifth part. And the last section is devoted to religion and religious controversies. It is hoped that this selection of a wide range of contemporary views of some aspects of life during Britain's age of change may prove of use to students of the period.

PART ONE

Society and its Mores

There is no country in which so absolute a homage is paid to wealth. In America there is a touch of shame when a man exhibits the evidences of large property, as if after all it needed apology. But the Englishman has pure pride in his wealth, and esteems it a final certificate. A coarse logic rules throughout all English souls; if you have merit, can you not show it by your good clothes and coach and horses? . . .

The ambition to create value evokes every kind of ability; government becomes a manufacturing corporation, and every house a mill. The headlong bias to utility will let no talent lie in a napkin—if possible will teach spiders to weave silk stockings. An Englishman, while he eats and drinks no more or not much more than another man, labors three times as many hours in the course of a year as another European; or, his life as a workman is three lives. He works fast. Every thing in England is at a quick pace . . .

Ralph Waldo Emerson (1803–82), *English Traits* (1856)

An Englishman takes a bath in the morning; walks with his children in the garden; eats leisurely his cheerful breakfast; learns all the news; goes to his business and works hard till four o'clock, and then his work for the day is over. He spends a full hour at his dinner table; rides a few miles with his wife and children; and devotes the evening to society. He is satisfied if he is slowly accumulating; takes life easy, and enjoys himself as he goes along.

Charles Edwards Lester (1815–90), *The Glory and Shame of England* (New York, 1841)

The general aspect of society is profound gravity. People look serious at a ball, at a dinner, on a ride on horseback or in a carriage, in Parliament or at Court, in the theatres or at the galleries. The great object in life is social position. To this end domestic establishments are sustained to rival each other.

Charles Francis Adams (1807–86), in 1861

The English do not appear to have a turn for amusing themselves.

Nathaniel Hawthorne (1804–64), *English Note Books* (ed. Randall Stewart, 1941)

. . . from ignorance, or from mismanagement in their preparation, the daily waste of excellent provisions almost exceeds belief. This waste is in itself a very serious evil . . . but the amount of *positive disease* which is caused amongst us by improper food, or food rendered unwholesome by a bad mode of cooking it, seems a greater evil still.

Mrs. Eliza Acton (1799–1859), *Modern Cookery for Private Families* (1845)

Of the beggars there are many distinct species. (1) The naval and the military beggars . . . (2) Distressed operative beggars . . . (3) Respectable beggars . . . (4) Disaster beggars . . . (5) Bodily afflicted beggars . . . (6) Famished beggars . . . (7) Foreign beggars . . . (8) Petty trading beggars . . . (9) Musical beggars . . . (10) Dependents of beggars . . .

Henry Mayhew (1812–87), *London Labour and the London Poor* (1861–2)

If we compare the prostitute at thirty-five with her sister, who perhaps is the married mother of a family, or has been the toiling slave for years in the over-heated laboratories of fashion, we shall seldom find that the constitutional ravages often thought to be a necessary consequence of prostitution exceed those attributable to the cares of a family and the heart-wearing struggles of virtuous labour.

William Acton (1813–75), *Prostitution considered in its Moral, Social and Sanitary Aspects* (1857)

. . . I have always thought that to sit in the British Parliament should be the highest object of ambition to every educated Englishman.

Anthony Trollope (1815–82), *An Autobiography* (1883)

Society is indeed a contract . . . it is a partnership in all science; a partnership in all art; a partnership in every virtue, and in all perfection. As the ends of such a partnership cannot be obtained in many generations, it becomes a partnership not only between those who are living, but between those who are living, those who are dead, and those who are to be born.

Edmund Burke (1729–97), *Reflections on the Revolution in France* (1790)

We live in an age when to be young and to be indifferent can be no longer synonymous. We must prepare for the coming hour. The claims of the future are represented by suffering millions; and the Youth of a Nation are the trustees of Posterity.

Benjamin Disraeli (1804–81), *Sybil: or The Two Nations* (1845)

Rank and Degree

Patrick Colquhoun (1745–1820), a Glaswegian who became a London stipendiary magistrate, was a pioneer statistician. His famous *Treatise on the Wealth, Power and Resources of the British Empire* (1814) became a textbook for economists and politicians. Colquhoun wrote at a time when earlier concepts of social divisions (generally based on a series of 'interests', each with a pyramidical range of orders) were starting to yield to notions of 'classes' (as yet, very imprecisely and hierarchically defined, though in the following table Colquhoun discerned some difference between 'the useful [and] the noxious members of the body politic'). The work was widely quoted by both liberal and socialist writers.

The population of the United Kingdom of Great Britain and Ireland, including the army and navy, admits of the following division into classes, viz.

		Heads of Families	*Total Persons comprising their Families*
	HIGHEST ORDERS		
1st	The Royal Family, the Lords Spiritual and Temporal, the Great Officers of State, and all above the degree of a Baronet, with their families	576	2,880
	SECOND CLASS		
2d	Baronets, Knights, Country Gentlemen, and others having large incomes, with their families	46,861	234,305

	Heads of Families	Total Persons comprising their Families
THIRD CLASS		
3d Dignified Clergy, Persons holding considerable employments in the state, elevated situations in the Law, eminent Practitioners in Physic, considerable Merchants, Manufacturers upon a large scale, and Bankers of the first order, with their Families	12,200	61,000
Carried forward	59,637	298,185
FOURTH CLASS		
4th Persons holding inferior situations in Church and State, respectable Clergymen of different persuasions, Practitioners in Law and Physic, Teachers of Youth of the superior order, respectable Freeholders, Ship Owners, Merchants and Manufacturers of the second class, Warehousemen and respectable Shopkeepers, Artists, respectable Builders, Mechanics, and Persons living on moderate incomes, with their families	233,650	1,168,250
FIFTH CLASS		
5th Lesser Freeholders, Shopkeepers of the second order, Inn-keepers, Publicans, and Persons engaged in miscellaneous occupations or living on moderate incomes, with their families	564,799	2,798,475

	Heads of Families	Total Persons comprising their Families
SIXTH CLASS		
6th Working mechanics, Artisans, Handicrafts, Agricultural Labourers, and others who subsist by labour in various employments, with their families	2,126,095	8,792,800
Menial Servants		1,279,923
SEVENTH, OR LOWEST CLASS		
7th Paupers and their families, Vagrants, Gipsies, Rogues, Vagabonds, and idle and disorderly persons, supported by criminal delinquency	387,100	1,828,170
Carried forward	3,371,281	16,165,803
THE ARMY AND NAVY		
Officers of the Army, Navy and Marines, including all Officers on half-pay and superannuated, with their families	10,500	69,000
Non-commissioned Officers in the Army, Navy, and Marines, Soldiers, Seamen, and Marines, including Pensioners of the Army, Navy, &C. and their families	120,000	862,000
TOTAL	3,501,781	17,096,803

Love of Titles

The growth of industry, the 1832 Reform Act and the repeal of the Corn Laws in 1846 were expected to destroy the importance of the landed aristocracy. They did not. Sizeable sections of the aristocracy and gentry became industrial entrepreneurs, as mineowners, ironmasters, harbour operators and railway directors. Furthermore, respect for aristocratic titles probably increased. In his *Collections and Recol-*

lections (1903) the raconteur G. W. E. Russell (1853–1919)—a relative of the ducal house of Bedford—gently mocked the national obsession with titles, which had been catered for by such catalogues of the titled classes as those produced by the Burke family, whose first *Peerage* was issued in 1826.

. . . Every constitutional Briton, whatever his political creed, has in his heart of hearts a wholesome reverence for a dukedom. Lord Beaconsfield, who understood these little traits of our national character even more perfectly than Thackeray, says of his favourite St. Aldegonde (who was heir to the richest dukedom in the kingdom) that "he held extreme opinions, especially on political affairs, being a Republican of the reddest dye. He was opposed to all privilege, and indeed to all orders of men except dukes, who were a necessity." That is a delicious touch. St. Aldegonde, whatever his political aberrations, "voiced" the universal sentiment of his less fortunate fellow-citizens; nor can the most soaring ambition of the British Matron desire a nobler epitaph than that of the lady immortalised by Thomas Ingoldsby:

She drank prussic acid without any water,
And died like a Duke-and-a-Duchess's daughter.

As, according to Dr. Johnson, all claret would be port if it could, so, presumably, every marquis would like to be a duke; and yet, as a matter of fact, that Elysian translation is not often made. A marquis, properly regarded, is not so much a nascent duke as a magnified earl. A shrewd observer of the world once said to me: "When an earl gets a marquisate, it is worth a hundred thousand pounds in hard money to his family." The explanation of this cryptic utterance is that, whereas an earl's younger sons are "misters", a marquis's younger sons are "lords". Each "my lord" can make a "my lady", and therefore commands a distinctly higher price in the marriage-market of a wholesomely-minded community. Miss Higgs, with her fifty thousand pounds, might scorn the notion of becoming the Honourable Mrs. Percy Popjoy; but as Lady Magnus Charters she would feel a laudable ambition gratified.

An earldom is, in its combination of euphony, antiquity, and association, perhaps the most impressive of all the titles in the peerage. Most rightly did the fourteenth Earl of Derby decline to be degraded into a brand-new duke . . .

But, magnificent and euphonious as an earldom is, the children of an earl are the half-castes of the peerage. The eldest son is "my lord", and his sisters are "my lady"; and ever since the days of Mr. Foker, Senior, it has been *de rigueur* for an opulent brewer to marry an earl's daughter; but the younger sons are not distinguishable from the ignominious progeny of viscounts and barons. Two little boys, respectively the eldest and the second son of an earl, were playing on the front staircase of their home, when the eldest fell over into the hall below. The younger called to the footman who picked his brother up, "Is he hurt?" "Killed, *my lord*," was the instantaneous reply of a servant who knew the devolution of a courtesy title.

As the marquises people the debatable land between the dukes and the earls, so do the viscounts between the earls and the barons . . . I hope I shall not be considered guilty of any disrespect if I say that ex-Speakers, ex-Secretaries of State, successful generals, and ambitious barons who are not quite good enough for earldoms, are "thrown into the common sink, which is viscounts." Not only heralds and genealogists, but every one who has the historical sense, must have felt an emotion of regret when the splendid title of twenty-third Baron Dacre was merged by Mr. Speaker Brand in the pinchbeck dignity of first Viscount Hampden.

After viscounts, barons . . . After the spiritual barons come the secular barons—the "common or garden" peers of the United Kingdom. Of these there are considerably more than three hundred; and of all, except some thirty or forty at the most, it may be said without offence that they are products of the opulent Middle Class. Pitt destroyed deliberately and for ever the exclusive character of the British peerage when, as Lord Beaconsfield said, he "created a plebeian aristocracy and blended it with the patrician oligarchy." And in order to gain admission to this "plebeian aristocracy" men otherwise reasonable and honest will spend incredible sums, undergo prodigious exertions, associate themselves with the basest intrigues, and perform the most unblushing tergiversations . . .

The Old Episcopate

The eighteenth-century tradition of aristocratic or aristocratically-nominated bishops long survived in the Church of England and, indeed, was often praised as giving stability to relations between Church and State. Such classical scholars were often remote but splendid grandees. In *Collections and Recollections* (1903) 'Gwe' Russell recalled the 'grand tradition of mingled splendour and profit' of early nineteenth century bishops, in the days of William Howley (1766–1848) at Canterbury (1828–48), E. V. Vernon-Harcourt (1757–1847) at York (1808–47), William van Mildert (1765–1836) at Durham (1826–36), B. E. Sparke (1759–1836) at Ely (1812–36) and C. R. Sumner (1790–1874) at Winchester (1827–69).

Few—and very few—are the adducible instances in which, in the reigns of George III, George IV, and William IV, a bishop was appointed for evangelistic zeal or pastoral efficiency.

But, on whatever principle chosen, the bishop, once duly consecrated and enthroned, was a formidable person, and surrounded by a dignity scarcely less than royal. "Nobody likes our bishop," says Parson Lingon in *Felix Holt*. "He's all Greek and greediness, and too proud to dine with his own father." People still living can remember the days when the Archbishop of Canterbury was preceded by servants bearing flambeaux when he walked across from Lambeth Chapel to what were called "Mrs. Howley's Lodgings". When the Archbishop dined out, he was treated with princely honours, and no one left the party till His Grace had made his bow. Once a week he dined in state in the great hall of Lambeth, presiding over a company of self-invited guests—strange perversion of the old archiepiscopal charity to travellers and the poor—while, as Sydney Smith said, "the domestics of the prelacy stood, with swords and bag-wigs, round pig and turkey and venison, to defend, as it were, the orthodox gastronome from the fierce Unitarian, the fell Baptist, and all the famished children of Dissent." When Sir John Coleridge, father of the late Lord Chief Justice, was a young man at the Bar, he wished to obtain a small legal post in the Archbishop's Prerogative Court. An influential friend undertook to forward his application to the Archbishop. "But remember," he said, "in writing your letter, that his Grace can only be approached on gilt-edged paper." Archbishop Harcourt never went from Bishopthorpe to York Minster except attended by his chaplains, in a coach and six, while Lady Anne was made to follow in a pair-horse carriage, to show her that her position was not the same thing among women that her husband's was among men. At Durham, which was worth £40,000 a year, the Bishop, as Prince Palatine, exercised a secular jurisdiction, both civil and criminal, and the Commission at the Assizes ran in the name of "Our Lord the Bishop". At Ely, Bishop Sparke gave so many of his best livings to his family that it was locally said that you could find your way across the Fens on a dark night by the number of little Sparkes along the road. When this good prelate secured a residential canonry for his eldest son, the event was so much a matter of course that he did not deem it worthy of special notice; but when he secured a second canonry for his second son, he was so filled with pious gratitude that, as a thank-offering, he gave a ball at the Palace of Ely to all the county of Cambridge. "And I think," said Bishop Woodford, in telling me the story, "that the achievement and the way of celebrating it were equally remarkable."

... The old Prince Bishops are as extinct as the dodo. The Ecclesiastical Commission has made an end of them. Bishop Sumner of Winchester, who died in 1874, was the last of his race ...

The New Economics

Adam Smith (1723–90), born in Kirkcaldy and educated at Glasgow University and Balliol College Oxford, was the most celebrated apostle of liberal economic doctrines. His *Inquiry into the Nature and Causes of the Wealth of Nations* (1776) became the 'bible' of liberal opponents of the mercantilist state. This influential and eminently readable work was written while Smith lectured at Edinburgh and Glasgow universities and tutored the 3rd Duke of Buccleuch (1746–1812) on a continental 'grand tour'. From 1778 Smith worked as a commissioner of Scottish customs. He proclaimed the social virtues of individualism and 'natural liberty' and minimised the rôle of the State.

The general industry of the society never can exceed what the capital of the society can employ. As the number of workmen that can be kept in employment by any particular person must bear a certain proportion to his capital, so the number of those that can be continually employed by all the members of a great society must bear a certain proportion to the whole capital of that society, and never can exceed that proportion. No regulation of commerce can increase the quantity of industry in any society beyond what its capital can maintain ...

Every individual is continually exerting himself to find out the most advantageous employment for whatever capital he can command. It is his own advantage, indeed, and not that of the society, which he has in view. But the study of his own advantage naturally, or rather necessarily, leads him to prefer that employment which is most advantageous to the society.

First, every individual endeavours to employ his capital as near home as he can, and consequently as much as he can in the support of domestic industry; provided always that he can thereby obtain the ordinary, or not a great deal less than the ordinary profits of stock.

. . . Secondly, every individual who employs his capital in the support of domestic industry, necessarily endeavours so to direct that industry that its produce may be of the greatest possible value.

. . . What is prudence in the conduct of every private family can scarce be folly in that of a great kingdom. If a foreign country can supply us with a commodity cheaper than we ourselves can make it, better buy it off them with some part of the produce of our own industry employed in a way in which we have some advantage . . .

The natural advantages which one country has over another in producing particular commodities are sometimes so great that it is acknowledged by all the world to be in vain to struggle with them . . .

Country gentlemen and farmers are, to their great honour, of all people, the least subject to the wretched spirit of monopoly. The undertaker of a great manufactory is sometimes alarmed if another work of the same kind is established within twenty miles of him . . .

'Mammonism'

In *Past and Present* (1843) the Scots writer Thomas Carlyle (1795–1881) condemned contemporaries' obsession with money and economic liberalism. The son of a Dumfriesshire mason, Carlyle became a schoolmaster, but moved to London in 1834 to begin a literary career, condemning contemporary materialism and injustice and praising the influence of 'strong' individuals.

The condition of England, on which many pamphlets are now in the course of publication, and many thoughts unpublished are going on in every reflective head, is justly regarded as one of the most ominous, and withal one of the strangest, ever seen in this world. England is full of wealth, of multifarious produce, supply for human want in every kind; yet England is dying of inanition . . .

. . . To whom, then, is this wealth of England wealth? Who is it that it blesses; makes happier, wiser, beautifuler, in any way better? Who has got hold of it, to make it fetch and carry for him, like a true servant, not like a false mock-servant; to do him any real service whatsoever? As yet no one. We have more riches than any Nation ever had before; we have less good of them than any Nation ever had before. Our successful industry is hitherto unsuccessful; a strange success, if we stop here! In the midst of plethoric plenty, the people perish . . .

. . . It must be owned, we for the present, with our Mammon-Gospel, have come to strange conclusions. We call it a Society; and go about professing openly the totalest separation, isolation. Our life is not a mutual helpfulness; but rather, cloaked under due laws-of-war, named 'fair competition' and so forth, it is a mutual hostility. We have profoundly forgotten everywhere that *Cash-payment* is not the sole relation of human beings; we think, nothing doubting, that *it* absolves and liquidates all engagements of man . . . Verily Mammon-worship is a melancholy creed . . .

Laisser-faire

J. R. McCulloch (1789–1864), a prominent author and 'classical economist', typified the new and dominant line of economists. The extract is from his *Statistical Account of the British Empire* (1837).

The absence of monopolies, and the non-interference of the government in industrious undertakings, undoubtedly conduce in no ordinary degree to the progress of industry. Every man is always exerting himself to find out how he may best extend his command over the necessaries and conveniences of life; and sound policy requires that he should, so long as he does not interfere with the rights and privileges of others, be allowed to pursue his own interest in his own way. Human reason is, no doubt, limited and fallible; we are often swayed by prejudices, and are apt to be deceived by appearances: still, however, it is certain that the desire to promote our own purposes contributes far more than any thing else to render us clear-sighted and sagacious.—"*Nul sentiment dans l'homme ne tient son intelligence éveillée autant que l'intérêt personnel. Il donne de l'esprit aux plus simples.*" The principle that individuals are, generally speaking, the best judges of what is most beneficial for themselves, is now universally admitted to be the only one that can be safely relied on. No writer of authority has, latterly, ventured to maintain the exploded and untenable doctrine, that governments may advantageously interfere to regulate the pursuits of their subjects. It is their duty to preserve order; to prevent one from injuring another; to maintain, in short, the equal rights and privileges of all. But it is not possible for them to go one step further, without receding from the principle of non-interference, and laying themselves open to the charge of acting partially by some, and unjustly by others.

Self-Help

Of all the Victorian 'virtues' the notion of 'self-help' was perhaps the most important liberal belief. Dr Samuel Smiles (1812–1904) was the most successful advocate of the notion that 'the spirit of self-help was the root of all genuine growth in the individual'. His book *Self-Help* (1859) primarily urged 'men to elevate and improve themselves by their own free and independent action', rather than be demoralised by external help.

. . . In many walks of life drudgery and toil must be cheerfully endured as the necessary discipline of life. Hugh Miller says the only school in which he was properly taught was "that world-wide school in which toil and hardship are the severe but noble teachers." He who allows his application to falter, or shirks his work on frivolous pretexts, is on the sure road to ultimate failure. Let any task be undertaken as a thing not possible to be evaded, and it will soon come to be performed with alacrity and cheerfulness. The habit of strenuous continued labour will become comparatively easy in time, like every other habit. Thus even men with the commonest brains and the most slender powers will accomplish much, if they will but apply themselves wholly and indefatigably to one thing at a time. Fowell Buxton placed his confidence in ordinary means and extraordinary application; realizing the scriptural injunction, "Whatsoever thy hand findeth to do, do it with all thy might"; and he himself attributed his own remarkable success in life to his practice of constantly "being a whole man to one thing at a time".

Nothing that is of real worth can be achieved without courageous working. Man owes his growth chiefly to that active striving of the will, that encounter with difficulty, which we call effort; and it is astonishing to find how often results apparently impracticable are thus made possible. An intense anticipation itself transforms possibility into reality; our desires being often but the precursors of things which we are capable of performing . . .

Free Trade

The Import Duties Committee of 1840, which was stage-managed by the Radical M.P. Joseph Hume (1777–1855) and furtively assisted by 'Free Trade' supporters in the Board of Trade, became an influential propagandist for the gathering campaign against Protectionist tariffs. Its *Report* was, in essence, a heavily prejudiced document.

The Tariff of the United Kingdom presents neither congruity nor unity of purpose; no general principles seem to have been applied.

The Schedule to the Act 3 & 4 Will. 4, c. 56, for consolidating the Customs Duties, enumerates no fewer than 1,150 different rates of duty chargeable on imported articles, all other commodities paying duty as unenumerated, and very few of such rates appear to have been determined by any recognised standard . . .

The Tariff often aims at incompatible ends; the duties are sometimes meant to be both productive of revenue and for protective objects, which are frequently inconsistent with each other . . .

. . . Your Committee . . . find on the part of those who are connected with some of the most important of our manufacturers, a conviction, and a growing conviction, that the protective system is not, on the whole, beneficial to the protected manufactures themselves . . .

Your Committee gather from the evidence that has been laid before them, that while the prosperity of our own manufactures is not to be traced to benefits derived from the exclusion of foreign rival manufacturers, so neither is the competition of continental manufacturers to be traced to a protective system. They are told that the most vigorous and successful of the manufactures on the Continent have grown, not out of peculiar favour shown to them by legislation, but from those natural and spontaneous advantages which are associated with labour and capital in certain localities, and which cannot be transferred elsewhere at the mandate of the Legislature, or at the will of the manufacturer. Your Committee see reason to believe, that the most prosperous fabrics are those which flourish without the aid of special favours . . .

Free Trade and Peace

Writing to Henry Ashworth, a major Lancashire cotton master, on 12 April 1842 the prominent free trade agitator Richard Cobden (1804–65) followed the Anti-Corn Law League's line that free trade would lead to peace. The extract is taken from John Morley, *The Life of Richard Cobden* (1910 edn.).

It has struck me that it would be well to try to engraft our Free Trade agitation upon the Peace movement. They are one and the same cause. It has often been to me a matter of the greatest surprise, that the Friends have not taken up the question of Free Trade as the means—and I believe the only human means—of effecting universal and permanent peace. The efforts of the Peace Societies, however laudable, can never be successful so long as the nations maintain their present system of isolation. The colonial system, with all its dazzling appeals to the passions of the people, can never be got rid of except by the indirect process of Free Trade, which will gradually and imperceptibly loose the bands which unite our Colonies to us by a mistaken notion of self-interest. Yet the Colonial policy of Europe has been the chief source of wars for the last hundred and fifty years. Again, Free Trade, by perfecting the intercourse, and securing the dependence of countries one upon another, must inevitably snatch the power from the *governments* to plunge their people into wars . . .

Free Trade and Liberty

The League lecturer Philip Harwood delivered some typical observations in his *Six Lectures on the Corn-Law Monopoly and Free Trade: delivered at the London Mechanics' Institution* (1843).

This is the prime, central, radical mischief of the Corn-Law. It stops the way of our foreign trade; that foreign trade which uses up the manufactures that employ and feed the people, that pays the revenue, that keeps society together. While this stoppage lasts, there is continuous destruction going on of national capital. Every mill that stops in the manufacturing towns makes the nation poorer: it turns producers into consumers, tax-payers into tax-eaters . . .

The cause of free trade is the cause of *civil liberty*. The right to buy food in the cheapest market and sell labour in the dearest market—what is it but the right of a man to do what he will with his own . . . ? . . . The cause of free trade is the cause of *political justice* . . .

The cause of free trade is the cause of *peace*; peace at home and peace abroad; peace between class and class, and between nation and nation. The very language of monopoly savours of war. The whole monopoly argument bristles with jealousy, suspicion and enmity . . .

A Protectionist Case

Against the well-financed and highly-organised Anti-Corn Law League the Protectionists were generally ineffective. Tory social reformers like Richard Oastler attempted to evolve a full social and political philosophy opposed to the liberal 'spirit of the times' and tenant farmers (principally in the wheat-producing counties) founded Protection Societies. But many landowners thought it inconceivable—until 1846—that Peel's Conservative ministry would 'desert' them. Their greatest venture (led by the Dukes of Richmond, Buckingham, Norfolk, Rutland and Cleveland, and the Earl of Yarborough) publicised its case in *Reasons for the Formation of the Agricultural Protection Society, addressed to the Industrious Classes of the United Kingdom* (1844), by Edward Stillingfleet Cayley (1802–62), Whig M.P. and North Yorkshire squire.

The custom of our forefathers appears to have been to consider the full employment of the people, and the busy interchange of their respective products among themselves, as the test of general prosperity. The practice with some of the present generation seems to be, to test the prosperity of the people, not by their comfort and employment, but by the number of millions of yards of manufactures exported; and by the quantity of foreign labour imported into this country in exchange, in the shape of foreign goods . . .

. . . If this country employed twenty millions of people in the cotton manufacture, no cotton manufacturer would be in favour of a free trade bringing in cheaper cotton than England could make . . .

To sacrifice a portion of the industrious classes, in a crusade after cheapness, without securing to them a new demand for their labour, is an injustice, great in proportion to the dependence of this class for a livelihood on their daily toil . . . In contending for protection to native industry, this Society contends for that state of things which, through the surest employment, will give the greatest comfort to the people . . .

Protection and Paternalism

Richard Oastler (1789–1861), the Tory leader of the Northern factory reform campaign, was always a staunch Protectionist. To his mind, a paternal State should protect both agriculture and industrial workers. The following extracts are taken from speeches at the 1832 election, subsequently printed in *Facts and Plain Words on Every-Day Subjects* (Leeds, 1833).

I am *not* of the present School of "Political Economists", "Free Traders", "Liberals", so called; "Emigration Boards and Committees" I detest—I contend that the Labourer has a *right* to live on his Native Soil; there is room enough and there may be food enough in our native Land for us all . . .

. . . The Altar, The Throne, and the Cottage, should share alike in the protection of the Law: the God of the Poor will never accept incense from the *first*, nor can there be stability in the *second*, if justice and mercy be withheld from the *third* . . . .

Shall the law refuse to protect the only property of the Poor, HIS LABOUR, because some few unjust, unprincipled men refuse to pay its value? . . . I maintain the Law *must* interfere . . .

. . . Whenever I hear a British artizan shout "cheap foreign corn", I always fancy I see his wife pulling his coat, and hear her crying out "low wages", "long labour", "bad profits". Is not that the case? I am sure I am right; is it not so? And when I hear a large mill-owner coaxing his workpeople with a promise of "cheap foreign corn", I fancy I see him shrugging his shoulders and saying, "more work for less money, that's all". Very well, then, my principle of legislation is this—to encourage home growth, home labour, home trade, and home consumption.

A Warning on Population

The Rev. Thomas Robert Malthus (1766–1834), an Anglican priest and teacher at the East India Company's College, first issued his *Essay on the Principles of Population* in 1798. Successive editions of this seminal work on the need to limit population provoked considerable controversy, and in 1830 Malthus published his little *Summary View of the Principle of Population*, to correct misinterpretations and re-state his views. Much of the *Summary* originally appeared as an article in the 1824 supplement to the *Encyclopaedia Britannica*.

In taking a view of animated nature, we cannot fail to be struck with a prodigious power of increase in plants and animals. Their capacity in this respect is, indeed, almost infinitely various, according with the endless variety of the works of nature, and the different purposes which they seem appointed to fulfil. But whether they increase slowly or rapidly, if they increase by seed or generation, their natural tendency must be to increase in a geometrical ratio, that is, by multiplication; and at whatever rate they are increasing during any one period, if no further obstacles be opposed to them, they must proceed in a geometrical progression.

. . . We see, that notwithstanding this prodigious *power* of increase in vegetables and animals, their actual increase is extremely slow; and it is obvious, that . . . long before a final stop was put to all further progress, their actual rate of increase must of necessity be very greatly retarded: as it would be impossible for the most enlightened human efforts to make all the soil of the earth equal in fertility to the average quality of land now in use; while the practicable approaches towards it would require so much time as to occasion, at a very early period, a constant and great check upon what their increase would be, if they could exert their natural powers.

Elevated as man is above all other animals by his intellectual facilities, it is not to be supposed that the physical laws to which he is subjected should be essentially different from those which are observed to prevail in other parts of animated nature. He may increase slower than most other animals; but food is equally necessary to his support; and if his natural capacity of increase be greater than can be permanently supplied with food from a limited territory, his increase must be constantly retarded by the difficulty of procuring the means of subsistence.

'The Two Nations'

Sybil, or The Two Nations (1845) by Benjamin Disraeli (1804–81), Tory M.P. and later twice Prime Minister, was the second of his 'Young England' trilogy of novels. Romantic, sentimental and 'aristocratic' in tone, it appealed for a revival of medieval chivalry to solve 'the condition of England problem'. It had a great success, though the 'Young England' group of Tories was soon to melt away. In a celebrated passage, Disraeli explained his concept of the 'two nations' into which England was divided in the mid-forties.

'There is so much to lament in the world in which we live,' said the younger of the strangers, 'that I can spare no pang for the past.'

'Yet you approve of the principle of their society; you prefer it, you say, to our existing life.'

'Yes; I prefer association to gregariousness.'

'That is a distinction,' said Egremont, musingly.

'It is a community of purpose that constitutes society,' continued the younger stranger; 'without that, men may be drawn into contiguity, but they still continue virtually isolated.'

'And is that their condition in cities?'

'It is their condition everywhere; but in cities that condition is aggravated. A density of population implies a severer struggle for existence, and a consequent repulsion of elements brought into too close contact. In great cities men are brought together by the desire of gain. They are not in a state of co-operation, but of isolation, as to the making of fortunes; and for all the rest they are careless of neighbours. Christianity teaches us to love our neighbour as ourself; modern society acknowledges no neighbour.'

'Well, we live in strange times,' said Egremont, struck by the observation of his companion, and relieving a perplexed spirit by an ordinary exclamation, which often denotes that the mind is more stirred than it cares to acknowledge, or at the moment is able to express.

'When the infant begins to walk, it also thinks that it lives in strange times,' said his companion.

'Your inference?' asked Egremont.

'That society, still in its infancy, is beginning to feel its way.'

'This is a new reign,' said Egremont, 'perhaps it is a new era.'

'I think so,' said the younger stranger.

'Well, society may be in its infancy,' said Egremont, slightly smiling; 'but, say what you like, our Queen reigns over the greatest nation that ever existed.'

'Which nation?' asked the younger stranger, 'for she reigns over two.'

The stranger paused; Egremont was silent, but looked inquiringly.

'Yes,' resumed the younger stranger after a moment's interval. 'Two nations; between whom there is no intercourse and no sympathy; who are as ignorant of each other's habits, thoughts, and feelings, as if they were dwellers in different zones, or inhabitants of different plants; who are formed by a different breeding, are fed by a different food, are ordered by different manners, and are not governed by the same laws.'

'You speak of—' said Egremont, hesitatingly.

'THE RICH AND THE POOR.'

Class Relationships

In her first novel, *Mary Barton* (1847), Mrs. Elizabeth Gaskell (1810–65) dealt with some of the problems facing the new industrialised society of Lancashire. She wrote from some experience, as the wife of a Unitarian minister in Manchester.

'Well, sir,' replied Job, 'it's hard to say: John Barton was not a man to take counsel with people; nor did he make many words about his doings. So I can only judge from his way of thinking and talking in general . . . You see he were sadly put about to make great riches and great poverty square with Christ's Gospel'—Job paused, in order to try and express what was clear enough in his own mind, as to the effect produced on John Barton by the great and mocking contrasts presented by the varieties of human condition. Before he could find suitable words to explain his meaning, Mr. Carson spoke.

'You mean he was an Owenite; for all equality and community of goods, and that kind of absurdity.'

'No, no! John Barton was no fool. No need to tell him that were all men equal to-night, some would get the start by rising an hour earlier to-morrow. Nor yet did he care for goods, nor wealth; no man less, so that he could get daily bread for him and his; but what hurt him sore, and rankled in him as long as I knew him (and sir, it rankles in many a poor man's heart far more than the want of any creature-comforts, and puts a sting into starvation itself), was that those who wore finer clothes, and eat better food, and had more money in their pockets, kept him at arm's length, and cared not whether his heart was sorry or glad; whether he lived or died—whether he was bound for heaven or hell. It seemed hard to him that a heap of gold should part him and his brother so far asunder. For he was a loving man before he grew mad with seeing such as he was slighted, as if Christ himself had not been poor. At one time, I've heard him say, he felt kindly towards every man, rich or poor, because he thought they were all men alike. But latterly he grew aggravated with the sorrows and suffering that he saw, and which he thought the masters might help if they would.'

'That's the notion you've all of you got,' said Mr. Carson. 'Now, how in the world can we help it? We cannot regulate the demands for labour. No man or set of men can do it. It depends on events which God alone can control. When there is no market for our goods, we suffer just as much as you can do.'

'Not as much, I'm sure, sir; though I'm not given to Political Economy, I know that much. I'm wanting in learning, I'm aware; but I can use my eyes. I never see the masters getting thin and haggard for want of food; I hardly ever see them making much change in their way of living, though I don't doubt they've got to do it in bad times. But it's in things for show they cut short; while for such as me, it's in things for life we've to stint. For sure, sir, you'll own it's come to a hard pass when a man would give aught in the world for work to keep his children from starving, and can't get a bit, if he's ever so willing. I'm not up to talking as John Barton would have done, but that's clear to me at any rate.'

'My good man, just listen to me. Two men live in a solitude; one produces loaves of bread, the other coats,—or what you will. Now, would it not be hard if the bread-producer were forced to give bread for the coats, whether he wanted them or not, in order to furnish employment to the other: that is the simple form of the case; you've only to multiply the numbers. There will come times of great changes in the occupation of thousands, when improvements in manufactures and machinery are made. It's all nonsense talking,—it must be so!'

Job Legh pondered a few moments.

'It's true it was a sore time for the hand-loom weavers when power-looms came in: them new-fangled things make a man's life like a lottery; and yet I'll never misdoubt that power-looms, and railways, and all such like inventions are gifts of God. I have lived long enough, too, to see that it is a part of His plan to send suffering to bring out a higher good; but surely it's also a part of His plan that so much of the burden of the suffering as can be should be lightened by those whom it is His pleasure to make happy and content in their own circumstances. Of course it would take a deal more thought and wisdom than me, or any other man has, to settle out of hand how this should be done. But I'm clear about this, when God gives a blessing to be enjoyed, He gives it with a duty to be done; and the duty of the happy is to help the suffering to bear their woe.'

'Still facts have proved, and are daily proving, how much better it is for every man to be independent of help, and self-reliant,' said Mr. Carson thoughtfully.

Squire and Man

In her last novel, *Wives and Daughters* (1866), Mrs. Gaskell pictured relations between a squire and an aged retainer.

Old Silas lay in a sort of closet, opening out of the family living room. The small window that gave it light looked right on to the "moor", as it was called; and by day the check curtain was drawn aside so that he might watch the progress of the labour. Everything about the old man was clean, of course; and, with Death, the leveller, so close at hand, it was the labourer who made the first advances, and put out his horny hand to the Squire.

"I thought you'd come, Squire. Your father came for to see my father as he lay a-dying."

"Come, come, my man!" said the Squire, easily affected, as he always was. "Don't talk of dying, we shall soon have you out, never fear. They've sent you some soup from the Hall, as I bade 'em, haven't they?"

"Ay, ay, I've had all as I could want for to eat and to drink. The young squire and Master Roger was here yesterday."

"Yes, I know."

"But I'm a deal nearer heaven to-day, I am. I should like you to look after th' covers in th' West Spinney, Squire; them gorse, you know, where th' old fox had her hole—her as give 'em so many a run. You'll mind it, Squire, though you was but a lad. I could laugh to think on her tricks yet." And, with a weak attempt at a laugh, he got himself into a violent fit of coughing, which alarmed the Squire, who thought he would never get his breath again. His daughter-in-law came in at the sound, and told the Squire that he had these coughing-bouts very frequently, and that she thought he would go off in one of them before long. This opinion of hers was spoken simply out before the old man, who now lay gasping and exhausted upon his pillow. Poor people acknowledge the inevitableness and the approach of death in a much more straightforward manner than is customary among the more educated. The Squire was shocked at her hard-heartedness, as he considered it; but the old man himself had received much tender kindness from his daughter-in-law; and what she had just said was no more news to him than the fact that the sun would rise to-morrow. He was more anxious to go on with his story.

Class Conflicts

In 1845 Friedrich Engels (1820–95) published his *Condition of the Working Class in England* in German. The first extract is quoted from this communist classic which was translated into English only in 1892, and the first accurate translation appeared as late as 1958. Engels, a German businessman managing a family mill in Manchester, had lived in Britain for only two years when he wrote his description of British workers—which, perhaps inevitably, was sometimes wildly inaccurate. Engels and Karl Marx (1818–83) issued *The Communist Manifesto*, the source of the second extract, as a call for European revolutions in 1848. It was first published in English in *The Red Republican*, 9 November 1850, an obscure journal edited by the Left-wing Chartist George Julian Harney (1817–97). To the founding-fathers of 'scientific' socialism the revolution seemed to be at hand.

(1) . . . The true intentions of the capitalists are vividly revealed in the working of the new poor law, for here the bourgeoisie is acting as a class and what it does cannot be hidden. The new Poor Law shows up the middle classes and throws into true perspective the other ways in which this class injures the proletariat. Support for the new Poor Law was not confined to a mere section of the bourgeoisie. The whole middle class is behind it. This can be proved, for example, by examining debates which took place in

Parliament in 1844. The Liberal party had been responsible for passing the new Poor Law. The Conservative party, led by Sir Robert Peel, defended the law and made only a few trifling changes in it when the Poor Law Amendment Act of 1844 was passed . . . And on both occasions the noble lords in the upper house gave their assent. In this way the exclusion of the proletariat from the state and from society has been made public. The middle classes have made it perfectly clear that they do not regard the workers as human beings and that they have no intention of treating them in a humane manner. We can confidently leave it to the British workers to regain their rights as human beings.

. . . The war of poor against rich in England—which is already being waged by individuals and also by all the workers by indirect means will [before long] be openly waged by the whole of the proletariat. It is too late for the parties concerned to reach a peaceful situation. The gulf between the two classes is becoming wider and wider. The workers are becoming more and more imbued with the spirit of resistance. The feelings of the proletariat against their oppressors are becoming more and more bitter. The workers are moving from minor guerilla skirmishes to demonstrations and armed conflicts of a more serious nature. Soon it will only be necessary to dislodge a stone and the whole avalanche will be set in motion. When the cry echoes throughout the country: "War to the mansion, peace to the cottage," then it will be too late for the wealthy to save their skins.

(2) The history of all hitherto existing society is the history of class struggles. Freeman and slave, patrician and plebeian, lord and serf, guildmaster and journeyman, in a word, oppressor and oppressed, stood in constant opposition to one another, carried on an uninterrupted, now open fight, a fight that each time ended, either in a revolutionary reconstitution of society at large, or in the common ruin of the contending classes.

In the earlier epochs of history, we find almost everywhere a complicated arrangement of society into various orders, a manifold gradation of social rank. In ancient Rome we have patricians, knights, plebeians, slaves; in the Middle Ages, feudal lords, vassals, guildmasters, journeymen, apprentices, serfs; in almost all of these classes, again, subordinate gradations.

The modern bourgeois society that has sprouted from the ruins of feudal society has not done away with class antagonisms. It has but established new classes, new conditions of oppression, new forms of struggle in place of the old ones.

Our epoch, the epoch of the bourgeoisie, possesses, however, this distinctive feature: it has simplified the class antagonisms. Society as a whole is more and more splitting up into two great hostile camps, into two great classes directly facing each other—bourgeoisie and proletariat.

... The distinguishing feature of Communism is not the abolition of property generally, but the abolition of bourgeois property. But modern, bourgeois property is the final and most complete expression of the system of producing and appropriating products that is based on class antagonisms, on the exploitation of some by others.

In this sense, the theory of the Communists may be summed up in the single sentence: Abolition of private property.

... The Communists disdain to conceal their views and aims. They openly declare that their ends can be attained only by the forcible overthrow of all existing social conditions. Let the ruling classes tremble at a Communist revolution. In it the proletarians have nothing to lose but their chains. They have a world to win.

WORKING MEN OF ALL COUNTRIES, UNITE!

High Society

Britain long remained an 'aristocratic' country, led in almost every field (but especially in politics, religion, sports, agriculture, local government and social life) by the 'great families'. In the first extract, G. W. E. Russell describes late eighteenth-century events (*Collections and Recollections*, 1903) and in the second portrays some aristocratic fashions. Disraeli's letters to his sister on the Season following Queen Victoria's Coronation form the third section (from *Home letters written by Lord Beaconsfield, 1830–1852*, 1928 edn.). In the fourth section C. C. F. Greville (1794–1865), the gossipy Whig secretary to the council, writes of the roué 3rd Marquess of Hertford (in his *Journal of the Reign of Queen Victoria*, ed. Henry Reeve, 1885). By contrast, in the fifth quotation Sir Edwin Hodder (*The Life and Work of the 7th Earl of Shaftesbury, K.G.*, 1887 edn.) describes the remarkable work of the great aristocratic, Evangelical social reformer.

(1) ... All testimony seems to me to point to the fact that towards the close of the eighteenth century Religion was almost extinct in

the highest and lowest classes of English society. The poor were sunk in ignorance and barbarism, and the aristocracy was honeycombed by profligacy. Morality, discarded alike by high and low, took refuge in the great Middle Class, then, as now, deeply influenced by Evangelical Dissent. A dissolute Heir-Apparent presided over a social system in which not merely religion but decency was habitually disregarded. At his wedding he was so drunk that his attendant dukes "could scarcely support him from falling." The Princes of the Blood were notorious for a freedom of life and manners which would be ludicrous if it were not shocking . . .

. . . The closing years of the eighteenth century witnessed the *nadir* of English virtue. The national conscience was in truth asleep, and it had a rude awakening. "I have heard persons of great weight and authority," writes Mr. Gladstone, "such as Mr. Grenville, and also, I think, Archbishop Howley, ascribe the beginnings of a reviving seriousness in the upper classes of lay society to a reaction against the horrors and impieties of the first French Revolution in its later stages." And this reviving seriousness was by no means confined to Nonconformist circles . . .

(2) . . . Lord Bathurst, who was born in 1791, told me that at his private school he and the other sons of peers sate together on a privileged bench apart from the rest of the boys. A typical aristocrat was the first Marquis of Abercorn. He died in 1818, but he is still revered in Ulster under the name of "The Owld Marquis". This admirable nobleman always went out shooting in his Blue Ribbon, and required his housemaids to wear white kid gloves when they made his bed. Before he married his first cousin, Miss Cecil Hamilton, he induced the Crown to confer on her the titular rank of an Earl's daughter, that he might not marry beneath his position; and when he discovered that she contemplated eloping, he sent a message begging her to take the family coach, as it never ought to be said that Lady Abercorn left her husband's roof in a hack chaise. By such endearing traits do the truly great live in the hearts of posterity.

. . . When Selina Countess of Huntingdon asked the Duchess of Buckingham to accompany her to a sermon of Whitefield's, the Duchess replied: "I thank your ladyship for the information concerning the Methodist preachers; their doctrines are most repulsive, and strongly tinctured with impertinence and disrespect towards their superiors, in perpetually endeavouring to level all ranks and do away with all distinctions. It is monstrous to be told you have a heart as sinful as the common wretches that crawl on the earth; and I cannot but wonder that your ladyship should relish any sentiments so much at variance with high rank and good breeding."

The exclusive and almost feudal character of the English peerage was destroyed, finally and of set purpose, by Pitt when he declared that every man who had an estate of ten thousand a year had a right to be a peer. In Lord Beaconsfield's words, "He created a plebeian aristocracy and blended it with the patrician oligarchy. He made peers of second rate squires and fat graziers. He caught them in the alleys of Lombard Street, and clutched them from the counting-houses of Cornhill." This democratization of the peerage was accompanied by great modifications of pomp and stateliness in the daily life of the peers. In the eighteenth century the Duke and Duchess of Atholl were always served at their own table before their guests, in recognition of their royal rank as Sovereigns of the Isle of Man; and the Duke and Duchess of Argyll observed the same courteous usage for no better reasons than because they liked it. The "Household Book" of Alnwick Castle records the amplitude and complexity of the domestic hierarchy which ministered to the Duke and Duchess of Northumberland; and at Arundel and Belvoir, and Trentham and Wentworth, the magnates of the peerage lived in a state little less than regal. Seneschals and gentlemen-ushers, ladies-in-waiting and pages-of-the-presence adorned noble as well as royal households . . .

(3) [July, 1838] There was a very brilliant ball at the Salisburys' the other night, with all the remarkables and illustrious in which London now abounds. I stayed till two o'clock; but there were no signs then of separation, and the supper-room only just open. By the bye, the Countess Zavodouska, for I believe that is her name, appears quite the reigning beauty of the season . . .

Yesterday, the day being perfect, there was a splendid review in Hyde Park. I saw it admirably from Mrs W[yndham] L[ewis]'s. The Delawares, Rolles, Lawrence Peels, and Dawsons were there, but no one was allowed to be on the drawing-room floor, lest there should be an appearance of a party, except old Lord Rolle and myself to be his companion. Lord R. sat in the balcony with a footman each side of him, as is his custom. The Londonderrys after the review gave a magnificent banquet at Holderness House. There were only 150 asked, and all sat down. Londonderry's regiment being reviewed, we had the band of the 10th playing on the staircase, the whole of the said staircase being crowded with orange-trees and cape jessamines. The Duke de Nemours, Soult, and all "illustrious strangers" were there—the banquet being in the gallery of sculpture.

(4) [19 March, 1842] . . . No man ever lived more despised or died less regretted. His life and his death were equally disgusting and revolting to every good and moral feeling. As Lord Yarmouth he was known as a sharp, cunning, luxurious, avaricious man of the world, with some talent, the favourite of George IV (the worst of kings) when Lady Hertford, his mother, was that Prince's mistress . . . He was a *bon vivant*, and when young and gay his parties were agreeable, and he contributed his share to their hilarity. But after he became Lord Hertford and the possessor of an enormous property he was puffed up with vulgar pride, very unlike the real scion of a noble race; he loved nothing but dull pomp and ceremony, and could only endure people who paid him court and homage . . . There has been, as far as I know, no example of undisguised debauchery exhibited to the world like that of Lord Hertford, and his age and infirmities rendered it at once the more remarkable and the more shocking. Between sixty and seventy years old, broken with various infirmities, and almost unintelligible from a paralysis of the tongue, he has been in the habit of travelling about with a company of prostitutes, who formed his principal society, and by whom he was surrounded up to the moment of his death, generally picking them up from the dregs of that class, and changing them according to his fancy and caprice. Here he was to be seen driving about the town, and lifted by two footmen from his carriage into the brothel, and he never seems to have thought it necessary to throw the slightest veil over the habits he pursued . . . And what a life, terminating in what a death! without a serious thought or a kindly feeling, lavishing sums incalculable on the worthless objects of his pleasures or caprices, never doing a generous or a charitable action, caring and cared for by no human being, the very objects of his bounty only regarding him for what they could get out of him; faculties, far beyond mediocrity, wasted and degraded, immersed in pride without dignity, in avarice and sensuality; all his relations estranged from him, and

surrounded to the last by a venal harem, who pandered to the disgusting exigencies *lassatae sed nondum satiatae libidinis* . . .

(5) "My lords," said the Duke of Argyll in a memorable speech in 1885 upon the political situation, "the social reforms of the last century have not been mainly due to the Liberal party. They have been due mainly to the influence, character, and perseverance of one man—Lord Shaftesbury."

"That," said Lord Salisbury, in endorsing this eloquent tribute, "is, I believe a very true representation of the facts" . . .

. . . He was the founder of a new order of men who, inspired by his example, and infected by his enthusiasm, followed and still follow in his footsteps. His life moved steadily along in one undeviating course, everything being brought into subjection to the self-imposed work he had undertaken, and nothing attempted but in an earnest and religious spirit. There was never any halting or hesitation in his opinions or purposes . . . He never stood aloof from any good work, by whomsoever proposed, nor from any fellow-worker, however humble; and he was as ready to lead an unpopular cause as a popular one. A man of singular unselfishness, of rare determination, perseverance, and courage, with an unfailing perception of right and wrong, and a wise and far-reaching sagacity, he had one single aim and purpose—to do good. That undaunted courage, that burning zeal, that tender sympathy, all sprang from deep-rooted convictions of the duties and responsibilities of life as revealed in the Holy Scriptures . . .

Snobbery

One consequence of the high social position of the aristocracy and the landed classes generally—and of their hierarchical hordes of retainers—was a strong consciousness of relative orders of preference in society. In the first extract *Punch*, xii (1847) gently describes the 'club snob'. In the second, George Eliot (Mary Ann Evans, 1819–80) gives the views of the rascally landlord Mr. Chubb (in her novel, *Felix Holt, The Radical*, 1866).

(1) As I came into the coffee-room at the No Surrender, old JAWKINS was holding out to a knot of men, who were yawning, as usual. There he stood, waving the *Standard*, and swaggering before the fire. "What," says he, "did I tell Peel last year? If you

touch the Corn Laws, you touch the Sugar Question; if you touch the Sugar, you touch the Tea. I am no monopolist. I am a liberal man, but I cannot forget that I stand on the brink of a precipice; and if we are to have Free Trade, give me reciprocity. And what was SIR ROBERT PEEL'S answer to me? MR. JAWKINS, he said"—

Here JAWKINS'S eye suddenly turning on your humble servant, he stopped his sentence, with a guilty look—his stale, old, stupid sentence, which every one of us at the Club have heard over and over again.

JAWKINS is a most pertinacious Club Snob. Every day he is at that fireplace, holding that *Standard*, of which he reads up the leading article, and pours it out, *ore rotundo*, with the most astonishing composure, into the face of his neighbour, who has just read every word of it in the paper . . . By evening-paper time he is at the Club . . .

(2) "Yes," said Felix, dryly; "I should think there are some sorts of work for which you are just fitted."

"Ah, you see that? Well, we understand one another. You're no Tory; no more am I. And if I'd got four hands to show at a nomination, the Debarrys shouldn't have one of 'em. My idee is, there's a deal too much of their scutchins and their moniments in Treby church. What's their scutchins mean? They're a sign with little liquor behind 'em; that's how I take it. There's nobody can give account of 'em as I ever heard."

The Hierarchy of Servants

Increasing middle-class prosperity was reflected in the ever-rising number of domestic servants. In 1861 Mrs. Isabella Beeton's celebrated *Book of Household Management* gave advice on 'the servant problem'. The work became a Victorian classic, first in monthly parts and later as a best-selling volume, during Mrs. Beeton's short life (1836–64).

THE NUMBER OF MEN-SERVANTS IN A FAMILY varies according to the wealth and position of the master, from the owner of the ducal mansion, with a retinue of attendants, at the head of which is the chamberlain and house-steward, to the occupier of the humbler house, where a single footman, or even the odd man-of-all-work, is the only male retainer. The majority of gentlemen's establishments probably comprise a servant out of livery, or butler, a footman and coachman, or coachman and groom, where the horses exceed two or three.

To a certain extent the number of men-servants kept is regulated by the number of women servants, this statement, of course, not applying to such out-door servants as coachman, groom, or gardener.

Occasionally a parlour-maid is kept instead of a second footman, or a kitchen or scullery-maid does the work in the way of boot-cleaning, etc., that would fall to a third footman or page. A man cook is now more rarely to be found in private service than formerly, women having found it expedient to bring their knowledge of the culinary art more to the level of the *chef* . . .

Mid-Century England

The post-office employee and novelist Anthony Trollope described mid-century attitudes in rural shires in his Barsetshire novels. The third 'chronicle', *Dr. Thorne* (1858), contained the following comment on the nature of mid-century English society.

. . . England is not yet a commercial country in the sense in which that epithet is used for her; and let us still hope that she will not soon become so. She might surely as well be called feudal England, or chivalrous England. If in western civilised Europe there does exist a nation among whom there are high signors, and with whom the owners of the land are the true aristocracy, the aristocracy that is trusted as being best and fittest to rule, that nation is the English. Choose out the ten leading men of each great European people. Choose them in France, in Austria, Sardinia, Prussia, Russia, Sweden, Denmark, Spain (?), and then select the ten in England whose names are best known as those of leading statesmen; the result will show in which country there still exists the closest attachment to, the sincerest trust in, the old feudal and now so-called landed interests.

England a commercial country! Yes; as Venice was. She may excel other nations in commerce, but yet it is not that in which she most prides herself, in which she most excels. Merchants as such are not the first men among us; though it perhaps be open, barely open, to a merchant to become one of them. Buying and selling is good and necessary; it is very necessary, and may, possibly, be very good; but it cannot be the noblest work of man; and let us hope that it may not in our time be esteemed the noblest work of an Englishman.

The 'Land Monopoly'

Cobden and his allies became increasingly hostile to the so-called 'land monopoly' of the great estates, protected by primogeniture and entail. On 1 October 1851 Cobden wrote, rather despairingly, to Bright on the subject (from Morley, *op. cit.*).

. . . We have made no progress upon the subject of primogeniture during the last twenty years. Public opinion is either indifferent or favourable to the system of large properties kept together by entail. If you want a proof, see how every successful trader buys an estate, and tries to perpetuate his name in connexion with 'that ilk' by creating an eldest son. It is probably the only question on which, if an attempt were made to abolish the present system, France could be again roused to revolution; and yet we are in England actually hugging our feudal fetters! But we are a Chinese people. What a lucky thing it is that our grandmothers did not deform their feet *à la Chinoise*! If so, we should have had a terrible battle to emancipate women's toes . . .

'Landlord Rule'

John Bright (1811–89) the Quaker Rochdale manufacturer and politician, shared Cobden's dislike of the landowning aristocracy. A typical attack was contained in his speech of 19 December 1845 to the Anti-Corn Law League rally in Covent Garden (here quoted from G. M. Trevelyan, *The Life of John Bright*, 1913).

We have had landlord rule longer, far longer than the life of the oldest man in this vast assembly and I would ask you to look at the results of that rule. The landowners have had unlimited sway in Parliament and in the provinces. Abroad the history of our country is the history of war and rapine: at home, of debt, taxes, and rapine too. In all the great contests in which we have been engaged we have found that this ruling class have taken all the honours, while the people have taken all the scars. No sooner was the country freed from the horrible contest which was so long carried on with the Powers of Europe, than this [corn] law, by their partial legislation, was enacted—far more hostile to British interests than any combination of foreign powers has ever proved. We find them legislating corruptly: they pray daily that in their legislation they may discard all private ends and partial affections, and after prayers they sit down to make a law for the purpose of extorting from all the consumers of food a higher price than it is worth, that the extra price may find its way into the pockets of the proprietors of land, these proprietors being the very men by whom this infamous law is sustained . . .

First View of England

Louis Simond (1767–1831) had emigrated from Lyons to the United States in 1789 and first visited Britain for an extensive 21-month tour in late 1809. He recorded his impressions in his *Journal of a Tour and Residence in Great Britain during the Years 1810 and 1811* (1815), from his arrival on Christmas Eve, 1809.

We found ourselves, on waking this morning early, anchored in the harbour of Falmouth, where we had arrived in the night, after a speedy and prosperous passage of twenty-one days from America, without a single storm to describe, or any extraordinary occurrence . . . The town of Falmouth—little, old, and ugly—was seen on our left, and another assemblage of little old houses on our right . . . The custom-house officers mustered in crowds about the ship, ransacking every corner—barrels and bags, boxes and hampers of half-consumed provisions, empty bottles and full ones, musty straw and papers, and all that the dampness of a ship, pitch and tallow, and the human species confined in a narrow space, can produce of offensive sights and smells, were exposed to open day. These custom-house officers have seized a certain surplus of stores beyond what a ship is allowed to bring in port, whether the voyage has been long or short. I overheard the head seizer asking the captain whether he preferred having his wine or his spirits seized; and the captain seemed to take the proposal in very good part, and told me afterwards the man was very *friendly* to him . . .

The houses, in a confused heap, crowd on the water; the tide washes their foundation; a black wall, built of rough stones, that stand on end, to facilitate the draining of the water, and steps, overgrown with sea-weeds, to ascend to the doors. Through one of these odd entrances I introduced my companions to the hotel—a strange, old, low building, extremely neat inside, with a tempting larder full in view, displaying, on shelves of tiles, fish of all sorts, fat fowls, &c. Well-dressed servants, civil and attentive, wait our commands . . . It is Sunday. The men are, many of them, in volunteer uniforms, and look well enough for citizen-soldiers; the women highly dressed, or rather highly undressed, in extremely thin draperies, move about with an elastic gait on the light fantastic patten, making a universal clatter of iron on the pavements. Ruddy countenances, and *embonpoint*, are very general and striking. Great astonishment was awakened at the sight of a sedan-chair; vibrating along on two poles. A monstrous carriage turned the corner of a street, overloaded with passengers—a dozen, at least, on the top, before, and behind; all this resting on four high slender wheels, drawn along full speed on a rough unequal pavement. We observed some men, in old-fashioned cocked-hats with silver lace, compelling a Quaker to shut his shop—which was opened again the moment they were gone. An elegant post-chaise and four stopped at the door. A young man, fat and fair, with the face and figure of a baby, six feet high, alighted from it; it was the first man of quality we had seen in England. He goes, we are told, to lounge away his *ennui* and his idleness beyond seas—a premature attack of the *maladie du pays* . . .

Dinner announced, suspended our observations; it was served in our own apartments. We had three small dishes, dressed very inartificially (an English cook only boils and roasts), otherwise very good. The table-linen and glass, and servants, remarkably neat, and in good order. At the dessert apples no bigger than walnuts, and without taste, which are said to be the best the country produces.

The London Rich and the London Poor

The Times of 12 October 1843 startlingly contrasted adjacent areas of the capital. Several contemporaries were equally horrified by reports by doctors and Poor Law officials on 'downtown' conditions.

. . . Within the precincts of wealth, gaiety, and fashion, nigh the regal grandeur of St. James, close on the palatial splendours of

Bayswater, on the confines of the old and new aristocratic quarters, in a district where the cautious refinement of modern design has refrained from creating one single tenement for poverty; which seems, as it were, dedicated to the exclusive enjoyment of . . . wealth . . . *there* want, and famine, and disease, and vice stalk in all their kindred horrors . . . Let all men remember this—that within the most courtly precincts of the richest city of God's earth, there may be found, night after night, winter after winter, women—young in years, old in sin and suffering—outcasts from society—ROTTING FROM FAMINE, FILTH AND DISEASE. Let them remember this, and learn not to theorize but to act. God knows there is much room for action nowadays.

Advertisements

In 1847 *Punch* (xii) protested against the growth of advertising. Founded in 1841, under the editorship of Mark Lemon the paper regularly commented on the social scene.

Advertisements are spreading all over England,—they have crept under the bridges—have planted themselves right in the middle of the Thames—have usurped the greatest thoroughfares—and are now just on the point of invading the omnibuses. Advertising is certainly the great vehicle for the age . . . We are haunted with advertisements enough in all shapes, tricks, and disguises. The Penny Post has increased the distribution of them most prolifically . . .

Let us be a nation of shopkeepers as much as we please, but there is no necessity that we should become a nation of advertisers . . .

The Army

Despite periodic reforms, military life remained bleak and ill-paid throughout the century. Long service, bad conditions and a severe disciplinary code remained normal. The following extract is taken from *Army Form B.50* (*Account Book*) (Calcutta, 1882). Some of its classic phrases will be familiar to recipients of much later Army pay books.

OBEDIENCE IS THE FIRST DUTY OF A SOLDIER

NOTES FROM THE ARMY ACT

For the following offences a soldier is liable at all times to the penalty of death or of any less punishment:—

Shamefully abandoning a post.

Shamefully casting away his arms, ammunition or tools in the presence of the enemy.

Treacherously holding correspondence with or assisting the enemy.

Doing anything to imperil the success of Her Majesty's forces.

Cowardice before the enemy.

Mutiny.

Personal violence to a superior, or disobedience to his lawful commands when in the execution of his office.

For the following offences, if committed on Active Service, a soldier is liable to the penalty of death or any less punishment, and if committed not on Active Service, to imprisonment, or any less punishment:—

Deserting, attempting to desert, or persuading any other person to desert. (N.B.—A soldier under orders for Active Service who deserts or attempts to desert is liable to the penalty of death).

Leaving his Commanding Officer or breaking into any house in search of plunder.

Leaving his guard, picquet, patrol or post without orders.

Forcing a safeguard, or sentry.

Impeding, or when called on, refusing to assist the Provost Marshal or any of his assistants.

Doing violence to a person bringing supplies to the Forces, or detaining stores proceeding to the Forces.

Intentionally occasioning false alarms, or treacherously giving up the countersign.

When a sentry, sleeping or being drunk on his post or leaving his post without orders.

Penal servitude, or any less punishment under all conditions of service, may be awarded the following offences:—

Deserting for the second or any subsequent time.

Fraudulent Enlistment for the second or any subsequent offence.

Stealing or embezzling any public money or goods.

When in command of a picquet or guard, releasing a prisoner without due authority.
Wilfully allowing a prisoner to escape.
Enlisting after having been discharged with disgrace.

On Active Service, Penal Servitude or any less punishment may be awarded if a soldier is found guilty of:—

Leaving the ranks without orders.
Wilfully destroying or damaging property.
Being taken prisoner through neglect.
Creating alarm or despondency.
Striking or offering violence to, or using threatening or insubordinate language to, or disobeying the order of a Superior.

All other offences, including any act to the prejudice of good order and military discipline not specially mentioned, may be punished by imprisonment depending on the nature and degree of the offence.

The following are some of the graver offences of this class:—

Traitorous words regarding the Sovereign.
Malingering or feigning disease.
Wilfully maiming himself or any other soldier.

A Military Crime

Alexander Somerville (1811–85), the son of a Scottish agricultural labourer joined the 2nd Royal North British Dragoons (the Scots Greys) in 1831 and was stationed in radical Birmingham in the following year. His regiment was prepared to put down reformers' risings during the crisis of 1832, but Somerville wrote to the ultra-radical *Weekly Dispatch* (of 27 May) declaring that while willing to 'put down . . . disorderly conduct', he and his fellow-troopers 'would have never, never, never raised an arm' against 'the liberties of their country'. A regimental court martial tried him ostensibly for refusing orders at the riding school. Somerville described the trial and the infliction of the sentence in his *Autobiography of a Working Man* (1848), using the court's minutes.

'*First evidence.*

'Lieutenant and Riding master Gillies being duly sworn, states to the court—

'That the prisoner, on the morning of the 28th inst., when taking his lesson in the riding school, turned in out of the ride and threw himself from his horse. Evidence asked him his reason for so doing. He, prisoner, told evidence, "because he could not ride the horse". He, evidence, told him it was his duty to teach him to ride his horse, and he, evidence, ordered him to mount the horse again, which the prisoner refused to do. Evidence then sent for the corporal and a file of the guard to take the prisoner to confinement, and on their arrival evidence again ordered the prisoner to remount his horse, which he again refused' . . .

'*Defence*

'The prosecution being here closed, the prisoner is put upon his defence, who states to the court that the horse he was riding was one upon which he never was before, and being unqualified to sit steady upon the horse, the prisoner found it to give way to the reins frequently, which he could not keep easy'.

'*Opinion*

'The court, having duly considered the evidence against the prisoner, are of opinion that he is guilty of the crime laid to his charge'. . . .

'*Sentence*

'The court, having found the prisoner "guilty" of the crime laid to his charge, the same being in breach of the Articles of War, do by virtue thereof sentence him, the prisoner, Alexander Somerville, to receive two hundred lashes in the usual manner of the regiment, at such time and place as the commanding officer may think fit—

M. J. FAWCETT, President. Approved, C. WYNDHAM, Major, commanding Second Dragoons'.

A Military Problem

A. W. Kinglake (1809–91) had become famous with the publication of *Eothen* (1844), a record of travels in the Ottoman empire during 1834 and 1835. In *The Invasion of the Crimea* (9 vols., 1877–88 edn.) he reported on the bureaucratic troubles of the Army during the Crimean War of 1854–56. British public opinion was shocked by the suffering of its Army, under the 1st Lord Raglan (1788–1855) and by the abominable provisions for medical and other supplies—as noted by *The*

Times reporter Dr. W. H. Russell (1820–1907) and the pioneer nursing reformer Florence Nightingale (1820–1910).

If the Director-General of the Army Medical Department wished to furnish to our hospitals in the East some kinds of supplies, as, for instance, wine, sago, arrowroot, he had to send his purpose revolving in an orrery of official bodies: for first, he well knew, he must move the Horse Guards, and the Horse Guards must move the Ordnance, and the Ordnance must set going the Admiralty, and the Admiralty must give orders to the Victualling Office, and the Victualling Office must concert measures with the Transport Office, and the Transport Office (having only three transports) must appeal to the private ship-owners, in the hope that sooner or later they would furnish the sea-carriage needed; so that then the original requisition becoming at last disentangled, might emerge after all from the labyrinth, and—resulting in an actual, visible shipment of wine, sago, arrowroot—begin to receive fulfilment.

PART TWO

The Land

It is in the country that the Englishman gives scope to his natural feelings. He breaks loose gladly from the cold formalities and negative civilities of the town; throws off his habit of shy reserve and becomes joyous and free-hearted . . . The taste of the English in the cultivation of land, and in what is called landscape gardening is unrivalled.

Washington Irving (1783–1859), *Sketch Book of Geoffrey Crayon, Gent.* (1865)

The true strength of the English Aristocracy and nationality abides in the many thousands of families of Landed Proprietors, and who, in virtue of their property, are the magistrates . . . They do not disdain, as the old French nobility did, to accept administrative, legislative, and judicial functions. Far from it—they have almost monopolised them . . .

Comte de Montalembert (1810–70), *The Political Future of England* (1856)

A regular country squire, fit for a novel—short, chubby, good-looking, shooting, fishing, hunting, hospitable, kindly, a magistrate, and not an ounce of brains!

Elizabeth Grant, *Memoirs of a Highland Lady* (Edinburgh, 1897)

It is only necessary to enter a labourer's cottage in England, and to compare it with one such as our cultivators mostly inhabit, to perceive a difference in the general comforts of the two people . . . The French peasant . . . does not live so well as the English farm-labourer. He is not so well clothed, less comfortably lodged, and not so well fed . . .

Léonce de Lavergne (1809–80), *Rural Economy of England, Scotland and Ireland* (Edinburgh, 1855)

Theirs is yon House that holds the Parish-Poor,
Whose walls of mud scarce bear the broken door;
There, where the putrid vapours, flagging, play,
And the dull wheel hums doleful through the day;
There Children dwell who know no Parents' care;
Parents, who know no Children's love, dwell there . . .

George Crabbe (1754–1832), 'The Village' (1783)

A lady's maid is a *very great* character *indeed*, and would be much more unwilling to take her tea with, or speak familiarly to, a footman or a housemaid than I should.

Elizabeth Davies Bancroft, *Letters from England 1846–9* (New York, 1904)

When they see poor folk sick or hungry before their eyes, they pull out their purses fast enough, God bless them; for they wouldn't like to be so themselves. But the oppression that goes on all the year round, and the filth, and the lying, and the swearing, and the profligacy, that go on all the year round, and the sickening weight of debt, and the miserable grinding anxiety from rent-day to rent-day, and Saturday night to Saturday night, that crushes a man's soul down, and drives every thought out of his head but how he is to fill his stomach and warm his back, and keep a house over his head, till he daren't for his life take his thoughts one moment off the meat that perishest—oh, sir, they never felt this . . .

Charles Kingsley (1819–75), *Yeast* (1848)

Agricultural Improvement

In 1770 the East Anglian farmer-journalist Arthur Young (1741–1820) described in his *Six Month's Tour through the North of England* the improvements effected on the great Wentworth Woodhouse estate in South Yorkshire by the 2nd Marquess of Rockingham (d. 1782). Young later became secretary to the first Board of Agriculture.

Upon turning his attention to agriculture, his Lordship found the husbandry of the *West Riding* of *Yorkshire* extremely deficient in numerous particulars: It was disgusting to him to view so vast a property, cultivated in so slovenly a manner; eager to substitute better methods in the room of such unpleasing as well as unprofitable ones, he determined to exert himself with spirit in the attempt; and he executed the noble scheme in a manner that does honour to his penetration.—A very few particulars, among many of the common practice, will shew how much this country wanted a *Rockingham* to animate its cultivation.

1. Large tracts of land, both grass and arable, yielded but a trifling profit, for want of draining . . .

2. The pastures and meadows of this country were universally laid down in ridge and furrow, a practice highly destructive of profit, and detestable to the eye . . .

3. The culture of turnips was become common, but in such a method that their introduction was undoubtedly a real mischief: *viz.* without hoeing . . .

4. The implements used in agriculture through this tract were insufficient for a vigorous culture . . .

. . . His Lordship's conduct was judicious and spirited. He has upwards of 2,000 acres of land in his hands; and began their improvement by draining such as were wet, rightly considering this part of husbandry as the *sine qua non* of all others . . .

The Rural Poor

In 1795 David Davies, Rector of Barkham in Berkshire, published *The Case of Labourers in Husbandry*, trying to account for current poverty in the countryside. Among other things, he blamed the enclosure movement.

The depriving the peasantry of all landed property has beggared multitudes. It is plainly agreeable to sound policy, that as many individuals as possible in a state should possess an interest in the soil; because this attaches them strongly to the country and its constitution, and makes them zealous and resolute in defending them. But the gentry of this kingdom seem to have lost sight of this wise and salutary policy. Instead of giving to labouring people a valuable stake in the soil, the opposite measure has so long prevailed, that but few cottages, comparatively, have *now* any land about them. Formerly many of the lower sort of people occupied tenements of their own, with parcels of land about them, or they rented such of others. On these they raised for themselves a considerable part of their subsistence, without being obliged, as now, to buy all they want at shops. And this kept numbers from coming to the parish . . .

The Speenhamland System

A general meeting of Berkshire justices, held in the Pelican Inn at Speenhamland on 6 May 1795, devised a new method of aiding the rural poor, as the *Reading Mercury* reported five days later. This wage-subsidy system spread to other counties.

Resolved unanimously, That the present state of the Poor does require further assistance than has been generally given them.

Resolved, That it is not expedient for the Magistrates to grant that assistance by regulating the wages of Day Labourers, according to the direction of the Statutes of the 5th Elizabeth and 1st James: But the Magistrates very earnestly recommend to the Farmers and others throughout the Country, to increase the pay of their Labourers in proportion to the present price of provisions; and agreeable thereto, the Magistrates now present, have unanimously resolved that they will, in their several divisions, make the following calculations and allowances for relief of all poor and industrious men and their families, who to the satisfaction of the Justices of their Parish, shall endeavour (as far as they can) for their own support and maintenance. That is to say, when the Gallon Loaf of Second Flour, weighing 8 lbs. 11 ozs. shall cost 1s., then every poor and industrious man shall have for his own support 3s. weekly, either produced by his own or his family's labour, or an allowance from the poor rates, and for the support of his wife and every other of his family 1s. 6d. When the Gallon Loaf shall cost 1s. 4d., then every poor and industrious man shall have 4s. weekly for his own, and 1s. 10d. for the support of every other of his family.

And so in proportion as the price of bread rises or falls, that is to say, 3d. to the man and 1d. to every other of the family, on every penny which the loaf rises above 1s.

Labourers in Leicestershire

Sir F. M. Eden (1766–1809), founder of the Globe Insurance Company, published his famous *State of the Poor* in 1797. It was 'a history of the labouring classes in England, with parochial reports.' The following extract is taken from the report on Ashby de la Zouch.

The war has been very injurious to the commercial interests of this town. Prices of provisions are: Beef, $3\frac{1}{2}$d. to 5d. per lb.; mutton, 5d.; veal, 3d. to 4d.; butter, 9d. to $10\frac{1}{2}$d.; bread flour, 4s. per st.; potatoes, 5d. per gall. (about autumn they are generally 2d. or 3d. per gall.); milk, $1\frac{1}{2}$d. per qt. Spinners of wool earn from 1s. 6d. to 3s. a week; wool combers from 12s. to 14s. a week; stocking weavers in general, 7s. to 17s. a week, but a few earn £1.15s.; hatters from 12s. to 20s.; labourers in husbandry, till within the last year, have 4s. a week in winter and 6s. in summer; now (1797) they have 6s. in winter, and 7s. to 9s. in summer, and victuals. Number of ale-houses reduced from 25 to 21 since 1794. There are 8 friendly societies, with 40 to 80 members apiece . . . Near four-fifths of the inhabitants now chargeable belong to the manufactories. Labourers in husbandry maintain their families much better than manufacturers, though their wages are lower. They are more economical and do not so much frequent the public house, so that they can support families of 3, 4 or 5 children without parish relief, while the manufacturers, having often drunken associates spend the money in ale-houses which should be applied to domestic uses, and having once applied for relief become totally regardless of that sense of shame, which is the best preservative of independence.

Enclosure in Cambridgeshire

Arthur Young welcomed the agricultural improvements following enclosure, but also often recorded the social changes which ensued. In *Annals of Agriculture* xiii (1804) he described Maulden in Cambridgeshire.

The common very extensive. I conversed with a farmer, and several cottagers: one of them said, inclosing would ruin England; it was worse than ten wars: Why, my friend, what have you lost by it? *I kept four cows before the parish was inclosed, and now I do not keep so much as a goose. And you ask me what I lose by it!* Their accounts of advantages, especially when they are gone, are not to be credited.

Patient Poor in Norfolk

James Woodforde (1740–1803) was the late eighteenth-century incumbent of Weston Longeville in Norfolk. His *Diary of a Country Parson* (ed. John Beresford 1924–31), is a classic account of quiet country life. There follows his entry for 22 December 1800.

We breakfasted, dined, &c. again at home. Yesterday being Sunday and St. Thomas's Day the Poor deferred going after their Christmas Gifts till this Morning. I had at my House fifty five, gave only to 53, the other two not living in the Parish. Gave in the Whole this Morn' at 6d. each in Number 53. 1.6.6. Dinner today, boiled Beef & a rost Chicken. I was but poorly to day after dinner, giddy &c. Sitting too long to day at one time I think. The Poor to day behaved extremely well indeed tho' times were extremely hard for them. They all appeared very patient and submissive. Mr. Press Custance sent us a Pheasant this Even'.

Distress in Suffolk

During the post-war depression the Board of Agriculture inquired into the state of the industry in 1816. From Suffolk Major Edward Moor reported on local agriculture. His account was printed in *Agricultural State of the Kingdom* (1816).

As a magistrate for this county, heretofore so wealthy and happy, no day, scarcely no hour of any day passes, without some occurrence bringing before me some instance of agricultural distress . . . I could fill my sheet with a detail of [farmers'] distresses. Small farmers coming to parish officers for work—all classes of farmers employing more men than they want, and would employ, if left to their own choice; though they can so ill afford this, it is better than maintaining able men to do nothing, and living upon the rates . . . It . . . appears to me that such of us as have capital are living on it; those who have not (or credit, which comes to the same thing) must sink. Those who were rich are virtually bankrupts. Those who were poor are paupers.

Change in the Countryside

William Cobbett (1762–1835), the Tory-Radical journalist, regularly condemned the passing of old ways in the countryside in his *Political Register*. His vivid descriptions of many counties were largely reprinted in *Rural Rides* (1830). In the following extracts (written at Burghclere in November 1821 and Reigate in October 1825) he typically attacks the passing of traditional habits among old gentry and socially-aspiring farmers.

(1) We intended to have a hunt; but the fox-hounds came across and rendered it impracticable. As an instance of the change which rural customs have undergone since the hellish paper-system has been so furiously at work, I need only mention the fact, that, forty years ago, there were *five* packs of fox-hounds and *ten* packs of *harriers* kept within *ten miles* of Newbury; and that now there is *one* of the former (kept, too, by *subscription*) and *none* of the latter, except the few couple of dogs kept by Mr. Budd! "So much the better," says the shallow fool, who cannot duly estimate the difference between a resident *native* gentry, attached to the soil, known to every farmer and labourer from their childhood, frequently mixing with them in those pursuits where all artificial distinctions are lost, practising hospitality without ceremony, from habit and not on calculation; and a gentry, only now-and-then residing at all, having no relish for country-delights, foreign in their manners, distant and haughty in their behaviour, looking to the soil only for its rents, viewing it as a mere object of speculation, unacquainted with its cultivators, despising them and their pursuits, and relying, for influence, not upon the good will of the vicinage, but upon the dread of their power.

(2) The land produces, on an average, what it always produced, but there is a new distribution of the produce. This 'Squire Charington's father used, I dare say, to sit at the head of the oak table along with his men, say grace to them, and cut up the meat and the pudding. He might take a cup of *strong beer* to himself, when they had none; but that was pretty nearly all the difference in their manner of living. So that *all* lived well. But the '*squire* had many *wine-decanters* and *wine-glasses* and "*a dinner set*", and a "*breakfast set*" and "*dessert knives*", and these evidently imply carryings on and a consumption that must of necessity have greatly robbed the long oak table if it had remained fully tenanted. That long table could not share in the work of the decanters and the dinner set. Therefore it became almost untenanted; the labourers retreated to hovels, called cottages; and, instead of board and lodging, they got money; so little of it as to enable the employer to drink wine; but, then, that he might not reduce them to *quite*

starvation, they were enabled to come to him, in the *king's name*, and demand food *as paupers*. And now, mind, that which a man receives in the *king's name*, he knows well he has *by force*; and it is not in nature that he should *thank* anybody for it, and least of all the party *from whom it is forced*. . . . Is it, in short, surprising, if he resort to *theft* and *robbery*?

An Old Squire

Sydney Smith (1771–1845), the witty Whiggish clergyman who had charmed London society with his liberal, gay talk, was obliged by the Clergy Residence Act of 1803 to live near the Yorkshire parish of Foston-le-Clay, to which he had been appointed by Whig aid in 1806, when Edward Venables-Vernon became Archbishop of York in 1808. Reluctantly settling at Heslington, he described the squire and his wife in a 'tale . . . heard by [his daughter, Lady Holland] at various times in detached portions.' Lady Holland published the account in her *Memoir of the Rev. Sydney Smith* (1869 edn.).

A diner-out, a wit, and a popular preacher, I was suddenly caught up by the Archbishop of York, and transported to my living in Yorkshire, where there had not been a resident clergyman for a hundred and fifty years. Fresh from London, not knowing a turnip from a carrot, I was compelled to farm three hundred acres, and without capital to build a parsonage house. I asked and obtained three years' leave from the Archbishop, in order to effect an exchange if possible; and fixed myself meantime at a small village two miles from York, in which was a fine old house of the time of Queen Elizabeth, where resided the last of the Squires with his lady, who looked as if she had walked straight out of the Ark, or had been the wife of Enoch. He was a perfect specimen of the Trullibers of old; he smoked, hunted, drank beer at his door with his grooms and dogs, and spelt over the county paper on Sundays. At first he heard I was a Jacobin and a dangerous fellow, and turned aside as I passed: but at length, when he found the peace of the village undisturbed, harvests much as usual, Juno and Ponto uninjured, he first bowed, then called, and at last reached such a pitch of confidence that he used to bring the papers, that I might explain the difficult words to him; actually discovered that I had made a joke, laughed till I thought he would have died of convulsions, and ended by inviting me to see his dogs.

A Fictional Squire

Charles Apperley (1779–1843) was a Denbigh soldier and farmer who (as 'Nimrod') became a popular writer for *The Sporting Record* and the historian of the rough, eccentric sporting squires who exchanged Latin tags while risking their lives hunting over high-hedged Leicestershire or racing coaches along newly-macadamised roads. His novel *The Life of A Sportsman* (1832) describes real events, but starts with a portrait of an idealised squire.

In the latter part of the last century, in one of the finest of the midland counties of England, lived Andrew Raby, a commoner of large possessions, and of very old English blood. When, however, I use the term 'possessions', I do not desire to convey the idea of his having an income sufficient to keep up a degree of pomp and dignity equal to that of his titled superiors, but such as enabled him fully to support the respectable and honourable station of an English country gentleman, and to indulge in all those pursuits which were congenial to his own taste, and, likewise, to exercise almost unbounded hospitality towards his friends. In fact, his rental was a little above ten thousand pounds per annum; which, when the usual drawbacks of agencies, repairs, and other heavy outgoings attendant on landed property, in addition to an annuity he paid to a sister, were deducted, left him—for he had no interest to pay to mortgagees . . . a clear annual income of seven thousand pounds; at least he reckoned not on more, on a fair average of years. With this comparatively limited income, he inhabited a house suitable for a man of twice his means . . . Planned after the fashion of the Elizabethan age, Amstead Abbey stood on an island, formed by a deep moat, and within the palings of an extensive and finely timbered park, containing a herd of deer sufficiently ample for the use of a private gentleman; the gardens, too, were large, no less than three hundred yards of "*glass*"—as forcing houses are technically denominated—being visible in them, exclusive of hot walls. A farm of three hundred acres of the best staple land of the county was in occupation, under the eye of a Scotch bailiff . . .

Mr. Raby's establishment consisted, indoors, of a butler and two footmen, with all the requisite females, and was only deficient in one respect—it wanted the *man cook* to aid the English kitchen-maid; but against this there was a prejudice which time has since removed . . .

There was one species of luxury—refinement, indeed, it may be termed, in reference to those times—in which Mr. Raby indulged; and this was the selection of his footmen and postillions. The first were London-bred; he declared that he never saw a country-bred footman who could bring a message into a room, or an under-butler of the same genus, who could clean a service of place . . . His postillions . . . were always Hounslow-bred ones; that is to say, sons of Hounslow post-boys, having had their education on the road . . .

The out-of-doors establishment was still more numerous. There was a pack of harriers in the kennel, six able coach-horses in one stable, ten hunters in another, besides a hack or two to go to post, or to carry "how do ye do's" about the country—no sinecure in those days: a capital team of spaniels for cock-shooting, pointers and setting dogs for partridges and hares, under the care of an experienced game-keeper, and a small kennel of greyhounds to contend for prizes at the neighbouring coursing meetings. One appendage to the present establishment of an English gentleman, however, was wanting: I mean a band of night-watchers to protect the game from poachers . . .

But the reader may well ask how all this was done on an income of seven thousand pounds.—By management, in the first place; and, in the next, by only occasionally visiting London for the season, Mr. Raby having little inclination for the bustle and hurry of a town life . . .

A Tory Squire

Anthony Trollope (1815–1882) described a variety of 'genteel' rural types—aristocrats, clergy and squires—in his Barsetshire novels, in the 1850s and 1860s. The future Liberal candidate for Beverley (in 1868) gently pictured an old-style Tory Protectionist squire and antiquarian in *Barchester Towers* (1857).

Wilfred Thorne, Esq., of Ullathorne, was the squire of St. Ewold's; or rather the squire of Ullathorne; for the domain of the modern landlord was of wider notoriety than the fame of the ancient saint. He was a fair specimen of what that race has come to in our days, which a century ago was, as we are told, fairly represented by Squire Western. If that representation be a true one, few classes of men can have made faster strides in improvement. Mr. Thorne, however, was a man possessed of quite a sufficient number of foibles to lay him open to much ridicule. He was still a bachelor, being about fifty and was not a little proud of his person. When living at home at Ullathorne there was not much room for such pride, and there therefore he always looked like a gentleman, and like that which he certainly was, the first man in his parish. But during the month or six weeks which he annually spent in London, he tried so hard to look like a great man there also, which he certainly was not, that he was put down as a fool by many at his club . . . He was a great proficient in all questions of genealogy, and knew enough of almost every gentleman's family in England to say of what blood and lineage were descended all those who had any claim to be considered as possessors of any such luxuries. For blood and lineage he himself had a most profound respect. He counted back his own ancestors to some period long antecedent to the Conquest.

Rural Society

William Busfeild Ferrand (1809–89), the Tory Protectionist M.P. for Knaresborough and squire of Harden Grange near Bingley, was an advocate of allotment schemes. In 1844, supported by Disraeli and Lord John Manners, he opened a Bingley scheme. His speech was reported in the *Leeds Intelligencer*, 19 October, and *The Times*, 14 October 1844.

When I inform the party here present that this is the proudest, if I do not say the happiest moment of my life, I can assure you that I utter a sincere truth, for if there be one position more than another in which an English country gentleman may stand proud and happy in his own parish, it is when he is surrounded by every grade of society within it, cheering him when his health is proposed at a vast meeting like the present. But let me tell you that the pride of the moment is enhanced in a tenfold degree when I recollect that this meeting is assembled for the purpose of so much rejoicing and when I also behold the operatives of our native parish placed for the evening on a level with ourselves . . . My friends, this is not the first time that such a glorious meeting has assembled in this parish. There has, God knows, too long been an intervening space between such cordial rejoicings. Shame on those who have neglected their duty in this respect, and on those who have neglected to inform them of their duty. The working classes of this parish have not hesitated to tell me what was my duty. I listened to their counsel; I followed their advice; and it is the working classes who have placed me where I am. Behold, my friends, the dawn of the sunshine of ancient days on our native land! Behold, this evening is new seed sown; some of you have already reaped the crops of former sowings. May God give the increase to all our fellow-countrymen!

A Free-Trader's Comment

Free-Trade manufacturers, angered by Lord Ashley's and other agricultural Tories' campaigns for factory reform, often retorted by condemning rural conditions. One of their agents was Alexander Somerville (1811–85), a radical ex-cavalry trooper, whose book *The Whistler at the Plough and Free Trade* (Manchester, 1852) largely consisted of reports on rural areas. Naturally, an early visit was made to the Ashley family's estates in Dorset.

I reached Cranbourne, and found a comfortable inn; talked with several people, who all agreed in stating that the labourers had a hard struggle to make a living.

All of them kept a pig or two; but they had to sell them to pay their rents.

There are cottage allotments of half an acre; but for various reasons . . . these are by no means as profitable as they might be.

Next morning . . . I found myself all at once in one of the sweetest little villages to be seen in England. It bears the name of St. Giles', and has a pleasant little church nestling among the lofty trees which overtop the entrance to Lord Shaftesbury's residence. A clear stream comes calmly along a green meadow, and the green meadow is fringed with houses, which are again surrounded with little gardens . . .

. . . The Rev. Mr. Moore, who holds the living, and who is possessed of considerable private property, is the chief promoter of the respectability . . . All the people residing there, and I conversed with many of them, speak most respectfully of the Earl of Shaftesbury, of Lord Ashley his son, and of the other members of the family; but though they were admitted to be kind to those immediately about them, the words spoken in praise of Mr. Moore were the most frequently and zealously expressed.

There is a free school, principally supported by Lord Shaftesbury, and the dwelling houses are let to the working people at £2 a-year, each having a little piece of garden ground. His Lordship lets them have wood for cheap fuel, and for those who are too poor to bring turf fuel from a common some miles off, he sends his carts to fetch it. Mrs. Moore and some of the Shaftesbury family have established a savings' bank, in which a penny a-week is deposited, to be drawn out at Christmas at which time they, the patronesses, double the amount of each deposit, and bring a travelling haberdasher to the village, who exchanges certain kinds of goods for the money in the bank.

Mr. Moore has given a field, his glebe I believe, to some of the families in half-acre allotments, at the moderate rent of twelve shillings each, which is, however, more by four or five shillings the acre than the farmers pay. Lord Shaftesbury has also given a few allotments, but several families are still without them, because of the hostility which the farmers evince to any such system; they will take no man as a regular labourer who has an allotment.

. . . The farm labourers are as badly provided on the St. Giles' estate as elsewhere, save those resident in the village, where the clergyman's benevolence is largely diffused.

. . . With all this charity, the people were no better provided than they ought to have provided for themselves without it. The comfort is not wholesome which is promoted by charity . . .

Moreover, this giving of charity causes the recipients to feel that they require it, and that they were not previously as well provided for as they should be. Those living within four hundred yards of Lord Shaftesbury's gate, which distance includes the village and living under the unusually benevolent superintendence of a clergyman, may not feel any very hard privations. His Lordship allows those who work in his park nine shillings a-week, which is a shilling more than the farmers give, and two shillings more than is given in other parts of the county; with this, and the perquisites, and the allotments, they may rub on pretty comfortably, being constantly employed; but his Lordship's estates extend far beyond the village of St. Giles, whereas the charity stops there. What the labourers require is real independence, not of wealth, to be above working, nor of relationship to a master, to be beyond obedience, but of agreement—an agreement which binds the master equally with the servant.

The Revolt of the Squires

Protectionists were slow to organise against the League's propaganda. They could not believe that their leader would desert; they preferred Parliamentary debate to hustings demagogy. But their anger—best expressed during the great Repeal debates of 1846 by Disraeli and Lord George Bentinck—know no bounds when Peel repealed the Corn Law, the symbol of the landed estate. On 25 June, as the Lords passed the Corn Bill, the Commons overturned the Ministry over an Irish Coercion Bill. The long-mute county members took their revenge: some 70 M.P.s voted against their former leader. In a masterly description Disraeli pictured the scene (*Lord George Bentinck. A Political Biography*) (1852), as Peel was defeated by 73 votes.

. . . It was impossible that he could have marked them, without emotion: the flower of that great party which had been so proud to follow one who had been so proud to lead them. They were men to gain whose hearts and the hearts of their fathers had been the aim and exultation of his life. They had extended to him an unlimited confidence and an admiration without stint. They had stood by him in the darkest hour, and had borne him from the depths of political despair to the proudest of living positions. Right or wrong, they were men of honour, breeding, and refinement, high and generous character, great weight and station in the country, which they had ever placed at his disposal. They had been not only his followers but his friends; had joined in the same pastimes, drank from the same cup, and in the pleasantness of private life had often forgotten together the cares and strife of politics.

He must have felt something of this, while the Manners, the Somersets, the Bentincks, the Lowthers, and the Lennoxes, passed before him. And those country gentlemen, "those gentlemen of England", of whom, but five years ago, the very same building was ringing with his pride of being the leader—if his heart were hardened to Sir Charles Burrell, Sir William Jolliffe, Sir Charles Knightley, Sir John Trollope, Sir Edward Kerrison, Sir John Tyrrell, he surely must have had a pang, when his eye rested on Sir John Yarde Buller, his choice and pattern country gentleman . . .

They trooped on: all the men of metal and large-acred squires, whose spirit he had so often solicited in his fine conservative speeches in Whitehall gardens: Mr. Bankes, with a parliamentary name of two centuries, and Mr. Christopher from that broad Lincolnshire which protection had created; and the Mileses and the Henleys were there; and the Duncombes, the Liddells, and the Yorkes; and Devon had sent there the stout heart of Mr. Buck—and Wiltshire, the pleasant presence of Walter Long. Mr. Newdegate was there . . . and Mr. Alderman Thompson was there . . . But the list is too long; or good names remain behind.

High Farming

Following the repeal of the Corn Laws, agriculturalists increasingly adopted the 'high farming' techniques most notably recommended by James Caird (1816–92), a Wigtownshire farmer, in 1849. Caird advocated a reduction in the wheat acreage and the extension of mixed rotations. A tour of 32 counties for *The Times* in 1850–51 confirmed the superiority of mixed farming in the North and West over the wheat farms of the South and East. Many of his reports were republished in *English Agriculture in 1850–51* (1852), which demonstrated the variety of English farming.

In the preceding letters the detail of good farming are given much more at length than instances of the reverse, as it was from the first only that instruction could be drawn. This was from no want of examples of antiquated farming; for if we spent one day in examining Sir John Conroy's farm in Arborfield, Mr. Hudson's at Castleacre, Mr. Beasley's at Overstone, or Lord Hatherton's at Teddesley, we were almost sure to be wandering on the next through the mazes of frequent hedgerows, gazing at five horses elaborately doing the work of two, manure suffered to go to waste, cattle insufficiently housed and fed, land undrained and unproductive, and farmers complaining, not without reason, of their want of success. One day we learned the processes by which Mr. Huxtable economises labour, manure, and food; and the next we saw in operation an antiquated fanning machine, precisely the same as Arthur Young described it eighty years ago, and worthy of the days before the Conquest; manure treated as a troublesome nuisance; and cattle wasting their substance and their food by being kept starving in the open fields in winter. The same day on which we saw the steam engine of Mr. Thomas of Lidlington in Bedfordshire, with which he is enabled to thrash his wheat crop for 1d. a bushel, we found other farmers paying four or five times as much for the same operation, not so well done by hand.

Northern Farming

In the Northern industrial area Caird found successful and profitable (though not always efficient) agriculture. The following description of Wharfedale was published in *The Times*, 26 December 1850.

Crossing from Lancaster to the West Riding by the new line of the North-Western Railway, the traveller is carried up the picturesque valley of the Lune, whence, after passing through a bleak high country, he begins to descend into the grassy dales of the upland district of Yorkshire. Here in the sheltered valleys of the mountain limestone the fields are completely inclosed, and though for many miles yet scarcely a ploughed field is to be seen, there is everywhere evinced a skilful and painstaking management of grass. The mixed breed of short-horns, long-horns, Irish, and polled Galloways, which satisfy the dairy farmers of Lancashire, now give place to the improved short-horns, which, with occasional exceptions, are the distinctive breed of this riding . . .

At Bingley is the estate of Mr. Ferrand, whose advocacy of the cause of protection cannot be charged to selfishness, inasmuch as his tenants, depending chiefly on grass, must be greatly benefited by the prosperity of their customers in the neighbouring mills, who buy all they have to sell, while the winter food for their dairy cattle is improved and cheapened by the choice afforded them in the different sorts of low priced grain now imported into the country . . . In the neighbourhood of all the manufacturing towns the system of husbandry is chiefly grass farming for the supply of the towns with milk and butter . . .

From what has been said, it will be easily seen that the manufacturing districts of the West Riding have an agriculture of their own, as little influenced by the price of corn, or dependent on it for success, as that of South Lancashire . . .

Landownership

A long radical campaign against the 'land monopoly' provoked landowners to deny that ownership was increasingly concentrated among fewer families. In 1872 the Government agreed to organise a 'New Domesday' survey by the Local Government Board and four years later the 'Return of Owners of Land' (P.P. 1874, lxxii) was issued. It showed that while 973,011 people owned something in England or Wales, only 43,000 had more than 100 acres and 710 owned more than a quarter of the country. Caird's book *The Landed Interest* (1878) included an examination and explanation of this phenomenon.

The distribution of landed property in England, so far as ownership is concerned, is by the growing wealth of the country, constantly tending to a reduction in the number of small estates. This tendency is further promoted by the law, which permits entails and settlements, thus hindering the natural sale of land so dealt with; and also by rights of primogeniture, which prevent subdivision of landed property among the family in case of intestacy. Cultivation thus passes out of the hands of small owners into those of tenant-farmers, causing a gradual decrease of the agricultural population, and a proportionate increase of the towns. This has been much accelerated by a policy of Free Trade, which has at once opened up the markets of the world for our commerce, and for the produce of our mines and manufactures. These are advantageously interchanged for the corn and other agricultural products of foreign lands . . . More than one-half of our corn is now of foreign growth, and nearly one-fourth of our meat and dairy produce; whilst year by year our cornland is giving place to the more profitable produce afforded by the milk and grazing and market-garden farms, which are gradually extending their circle. Such produce renders the land more valuable, more tempting prices are offered for it to the small landowners, and their numbers decrease. Wealthy men from the mines and manufactories and shipping and colonial interests, and the learned professions, desire to become proprietors of land; and some competition exists between them and those landowners whose increasing wealth tempts them on suitable opportunities to enlarge the boundaries of their domains. Thus small proprietors are bought out, and agricultural landowners diminish in number; while, side by side with them, vast urban populations are growing up, having little other connection with the land than that of affording the best market for its produce.

A Squire's Finances

The best amendment to and synopsis of the 'Return' was *The Great Landowners of Great Britain and Ireland* (1878, 1879, 1883) by John Bateman (1839–1910), a small Essex squire. In the 1883 edition Bateman added further information and comments.

One reviewer in his critique says plaintively that "many who answer the requirements of Mr. Bateman's 3,000 acres and 3,000*L.* a-year by no means as an actual fact are in receipt of that income." True words, forsooth! For the benefit of guileless fundholders who have not as yet dabbled in land, I will give them what I consider a fair specimen of what a "landed income" of 5,000*L.* a-year means when analysed. My typical 5,000*L.* a-year squire shall be called—

STEADYMAN, JOHN, of Wearywork Hall, Cidershire
b. 1825, s. 1860, m. 1851

	acres		*g. an. Val.*
	3,500		5,000
		£	
Deduct for value in the rate-books put upon mansion, grounds, fishponds, etc.		220	
Deduct also the value put upon cottages lived in rent free by old workmen and pensioners of the late Mr. Steadyman		30	
		—	250
Leaving a clear rent roll of			£4,750

Now deduct as under:	£
His late father's two maiden sisters, Jane and Esther Steadyman, who each have a rent charge of 180*L.* per annum (*N.B.*—Both these old ladies seem immortal)	360
His mother, Lady Louisa Steadyman, a rent charge of	700
His sisters, Louisa, Marian, and Eva (all plain), each 150*L.*	450
His brother, Wildbore Steadyman, who was paid off and emigrated, but almost annually comes down on the good-natured head of the family for say	50
Mortgage on Sloppyside Farm and Hungry Hill (started when his father contested the county), interest	650
Do. on Wearywork End (started when his one pretty sister married Sir Shortt Shortt, Bart., and was paid off), interest	150

	£
His estate agent, Mr. Harrable, salary	150
Keep of a horse for do., 35*L.*; house for do. 45*L.*	80
Average of lawyer's bill (settlements, conveyances, etc.)	60
Average cost of farm repairs, etc.	350
Draining tiles furnished gratis to the tenants	40
Repairs to the family mansion	70
Voluntary church rate, school at Wearywork, do. at Wearywork End, pensions, and purely local charities (*N.B.*—If Mr. S. is a Roman Catholic, which I do not think he is, a private chaplain, chapel, school, etc. would increase this to at least 225*L.*)	175
Subscription to county (Liberal or Tory) registration Fund	10
Do. to the Cidershire Foxhounds (25*L.*) and Boggymore Harriers (5*L.*)	30
Do. to the Diocesan—? (everything now-a-days is Diocesan, we shall soon be taking pills from Diocesan dispensaries)	25
Other county subscriptions—hospitals, flower shows, races, &c.	35
Returned 15 per cent. of rents in "hard times", averaging perhaps one year in five (would that we could say so now, 1882)	150
Loss on occasional bankrupt tenants (Mr. Harrable dislikes distraint) average	30
Arrears of rent, say annually 300*L.*, loss of interest thereon at 5 per cent	15
Income-tax at 4*d.* in the pound on rents paid and unpaid	83
Insurance on all buildings	55
	£3,718

Leaving our worthy squire the magnificent annual sum of 1,032*L.* to live upon. The subscriptions, I think I may say, are hardly over painted—being, as folks say, "the least that can be expected from a person in Mr. S's position."

The New-Style Squire

Punch often assailed allegedly niggardly squires. 'The Fine Old English Gentleman of the Present Time' (*Punch*, xii, 1847) is typical.

I'll sing you a fine old song, improved by a modern pate,
Of a fine Old English Gentleman, who owns a large estate,
But pays the labourers on it at a very shabby rate.
Some seven shillings each a week for early work and late,
  Gives this fine Old English Gentleman, one of the present time.

His hall so brave is hung around with pictures, all in rows,
Of oxen that have gained the prize at agricultural shows,
And pigs so fat that they can't see an inch before their nose;
For the whole of his attention on his cattle he bestows,
  Like a fine Old English Gentleman, one of the present time.

In winter's cold, when poor and old for some assistance call,
And come to beg a trifle at the portals of his hall,
He refers them to the workhouse, that stands open wide for all;
For this is how the parish great relieve the parish small,
  Like this fine Old English Gentleman, one of the present time.

But rolling years will onwards flow, and time, alas! will fly,
And one of these fine days this fine Old Gentleman must die.
Ah! will he then bethink him, as he heaves life's latest sigh,
That he has done to others quite as he would be done by,
  As the true Old English Gentleman did in the olden time?

Aristocratic Society: An American View

At the top of the social hierarchy, great noblemen lived in splendid state in both the country and the metropolis. In his *Journal* the American Louis Simond described visits to (1) Chatsworth under the 6th Duke of Devonshire (1790–1858), (2) Blenheim Palace under the 3rd Duke of Marlborough (1733–1817) and (3) the Petworth of the 3rd Earl of Egremont (1751–1837).

(1) From the inn at Chatsworth, we walked across the park to the house, which is extremely handsome and palace-like, more so indeed than any house we have seen in England, although not so large as some others . . .

The domestics of these noble houses are generally as obsequious as inn-keepers, and from the same motives. Porters, footmen, gardeners, waited upon us immediately. The apartments have nothing remarkable; Gobelin tapestry, old, faded, and in wretched taste; and numerous pictures still worse. It is quite inconceivable that a person of so cultivated a taste as the last Duchess should have been able to bear the sight of these daubs. We hear, indeed, that for many years she did not come here. The household seemed to have great hopes from their young master, who, the gardener informed us, cares more about the beauties of the place than his father.

(2) The seventh guide was a coxcomb of an upper servant, who hurried us through the house. The entrance-hall is very fine. The apartments exhibit Gobelin tapestry, in very bad taste, as usual; a multitude of indifferent pictures, and some good ones. Nothing can be more magnificent than the library . . . [which] contains 20 or 25,000 volumes . . . The fees of all our different guides amounted to nineteen shillings. The annual income of the Duke of Marlborough is L.70,000. There are eighty house-servants; one hundred out of doors, of whom thirty are for the pleasure-grounds.

(3) Lord E[gremont] is represented by the people of the country as a plain man, rather shy, odd, and whimsical; which is saying a great deal in a country where this disposition is common enough to escape observation. He suffers the peasants of his village to play bowls and cricket on the lawn before the house; to scribble on the walls, and even on the glass of his windows; yet he has just turned away a gardener for selling some vegetables out of a garden which might supply the country ten miles round, and I dare say does. This nobleman has a numerous family of children, the last two only legitimate; the latter died, and the title will pass to a collateral heir, with as small a portion as he can of an income of L.80,000 a-year. There are many men in England who are libertines out of modesty, or rather *mauvaise honte*, unable to control their awe of modest women; and I understand this disposition is particularly common among the nobility. It is probably the consequence of a late university education, and being kept too long out of general society.

Aristocratic Society: A British View

Greville visited great palaces not as a tourist but as a welcome guest and family friend. The following extracts describe (1) a fête at Petworth in 1834 (*Journal of the Reigns of George IV and William IV* (1875) iii), (2) the birthday celebrations of the 5th Duke of Rutland (1778–1857) at

Belvoir Castle in 1838 and (3) visits to the 7th Duke of Bedford (1788–1861). (*Journal . . . Queen Victoria* (1885) i, ii).

(1) Plum puddings and loaves were piled like cannon balls, and innumerable joints of boiled and roast beef were spread out, while joints were prepared in the kitchens, and sent forth as soon as the firing of guns announced the hour of the feast . . . It was one of the gayest and most beautiful spectacles I ever saw, and there was something affecting in the contemplation of that old man—on the verge of the grave, from which he had only lately been reprieved, with his mind as strong and his heart as warm as ever—rejoicing in the diffusion of happiness, and finding keen gratification in relieving the distress and contributing to the pleasures of the poor.

(2) [4 Jan. 1838] . . . To-day (the cook told me) nearly four hundred people will dine in the Castle. We all went into the servants' hall, where one hundred and forty-five retainers had just done dinner and were drinking the Duke's health, singing and speechifying with vociferous applause, shouting, and clapping of hands. I never knew before that oratory had got down into the servants' hall, but learned that it is the custom for those to whom 'the gift of the gab' has been vouchsafed to harangue the others, the plum of eloquence being universally conceded to Mr. Tapps, the head coachman, a man of great abdominal dignity, and whose Ciceronian brows are adorned with an ample flaxen wig, which is the peculiar distinction of the functionaries of the whip. I should like to bring the surly Radical here who scowls and snarls of 'the selfish aristocracy who have no sympathies with the people', and when he has seen these hundreds feasting in the Castle, and heard their loud shouts of joy and congratulation, and then visited the villages around, and listened to the bells chiming all about the vale, say whether 'the greatest happiness of the greatest number' would be promoted by the destruction of all the feudality which belongs inseparably to this scene, and by the substitution of some abstract political rights for all the beef and ale and music and dancing with which they are made merry and glad even for so brief a space. The Duke of Rutland is as selfish a man as any of his class—that is, he never does what he does not like, and spends his whole life in a round of such pleasures as suit his taste, but he is neither a foolish nor a bad man, and partly from a sense of duty,

partly from inclination, he devotes time and labour to the interest and welfare of the people who live and labour on his estate. He is a Guardian of a very large Union and he not only attends regularly the meetings of Poor Law Guardians every week or fortnight, and takes an active part in their proceedings, but he visits those paupers who receive out-of-door relief, sits and converses with them, invites them to complain to him if they have anything to complain of, and tells them that he is not only their friend but their representative at the assembly of Guardians, and it is his duty to see that they are nourished and protected. To my mind there is more 'sympathy' in this than in railing at the rich and rendering the poor discontented, weaning them from their habitual attachments and respects, and teaching them that the political quacks and adventurers who flatter and cajole them are their only real friends.

(3) [27 Sept. 1841] . . . It is very pleasant to be at Woburn, with or without society, a house abounding in every sort of luxury and comfort, and with inexhaustible resources for every taste—a capital library, all the most curious and costly books, pictures, prints, interesting portraits, gallery of sculpture, garden with the rarest exotics, collected and maintained at a vast expense—in short, everything that wealth and refined taste can supply.

[5 Oct. 1842] . . . I have been at Woburn for a couple of days . . . The Duke is well and wisely administering his estate and improving his magnificent place in every way. I never saw such an abode of luxury and enjoyment, one so full of resources for all tastes. The management of his estate is like the administration of a little kingdom. He has 450 people in his employment on the Bedfordshire property alone, not counting domestic servants. His pensions amount to 2,000 *L.* a year. There is order, economy, grandeur, comfort, and general content.

A French View of English Agriculture

The French agricultural writer Léonce de Lavergne published his *Rural Economy of England, Scotland and Ireland* at Edinburgh in 1855. He greatly praised British (especially English) superiority to French farming in almost every respect.

The fact is that English agriculture, taken as a whole, is at this day the first in the world; and it is in the way of realising further progress . . . One has only to pass through any of the English counties, even by railway, to discover that England feeds a proportionately greater number of sheep than France . . . The superiority of British husbandry to ours is not quite so great in cattle as it is in sheep. There is still, however, a sensible difference . . . By the sole fact of the almost entire abandonment of tillage by oxen, the soil of Britain, even including Scotland and Ireland, has in cattle reached a production double that of ours.

A Businessman-Squire

Many Victorian landowners were closely involved in business ventures; the dichotomy between landed and industrial interests imagined by some radicals had little validity. Extracts from the diaries of William Aldam (1813–90), squire of Frickley Hall in South Yorkshire, a railway and inland navigation director, illustrated the variety of interests of some country gentlemen. Aldam was Liberal M.P. for Leeds in 1841–47.

[24 March 1849] At Doncaster. A warrant granted against a man refusing to pay under a bastardy order. The beech tree near the carriage road to the front door, cut down, by which a large opening is made. The fallows have been well worked throughout the week—on the land for potatoes and turnips and mangold, the wicks collected and burnt, the whole dragged several times, most of the latter part after dragging and rolling again ploughed. Hopland last week was discovered stealing turnips. Several similar appear to have been committed by him. He is to forfeit his homestead—several applications have been made for it.

[12 April] Read a new number of Quarterly, the admirable article on cattle and the review of Macaulay's History. Found Moore rapidly finishing the Middle West Close on Oldbeck. Rode round the country. Weather fair, wind West—unsettled rather. Harrison diking.

[13 April] L[eeds] and L[iverpool] C[anal] meeting Bradford 11 o'clock. Attended the Dispensary Ball at Doncaster last night.—got home at 3 o'clock. Left by the early train for Bradford. It seems probable that the dividend declared at this meeting will be the last £30 dividend. Saw Hailstone's allotment of sewers at noon.

[14 April] Came from Leeds by the first train. At the Court of

Sewers a bill of indictment against the participants on account of bad drainage . . . was presented to the Grand Jury, and by them found. Much confusion about the mode of procedure of the Court.

[18 May] At Huddersfield. The question of the Delph branch disposed of by a reference to the L[ondon] and N[orth] W[estern Railway] Board, with a request to commence immediately. £500 paid Nicholson by Lee's advice. Brooke on the point of leaving for Germany. Left my Huddersfield [Canal] certificates to be exchanged for L. & N.W. stock.

[19 May] At Doncaster. Several lay cases occupying to 5 o'clock. Some appeals in which navvies were partners; some game cases; and applications for bastardy orders. A case in which I gave a summons postponed from misnomers.

[22 May] Rained in the morning heavily, then bright and hot. Vegetation progressing with immense rapidity. Mapped the Bottom Close, using colour for the first time. My father dined here. The Heatons came to spend a day or two—music in the evening . . .

[23 May] Made a general survey of all the fields which had been drained . . .—generally well satisfied, except in Gouldings, where the produce is insufficient. The drains were running. I. Heaton accompanied me, and seemed to enjoy the day.

[9 June] At Doncaster. An application for a bastardy order from sluttish looking girl from Hatfield Moor rejected for want of corroboration.—a 9d. order made for a scholarship at Stainforth. Went to Warmsworth. My father not very well. Going to Darlington on Wednesday the 13th. The bridge over the river L. made unpracticable.

[20 June] The [canal] committee meeting held at the office. The dues on coal into Liverpool reduced from ½d. to ¼d.—2s. 7d. per ton, now the entire charge for dues, boat, haulage, etc. from Wigan to Liverpool: railway charges same. Went over Birkenhead . . .

[21 June] The new park kept in very good order. Came to Stalybridge—thence by engine along the Huddersfield line . . .—went very well, 6¾ minutes through tunnel. Examined some questions on the way. Afterwards an engineering committee meeting.

[27 June] Partly arranged my chemical instruments, investigated the use of the sextant and measured the height of some trees. Inspected Thickett's middle field, to map it. Howing turnips. A lad weeding potatoes. The Doncaster horticultural show. Read report as to traffic of Huddersfield railway.

[12 July] Prepared for tomorrow at Huddersfield. Very hot weather. Frank ploughing the tare piece. Rode round by Broad Lane to see the crops.—ordered two men to be got to thrash oats. Drove to Bilham.

[13 July] At Huddersfield. We had the Directors' opening. A fine sunny day with a good breeze. The two trains each drawn by two engines—50 carriages in all. Picnicked in a field adjoining the railway in Saddleworth. In returning about 1200–1300 people. Dined at Huddersfield, speechifying after the usual fashion . . .

Younger Sons

Count Alexis de Tocqueville (1805–59), the French philosopher and politician, regretted the disparities of wealth in Britain during successive visits. In May 1835 he discussed the rôles of younger sons, barred from aristocratic succession by entail and primogeniture, in a conversation with Henry Reeve (1813–95). The extract is from his *Journeys to England and Ireland* (ed. J. P. Mayer, 1958).

Q. What are the openings for the younger branches of the aristocracy?

A. *Firstly*, the Established Church; generally the great landowners have rights of nomination to some well-endowed livings.

Secondly, the Bar; one must start by being quite rich to qualify. The rich landowner makes this initial expenditure for his son, and by this means the son finds himself in an élite body, where competition is necessarily limited as great means are required to enter into it.

Thirdly, the army; commissions are bought; a soldier almost never becomes an officer.

Fourthly, the great resort is India. India offers quite a large number of positions at enormous salaries, £10,000 for example; the aristocracy pushes its younger sons in that direction. It is an inexhaustible resource for it, all the more because the climate is so deadly that the odds are three to one that an Englishman will die there; but if he does not die, he is *sure* of getting rich . . .

PART THREE

Inland Transport

The Duke of Bridgewater's Canal . . . takes clay and flints to the potteries, groceries and West Indian produce to every part of the island, and returns loaded with the products and manufactures of almost all the countries to the South of the Humber, Mersey etc.

Gore's Liverpool Directory (1805)

There are no stage-coaches in the Highlands. We now meet them on the roads, and the absurdity of their construction strikes us anew. There are twelve or fifteen people on top, besides baggage, and accidents are frequent.

Louis Simond (1767–1831), *Journal of a Tour and Residence in Great Britain* (Edinburgh, 1815)

The Leeds and Liverpool canal, which skirts the town of Skipton on the south-west side, affords great facility to trade, and connects it with both the eastern and western sea.

Edward Baines (1774–1848), *History, Directory and Gazetteer of the County of York* (Leeds, 1822)

We have no doubt that railways will ultimately prove a great public and private benefit, but we hope that as little money as possible will be squandered in premature and ill-judged efforts to establish them.

Leeds Mercury, 24 Dec. 1824

In the early part of the day, the carriage of Mr. Robert Stephenson, of Newcastle, attracted great attention. It ran, without any weight attached to it, at the rate of 24 miles in the hour, rushing past the spectators with amazing velocity.

Liverpool Times, 13 Oct. 1829

Thus was opened this great national undertaking [the Liverpool and

Manchester Railway], which is to shorten distances and facilitate communication in a manner which a few years back it had not entered into the mind of man even to conceive.

Morning Post, 18 Sept. 1830

Railroad travelling is a delightful improvement of human life. Man is become a bird . . . Everything is near, everything is immediate—time, distance, and delay are abolished. But . . . we must shut our eyes to the price we shall pay for it. There will be every three or four years some dreadful massacre . . .

Sydney Smith (1771–1845) to *Morning Chronicle*, 7 June 1842

The Extension to the East will accommodate the richest agricultural district in Scotland with timber, slate, coal, lime and other minerals . . . while the Western Extension of the Caledonian, as well as the trunk line, intersect tracts of country remarkable for their mineral resources, but requiring a supply of agricultural produce from the East . . .

Prospectus of the Caledonian Extension Railway (1845)

These banditti, known in some parts of England by the name of 'Navies' or 'Navigators', and in others by that of 'Bankers', are generally the terror of the surrounding country; they are as completely a class by themselves as the Gipsies. Possessed of all the daring recklessness of the Smuggler, without any of his redeeming qualities, their ferocious behaviour can only be equalled by the brutality of their language.

Peter Lecount, to Select Committee on Railway Labourers (1846)

In my whole experience I have never known a case where the railways have caused the value of property to fall.

Robert Stephenson (1803–59), in Samuel Salt, *Railway Commercial Information* (1850)

As if the old mail coach rate of eight miles an hour was not fast enough for the march of civilisation, the devil has been raised in the shape of steam to impel us at his own pace . . . My pleasantest, or I might better say happiest, travels have been either at a mule's footpace, or with a knapsack on my own shoulders.

Robert Southey (1774–1843), in *Selections from the Letters of Robert Southey* (1856)

I detest railways. Your railway has cut through and spoiled some of the loveliest bits of scenery in the country.

John Ruskin (1819–1900), in E. T. Cook and A. Wedderburn (eds.), *Works of John Ruskin* (1907) xxvii

Turnpikes

The road system—under often lethargic parochial control from Tudor times—was considerably improved in some areas during the eighteenth century by turnpike trusts, composed of local landowners and businessmen, who charged users of their stretch of highway. As Arthur Young noted (1) in his *Six Weeks' Tour through the Southern Counties of England and Wales* (1768), turnpiked roads varied greatly; and in the nineteenth century the road system was to deteriorate rapidly. A year later Thomas Pennant (1726–98) in his *Journal of a Tour in Scotland* described the bad state of the unimproved Blair Atholl-Braemar road (2).

(1) The road from Witney to North Leach is, I think, the worst turnpike I ever travelled in; so bad, that it is a scandal to the country. They mend and make with nothing but the stone which forms the under stratum all over the country, quite from Tetsford the other side of Oxford . . .

. . . From Chepstow to the half-way house between Newport and Cardiff, they continue mere rocky lanes, full of hugeous stones as big as one's horse and abominable holes. The first six miles from Newport, they were so detestable, and without either direction-posts, or mile-stones, that I could not well persuade myself I was on the turnpike, but had mistook the road; and therefore asked everyone I met, who assured me, to my astonishment, Ya-as . . .

I chiefly travelled upon turnpikes; of all which, that from Salisbury, to four miles the other side of Romsy, towards Winchester is, without exception, the finest I ever saw. The trustees of that road, highly deserve all the praise that can be given, by every one who travels it, for their excellent management: to management the goodness of it must be owing; for fine as their materials are, yet I have in other counties met with as fine; but never with any that were so firmly united, and kept so totally free from loose stones, rutts and water . . . To conclude the whole, it is every where broad enough for three carriages to pass each other; and lying in straight lines, with an even edge of grass the whole way, it has more the appearance of an elegant gravel walk, than of an high-road.

(2) The road is the most dangerous and horrible I have ever travelled; a narrow path so rugged that our horses were often obliged to cross their legs in order to pick a secure place for their

feet; while, at a considerable and precipitous depth below, roared a black torrent, rolling through a bed of rock, solid in every part, but where the antient Tilt had worn its way.

Risks and Delights on the Road

Royal Mail and post coaches developed a large network of services between hundreds of eighteenth-century inns, and men of substance maintained large personal carriages and a variety of smaller vehicles. Some of the hazards and pleasures of road journeys are described in contemporary and later accounts. The first extract is from G. W. E. Russell, *op. cit.* The second describes a family journey from London to Scarborough, made by Elizabeth Grant of Rothiemurchus (1797–1885) in 1803 (*Memoirs of a Highland Lady*, 1898). The third is from J. P. Malcolm, *Excursions* (1807). In the fourth Charles Dickens describes a celebrated fictional ride (*Pickwick Papers*, 1837) and in the fifth the American Simond (*op. cit.*) describes the Bath-London road in January 1810. In the final extract George Eliot (*op. cit.*) looks back sentimentally to the coaching system of about 1831–32.

(1) Stories of highwaymen are excellent Links with the Past, and here is one. The fifth Earl of Berkeley, who died in 1810, had always declared that anyone might without disgrace be overcome by superior numbers, but that he would never surrender to a single highwayman. As he was crossing Hampstead Heath one night, on his way from Berkeley Castle to London, his travelling carriage was stopped by a man on horseback, who put his head in at the window and said, "I believe you are Lord Berkeley?" "I am". "I believe you have always boasted that you would never surrender to a single highwayman?" "I have". "Well," presenting a pistol, "I am a single highwayman, and I say, 'Your money or your life'." "You cowardly dog," said Lord Berkeley, "do you think I can't see your confederate skulking behind you?" The highwayman, who was really alone, looked hurriedly round, and Lord Berkeley shot him through the head. I asked Lady Caroline Maxse (1803–1886), who was born a Berkeley, if this story was true. I can never forget my thrill when she replied, "Yes; and I am proud to say that I am that man's daughter."

(2) My mother had been alarmingly ill . . . [and] it was resolved that she and we should have a few weeks of sea-bathing at Scar-

borough on our way; a sort of couch was contrived for her, on which she lay comfortably in the large *berline* we had hitherto used, and which the four horses must have found heavy enough when weighted with all its imperials, hat boxes, and the great hair trunk that had been poor William's terror. Mrs. Lynch and Mackenzie, who had been my father's valet before he married, were on the outside; my father, Jane and I within with my mother, and we travelled with our own horses ridden by two postillions in green jackets and jockey caps, leaving London, I think, in July. In the heavy post-chariot behind were the two nurses, the baby in a swinging cot, William who was too riotous to be near my mother, and a footman in charge of them. What it must have cost to have carried such a party from London to the Highlands! and how often we travelled that north road! Every good inn became a sort of home, every obliging landlord or landlady an old friend. We had cakes here, a garden with a summer-house there, a parrot farther on, all to look forward to on every migration, along with the pleasant flatteries on our growth and our looks of health; as if such a train would not have been greeted joyously by every publican! We travelled slowly, thirty miles a day on an average, starting late and stopping early, with a bait some after noon, when we children dined . . .

(3) The disadvantages attending travelling in the mail are not numerous, yet those are of some importance: the fatigue is considerable, and the intervals of rest much too short; besides, the rapidity of their motion sometimes occasions an overturn. I observed our coach appeared to be perfectly new; but I felt the more secure on reflection, till the cause was explained by the self-congratulation of a gentleman, who said he should doze the night away in security, as he had never heard of the overturning of the *same person* a second time in the space of three days.

(4) The coachman mounts to the box, Mr. Weller jumps up behind, the Pickwickians pull their coats round their legs and their shawls over their noses, the helpers pull the horse-cloths off, the coachman shouts out a cheery "All right," and away they go. They have rumbled through the streets, and jolted over the stones and at length reach the wide and open country. The wheels skim over the hard and frosty ground; and the horses bursting into a canter at a smart crack of the whip, step along the road as if the load

behind them: coach, passengers, codfish, oyster barrels, and all; were but a feather at their heels. They have descended a gentle slope, and enter upon a level, as compact and dry as a solid block of marble, two miles long. Another crack of the whip, and on they speed, at a smart gallop . . .

And now the bugle plays a lively air as the coach rattles through ill-paved streets of a country town . . . Mr. Winkle, who sits at the extreme edge, with one leg dangling in the air, is nearly precipitated into the street, as the coach twists round the sharp corner by the cheesemonger's shop and turns into the market-place; and before Mr. Snodgrass, who sits next to him, has recovered from his alarm, they pull up at the inn yard, where the fresh horses, with cloths on, are already waiting. The coachman throws down the reins and gets down himself, and the other outside passengers drop down also: except those who have no great confidence in their ability to get up again: and they remain where they are, and stamp their feet against the coach to warm them.

(5) The country is beautiful, rich, and varied, with villas and mansions, and dark groves of pines—shrubs in full bloom, evergreen lawns, and gravel walks so neat—with porters' lodges, built in rough-cast, and stuck all over with flints, in their native grotesqueness; for this part of England is a great bed of chalk, full of this singular production (flints). They are broken to pieces with hammers, and spread over the road in deep beds, forming a hard and even surface, upon which the wheels of carriages make no impression. The roads are now wider; kept in good repair, and not deep, notwithstanding the season. The post-horses excellent; and post-boys riding instead of sitting. Our rate of travelling does not exceed six miles an hour, stoppages included; but we might go faster if we desired it. We meet with very few post-chaises, but a great many stage-coaches, mails, &c. and enormous broad wheel waggons. The comfort of the inns was our incessant theme at night—the pleasure of it is not yet worn out.

January 11.—We arrived yesterday at Richmond. This morning I set out by myself for *town*, as London is called *par excellence*, in the stage-coach, crammed inside, and *herissé* outside with passengers, of all sexes, ages, and conditions. We stopped more than twenty times on the road—the debates about the fare of way-passengers—the settling themselves—the getting up, and the getting down, and damsels showing their legs in the operation, and tearing and muddying their petticoats—complaining and swearing—took an immense time. I never saw any thing so ill managed . . .

(6) Five-and-thirty years ago the glory had not yet departed from the old coach-roads; the great roadside inns were still brilliant with well-polished tankards, the smiling glances of pretty barmaids, and the repartee of jocose ostlers; the mail still announced itself by the merry notes of the horn; the hedge-cutter or the rick-thatcher might still know the exact hour by the unfailing yet otherwise meteoric apparition of the pea-green Tally-ho or the yellow Independent; and elderly gentlemen in pony-chaises, quartering nervously to make way for the rolling swinging swiftness, had not ceased to remark that times were finely changed since they used to see the pack-horses and hear the tinkling of their bells on this very highway.

The Canals

John Hassell (d. 1825), a popular London publisher of tour books, issued his *Tour of the Grand Junction Canal* in 1819 as an enthusiastic introduction to the pleasures of canal travel.

Deviating from the tedious monotony of the turnpike road, the course of the stream destined for inland navigation must necessarily be directed through a succession of the richest scenery—whether stealing through the glades and glooms of rural retirement, winding round the brows of hills, or gliding through the valleys by which they are surrounded, alternately visiting the recesses of pictorial abode, or the populous town, and the "hum of men" . . .

In 1818, the annual gross revenue of the canal amounted to the sum of £170,000; it possesses 1,400 proprietors; and its shares of £100 have recently sold at from £240 to £250 each. Many of the first capitalists in the kingdom are its proprietors, and its usual routine of business is so conducted as to give satisfaction to all who are connected with it . . .

Inland navigation, to a manufacturing country, is the very heart's blood and soul of commerce, nor can we easily estimate the utility and importance of this mode of conveyance, in obviating the expense and tediousness of land carriage, or the more protracted delays invariably attendant on opposite winds and tides.

The Advantages of Canals

The late eighteenth century saw the development of the 'canal mania' and a rapid spread of the canal and inland waterway network. By 1831 Joseph Priestley (c. 1767–1852), an official of the great Aire & Calder Navigation, could record details of hundreds of ventures in his *Historical Account of the Navigable Rivers, Canals, and Railways of Great Britain.* The extracts typify some of Priestley's claims for particular ventures.

[Aberdare Canal]

The chief object of this navigation is the export of the produce of the iron furnaces, coal mines and limestone quarries, which abound in the immediate vicinity.

[Aberdeenshire Canal]

The chief article of conveyance of this canal is granite, great quantities of which are annually exported from the quarries on its banks to London and other parts of the country, by means of its communication with the harbour of Aberdeen . . .

[The Duke of Bridgewater's Canal]

The primary object of "The Father of British Inland Navigation," as the Duke of Bridgewater has been justly styled, was to open his valuable collieries at Worsley, and to supply the town of Manchester with coal, at a much cheaper rate than could be done by the imperfect navigation of the Mersey and Irwell.

[Caledonian Canal]

This canal, or rather series of canals and navigable lochs, forms one of the most magnificent inland navigations in the world; and its execution has been justly accounted one of the brightest examples of what the skill and perseverance of our engineers can accomplish . . . This canal, which was projected and commenced chiefly with the view of giving facilities to the Baltic Timber Trade, was opened in October, 1822.

[Chesterfield Canal]

The chief objects of this canal are the export of coal, lime, and lead from Derbyshire, and of the produce of the iron furnaces in the neighbourhood of Chesterfield; and corn, deals, timber, groceries, &c. on the other hand, are conveyed into the county of Derby.

[Forth and Clyde Canal]

The original project proposed by this canal was to open a communication between those important rivers, the Forth and Clyde, and between the northern metropolis and the manufacturing towns of Glasgow and Paisley; and whether as respects the utility of the work, the magnitude of the undertaking, or the skill and ingenuity with which it was designed and executed, the Forth and Clyde Canal will ever hold a distinguished place amongst the most important branches of our inland navigation.

[Kennet and Avon Canal]

. . . The traffic on it in coal, corn, stone, copper and iron, is of very considerable extent, and, from the almost daily addition to its communication with different parts of the kingdom, by connecting canals and railroads, must continue to increase as long as Great Britain maintains its character as a commercial nation.

[Lancaster Canal]

It would be almost impossible to enumerate all the advantages accruing to the public from the execution of this undertaking. The interchange of the coals and cannel of Wigan and the southern extremity of the line, with the stone, lime and slate of its northern parts, is not amongst the least beneficial effects of its completion; whilst liquors and various other articles of foreign merchandize introduced at the port of Lancaster, are by its means conveyed with expedition and at a trifling expense to the various populous manufacturing places on its line.

[Leeds and Liverpool Canal]

This gigantic concern, which was no less than forty-six years in executing, and which has cost £1,200,000, has proved highly beneficial to the country through which it passes, giving facility to the transport of coal, limestone, lime for manure, and all agricultural produce, connecting the trade of Leeds with Liverpool and with Manchester, Wigan, Blackburn, Burnley, Colne, Skipton, Keighley, Bingley and Bradford . . .

. . . Upon inspection of the map, it will appear that this canal connects the Irish Sea with the German Ocean, and the great ports of Liverpool and Hull, by which a cheap and ready transit is afforded to the Foreign Trade to and from the Baltic, Holland, Hanseatic Towns, the Netherlands, France and Germany; also with Ireland, the West Indies and America. Besides, the public are greatly benefited by the ease with which the interior trade is carried from Leeds and the West Riding into the manufacturing districts of Lancashire and to Liverpool, and *vice versa*. Moreover, upon the banks of this canal are found immense quantities of stone for paving and building, limestone for repairs of roads and for burning into lime for manure; inexhaustible beds of coal, which not only supply the neighbouring districts, but furnish an abundance for exportation at Liverpool; in short no part of the kingdom is more benefited by a public work of this kind than the country, through which the Leeds and Liverpool canal passes.

The Decline of the Roads

The coming of the railways inevitably led to a decline of road transport. In 1839 Edward Sherman, an inn and coach proprietor whose business had declined severely, told the Select Commitee on Turnpike Trusts (*P. P.* 1839, ix) that turnpike tolls and taxation of stage coaches worsened the position (1). The decline of road services ruined not only the great coaching businesses but also many coaching inns and ancillary services. The second extract is the poetic 'Lament and Anticipation of a Stage Coachman' (1843) by the celebrated Thomas Cross, a veteran driver of the Lynn Union coach.

(1) Would you state to the Committee whether or not of late years, say within the last two or three years, you have experienced any result from the formation of railroads?—I have a reduction on the North road, since the opening of the railroad, of 15 coaches daily.

From what period?—From the opening of the railroads . . .

You are now working two coaches?—Yes, between London and Birmingham.

How many did you work before the railroad opened?—Nine, which I had for the whole year previously . . .

Do you conceive there is any legislative assistance you could receive that would enable you to compete with the railroads?—No, there is nothing but great reductions that would enable us to compete with them; it is not fair competition as we are now.

But a reduction of duty and a reduction of tolls would materially assist you?—To satisfy that part of the public who are timid, and not disposed to go by the railroad; some portion would rather go by coach; not many, very few . . . what we carry now are mostly people who are timid people, and do not like to go by the railroad, except . . . when we go with very low fares indeed; that induces the lower orders of people; the people we carry are so poor, the coachmen and guards say they get nothing besides the passage-money; their places are not worth having.

(2) The smiling chambermaid, she too forlorn,
The boots, gruff voice, the waiter's busy jest,
The ostler's whistle, or the guard's loud horn,
No more shall call from their places of rest.

The next we heard some new-invented plan,
Had in Union lodged our ancient friend,
Come here and see, for thou shall see the man,
Doom'd by the railroad to so sad an end.

The Liverpool and Manchester Railway

Frances Anne Keble (1809–93), the celebrated actress, fell in love with both railways and the pioneer engineer George Stephenson (1781–1848) after an escorted trip along the Liverpool and Manchester line in August 1830. Her diary for 26 August was published in *Records of a Girlhood* (1878).

You can't imagine how strange it seemed to be journeying on thus, without any visible cause of progress other than the magical machine, with the flying white breath and rhythmical unvarying pace, between these rocky walls, which are already clothed with moss, and ferns, and grasses; and, when I reflected that these great masses of stone had been cut asunder to allow our passage thus far below the surface of the earth, I felt as if no fairy tale was ever half so wonderful as what I saw . . .

. . . The engine having received its supply of water, the carriage was placed behind it, for it cannot turn, and was set off at its utmost speed, thirty-five miles an hour; swifter than a bird flies (for they tried the experiment with a snipe). You cannot conceive what that sensation of cutting the air was; the motion is as smooth as possible too . . .

An Early Journey

Travel on early railways was something of an adventure. Thomas Creevey (1768–1838), the gossipy Whiggish correspondent, lawyer,

M.P. and sinecurist, was an early but doubtful traveller on the (then incomplete) Liverpool & Manchester Railway on 14 November 1829. He reported the event to his step-daughter, Miss Ord (Sir Herbert Maxwell, ed., *The Creevey Papers*, 1903).

Today we have had a *lark* of a very high order. Lady Wilton sent over yesterday from Knowsley to say that the Loco Motive machine was to be upon the railway at such a place at 12 o'clock for the Knowsley party to ride in if they liked, and inviting this house to be of the party. So of course we were at our post in 3 carriages and some horsemen at the hour appointed. I had the satisfaction, for I can't call it *pleasure*, of taking a trip of five miles in it, which we did in just a quarter of an hour—that is, 20 miles an hour . . . But observe, during these five miles, the machine was occasionally made to put itself out or *go it*; and then we went at the rate of 23 miles an hour, and just with the same ease as to motion or absence of friction as the other reduced pace. But the quickest motion is to me *frightful*: it is really flying, and it is impossible to divest yourself of the notion of instant death to all upon the least accident happening. It gave me a headache which has not left me yet . . . Altogether I am extremely glad indeed to have seen this miracle, and to have travelled in it. Had I thought worse of it than I do, I should have had the curiosity to try it; but, having done so I am quite satisfied with my *first* achievement being my *last*.

Birmingham to Lancashire

Greville first travelled by rail in July 1837, when visiting Knowsley (the Lancashire seat of the Earl of Derby). His comments appeared in his *Journal of the Reign of Queen Victoria* (1885) i. The Grand Junction line from Birmingham to Liverpool had just been opened.

Tired of doing nothing in London, and of hearing about the Queen, and the elections, I resolved to vary the scene and run down here to see the Birmingham railroad, Liverpool, and Liverpool races. So I started at five o'clock on Sunday evening, got to Birmingham at half-past five on Monday morning, and got upon the railroad at half-past seven. Nothing can be more comfortable than the vehicle in which I was put, a sort of chariot with two places, and there is nothing disagreeable about it but the occasional whiffs of stinking air which it is impossible to exclude altogether. The first sensation is a slight degree of nervousness and feeling of being run away with, but a sense of security soon supervenes, and the velocity is delightful. Town after town, one park and *château* after another are left behind with the rapid variety of a moving panorama, and the continual bustle and animation of the changes and stoppages make the journey very entertaining. The train was very long, and heads were continually popping out of the several carriages, attracted by well-known voices, and then came the greetings and exclamations of surprise, the 'Where are you going?' and 'How on earth came you here?' Considering the novelty of its establishment, there is very little embarrassment, and it certainly renders all other travelling irksome and tedious by comparison. It was peculiarly gay at this time, because there was so much going on. There were all sorts of people going to Liverpool races, barristers to the assizes, and candidates to their several elections.

Royal Interest

Queen Victoria was the first monarch to travel by rail, eventually using a special train. Her early correspondence, published in *The Letters of Queen Victoria . . . 1837–1861* (ed. A. C. Benson and Viscount Esher, 1908) i, includes (1) a letter from Viscount Melbourne (of 29 December 1841) on a railway accident near Reading five days earlier and (2) her letter (of 14 June 1842) to her uncle, King Leopold I of the Belgians, on her first railway journey, from Windsor to London on the Great Western line.

(1) The railway smash is awful and tremendous, as all railway mishaps are, and Lord Melbourne fears must always be. These slips and falls of earth from the banks are the greatest danger that now impends over them and if they take place suddenly and in the dark, Lord Melbourne does not see how the fatal consequences of them are to be effectually guarded against. They are peculiarly likely to happen now, as the cuttings have been recently and hastily made, the banks are very steep, and the season has been peculiarly wet, interrupted by severe frosts.

(2) We arrived here yesterday morning, having come by the railroad, from Windsor, in half an hour, free from dust and crowd and heat, and I am quite charmed with it.

Railway Classes

Early railways were notoriously class-conscious and there was considerable reluctance to provide roofs or seats for 3rd-class passengers. *Punch* (viii, 1845) commented on companies' behaviour.

The classification adopted in the management of Railways is not confined to the carriages; but the distinctions of first, second, and third classes are scrupulously observed in the degree of politeness shown by the servants of the company to the passengers. The old maxim that civility costs nothing, seems to be utterly repudiated by Railway Directors, who calculate no doubt that politeness at all events takes time; and as time is money, the servants of the company are not justified in giving it without an equivalent. Any one who doubts the fact of the distinction to which we have alluded being drawn, has only to present himself at different times as an applicant for information at a Railway Terminus in the different characters of a first, second, and a third class passenger.

. . . In fact, there are short answers as well as short trains, and each class has a set of rules of politeness applied to it, which the officers are bound to obey as scrupulously as they do the Railway signals.

Hostile Landowners

Some landowners were hostile to railway developments because of their effects on rural sports, farm lay-outs and drainage schemes. John Francis' *History of the English Railway* (1851) instanced examples of early disagreements. The eccentric Waldo Sibthorp (1783–1855), M.P. for Lincoln, considered that 'next to a civil war, railways were the greatest curse to the country'. But many landowners were closely involved in railway promotion, shareholding and direction.

"Landowners," wrote *Fraser's Magazine*, "were kept in a constant state of anxiety by rumours of the course each railway was likely to pursue. Young men with theodolites and chains marched about the fields; long white sticks with bits of paper attached were carried ruthlessly through fields, gardens, and sometimes even through houses." Colonel Sibthorp said, "The injuries done by the engineers of railway companies to the property of private individuals was most unjust. Not content with making encroachments in the day-time, these marauders of engineers took advantage of the darkness to commit those trespasses which their modesty would not suffer them to do at another time. An honourable friend of his rose one morning and actually found a flag stuck up before his very door." There can be no doubt that the insolent assurance of many connected with railroads was unbounded. One proprietor, when he asked the promoters what would be given him for the land which a line was to traverse, was informed "they would tell him when the bill was passed into a law. That they did not care whether he consented or not; that the railway department of the board of trade had already reported in favour of the line, and it would be the worse for him if he offered opposition." Another was told that if he objected to the rail passing near his lawn, it would be taken through his kitchen.

Sunday Trains

Sabbatarians were regularly angered by proposals for Sunday trains. A famous protest was delivered to the Eastern Counties Railway in 1851 by the Rev. George Corrie (1793–1885), the Master of Jesus College, Cambridge in 1849–85 (as reported in the *Cambridge Chronicle*).

He expressed his pain that they had made arrangements for conveying foreigners and others to Cambridge at such fares as might be likely to tempt persons who having no regard for Sunday themselves would inflict their presence on the University on that day of rest . . . The contemplated arrangements were as distasteful to the University authorities as they must be offensive to Almighty God and to all right minded Christians.

Railways and the Countryside

Country-lovers often protested against railways desecration of rural scenes. *Punch* (ix, 1845), always critical of railway habits, apparently supported their case.

RAILWAY PASTORALS

The iron hand of Railway enterprise is fast tearing up by the roots all the pastoral and poetical associations of our youth, and cottages near woods, as well as mossy cells or leafy nooks, are being superseded by Railway termini. Where the cow once lowed, the engine now screams, and the pipe of the gentle CORYDON is completely put out by the funnel of the locomotive. PHILLIS is sent flying by the power of steam, and the hermit of the dale is compelled to break his staff or cut his stick, to make way for the immense staff of officials required on the Railways.

Railways in Lakeland

William Wordsworth (1770–1850), the Lakeland poet, was 'not against Railways but against the abuse of them'; he was, indeed an investor. But the proposed Kendal and Windermere line infuriated him in 1844: he published two sonnets asking

> Is then no nook of English ground secure
> From rash assault?

protested to the Cumbrian M.P.s and in the *Morning Post* and wrote to W. E. Gladstone (1809–98), the President of the Board of Trade.

Rydal Mount, Oct. 15th, 1844.

My Dear Mr. Gladstone,

We are in this neighbourhood all in consternation, that is every man of taste and feeling, at the stir which is made for carrying a branch Railway from Kendal to the head of Windermere. When the subject comes before you officially, as I suppose it will, pray give it more attention than its apparent importance may call for. In fact, the project if carried into effect will destroy the *staple* of the Country which is its beauty, and, on the Lord's day particularly will prove subversive of its quiet, and be injurious to its morals . . .

Believe me my dear Mr. Gladstone
faithfully your much obliged
Wm. Wordsworth.

The Railway Organiser

Interest in the technical achievements of the pioneer engineers has often led to virtual neglect of the work of railway promoters, planners and directors. George Henry Gibbs (1785–1842), London banker and Great Western Railway director, recorded his own involvement in a diary published by his grandson, the 2nd Lord Aldenham, under the title of *The Birth of the Great Western Railway* (1910).

March 1836. The affairs and prospects of the Great Western Railway have very much engrossed my mind for the last fortnight. I have taken an active part in all the proceedings connected with it from the first formation of the London Committee two years and a half ago, when it was looked upon by the public, with apathy and distrust, to the present moment, when it occupies so great a portion of public attention. I regard it as a great national work calculated to effect an important change in our internal relations and to produce a great balance of good; and, having shown my confidence in the undertaking by becoming a large shareholder, my mind has been more particularly engrossed with the subject lately in consequence of the rapid rise which has taken place in the value of shares . . .

2 June [1838]. Drove to the depôt, where they reported that all was ready for Monday morning. Eton College applied yesterday for an injunction to prevent our stopping at Slough. The application was dismissed with costs.

4 June. Our railway opened to the public this morning. I went to Maidenhead by the first train and came back by the third, which started from Maidenhead at 10.15. I was disappointed with regard to the speed, as we were 1 hour and 20 minutes going down and 1 hour and 5 minutes coming up. If from the 65 minutes we deduct 4 lost at Drayton, 3 at Slough, and 4 between the two places and in slackening and getting up speed, there remains 54 minutes for 23 miles, or 25½ miles per hour. We carried altogether today 1,479 people and took £229.

King Hudson and Greed

George Hudson (1800–71) of York became the most notorious manipulator of railway promotions, mergers and finances, before his exposure and downfall in 1848–49. Thomas Carlyle (1795–1881) published his essay on 'Hudson's Statue' in *Latter-Day Pamphlets* (1850). At the peak of his power Hudson had been a considerable landowner and M.P. for Sunderland.

Hudson the railway king, if Popular Election be the rule, seems to me by far the most authentic king extant in this world. Hudson has been 'elected by the people' so as almost none other is or was. Hudson solicited no vote; his votes were silent voluntary ones, not liable to be false; he *did* a thing which men found, in their inarticulate hearts, to be worthy of paying money for; and they paid it. What the desire of every heart was, Hudson had or seemed to have produced: scrip out of which profit could be made. They 'voted' for him by purchasing his scrip with a profit to him . . . What their appetites, intelligence, stupidities, and pruriences had taught these men, they authentically told you there. I beg you to mark that well. Not by all the ballot-boxes in Nature could you have hoped to get, with such exactness, from these men, what the deepest inarticulate voice of the gods and of the demons in them was, as by this their spontaneous purchase of scrip. It is the ultimate rectified quintessence of these men's 'votes': the distillation of their very souls; the sincerest sincerity that was in them. Without gratitude to Hudson, or even without thought of him, they raised Hudson to his bad eminence, not by their voice given once at some hustings under the influence of balderdash and beer, but by the thought of their heart, by the inarticulate, indisputable dictate of their whole being. Hudson inquired of England: "What precious thing can I do for you, O enlightened Countrymen; what may be the value to you, by popular election, of this stroke of work that lies in me?" Popular election . . . has answered: "Pounds sterling to such and such amount; that is the apparent value of thy stroke of work to *us*,—blockheads as we are." Real value differs from apparent to a frightful extent in this world, try it by what suffrage you will!

The Triumph of the Railway

The Liverpool & Manchester soon demonstrated the possibilities—not least for passengers—of the railways. *The Annual Register* (1832) summarised its early achievements.

Before the establishment of the Liverpool and Manchester railway, there were twenty-two regular and about seven occasional extra coaches between those places, which, in full, could only carry per day 688 persons. The railway, from its commencement, carried 700,000 persons in eighteen months being an average of 1,070 per day. It has not been stopped for a single day. There has occurred but one fatal accident on it in eighteen months. The fare by coach was 10s. inside and 5s. outside—by railway it is 5s. inside, and 3s. 6d. outside. The time occupied in making the journey by coach was four hours—by railway it is one hour and three quarters. All the coaches but one have ceased running, and that chiefly for the conveyance of parcels. The mails all travel by the railway, at a saving to government of two-thirds of the expense. The railway coaches are more commodious than others. The travelling is cheaper, safer, and easier. A great deal of traffic, which used to go by other roads, comes now by railway . . . A regiment of soldiers has been carried by the railway from Manchester to Liverpool in two hours. Gentlemen's carriages are conveyed on trucks by the railway. The locomotives travel in safety after dark. The rate of carriage of goods is 10s. per ton; by canal it used to be 15s. per ton. The time occupied in the journey by railway is two hours; by canal it is twenty hours. The canals have reduced their rates 30 per cent . . . The saving to manufacturers in the neighbourhood of Manchester, in the carriage of cotton alone, has been 20,000*l.* per annum. Some houses of business save 500*l.* a year in carriage . . . The railway is assessed to the parochial rates in all the parishes through which it passes; though only thirty-one miles, it pays between 3,000*l.* and 4,000*l.* per annum in parochial rates. Coal pits have been sunk, and manufactories established on the line, giving great employment to the poor . . . It is found advantageous for the carriage of milk and garden produce . . . A great deal of land on the line has been let for garden ground, at increased rents . . . No inconvenience is felt by residents from smoke or noise; and, on the contrary, great advantage is experienced by means of travelling, to and fro, distances of ten miles in half an hour for 1s. and without any fatigue.

Consequences of the Railway

When the barrister William Johnston published his book on *Britain As It Is* (1851) there were some 5,500 miles of track open and railways were carrying some sixty million passengers. Johnston did not entirely approve of the results.

The most important event of the last quarter of a century in British history is the establishment of Railroads. The stupendous magnitude of the capital they have absorbed—the changes they have produced in the habits of society—the new aspect they have given, in some respects, to the affairs of government—the new feelings of power they have engendered—the triumphs and the disappointments of which they have been the cause—above all, the new and excessive activities to which they have given rise—must lead all who reflect upon the subject to admit that the importance of the general result of these great undertakings can scarcely be exaggerated. They have done much towards changing the old deliberative and thoughtful habits of Englishmen. People who breakfast at York, and dine in London—who may be summoned from Liverpool to the metropolis in three or four minutes by the electric telegraph, and answer the summons in person within six or seven hours by the express train—acquire a habit of pressure and velocity in all they do . . .

. . . It appears to me that, if the legislature had wisely governed the expenditure of capital upon railways, such a source for the gradual and profitable investment of profits and savings would have been an immense national advantage, whereas allowing the public to rush headlong into undertakings which they had not the means to complete, and for which the country had no pressing occasion, has been productive of great private distress, and has no doubt operated most prejudicially upon the public finances . . .

An Excursion

Railways made possible the 'day-trip' excursion to the sea, on public holidays. An early example was the notice of the Leeds & Selby Railway of 1830 for railway travel to Selby, continuing by packet boat to Hull. The L. & S. Line was opened in 1834, and the Selby & Hull company of 1834 completed the Leeds-Hull line in 1840.

TO HULL AND BACK THE SAME DAY.

GOOD FRIDAY,

BY RAILWAY AND STEAM PACKET.

THE PUBLIC are informed that Arrangements have been made for carrying passengers to HULL and BACK, *on Friday, the Thirteenth Instant*, also to Booth Ferry, Howden Dike, or any other intermediate places. The train will leave the Depot, Marsh Lane, at SEVEN in the MORNING, and parties will arrive in Hull by Packet about One o' Clock. The packet will leave Hull again about Five and arrive in Leeds by Railway at Ten. Fares to Hull and back,—

First Class and Best Cabin . . . . 9s.
Second Ditto and Common Ditto . . . . . . 6s.

WILLIAM SIMPSON, Superintendent.

Railway Office, April 6th, 1838.

Birth of a Travel Agency

Thomas Cook (1808–92), a Baptist preacher in Derbyshire, started his great travel agency by organising Midland Counties rail transport to a Temperance rally in 1841. He recalled his first experience of the business in *Leisure Hour* (1852).

I was an enthusiastic temperance man, and the secretary of a district association, which embraced parts of the two counties of Leicester and Northampton. A great meeting was to be held at Leicester . . . From my residence at Market Harborough I walked to Leicester (fifteen miles) to attend that meeting. About midway between Harborough and Leicester—my mind's eye has often reverted to the spot—a thought flashed through my brain, what a glorious thing it would be if the newly-developed powers of railways and locomotion could be made subservient to the promotion of temperance! . . . I broached the idea of engaging a special train to carry the friends of temperance from Leicester to Loughborough and back to attend a quarterly delegate meeting . . . On the day appointed about five hundred passengers filled some twenty or twenty-five open carriages . . . All went off in the best style, and in perfect safety we returned to Leicester; and thus was struck the keynote of my excursions, and the social idea grew upon me.

The Size of the Rail Network (1)

George Bradshaw (1801–53), a Manchester printer, first issued his celebrated *Railway Time Tables and Assistant to Railway Travelling* in 1839. He later issued a series of manuals, directories and shareholders' guides to the railway companies. The following details are taken from *Bradshaw's Railway Manual, Shareholders' Guide, and Official Directory for 1869*, xxi (1869).

. . . Up to 1867 there had been a progressive increase, not merely in the extent of mileage brought into operation, but in the number of companies owning the properties. The highest number of separate undertakings in the three kingdoms we have had to record (in the volume commencing 1867) was 476, but in that year the number, by amalgamations, had decreased to 463; and a further diminution, not merely by amalgamation but by abandonments during 1868, reduces the number of separate companies of which we can take cognisance to 455. A still greater reduction may be anticipated for 1869, not alone in consequence of the paucity of new companies for the current year, but also on account of abandonments and amalgamations which are to be brought before Parliament during the forthcoming session.

But, although the number of separate undertakings gives promise to be annually on the decrease, the actual mileage brought under traffic is making steady progress. In 1866 the number of miles in operation extended to 13,854, of which 7,711 were double lines, and 6,143 single. During 1869 this mileage had increased to 14,247, of which 7,844 were double and 6,403 single. The increase for the latter year was therefore 133 of double lines, and 260 of single, making a total of 393 additional miles . . .

It will be observed from our customary compilation of new mileage brought under traffic during 1868, that the openings extend to 315 miles, of which at least one half may be regarded as composed of single lines.

. . . The growth of capital, notwithstanding the enormous financial difficulties which companies have had to encounter, has still been comparatively enormous. In our preface for last year we gave an outline of the growth of capital and revenue since 1855. For that year and for 1865, the progress of ten years was thus exemplified:—

	Capital	Revenue
1855	£297,584,709	£21,507,599
1865	455,478,143	35,751,655
Increase	£157,893,434	£14,244,056

The Size of the Rail Network (2)

Samuel Smiles first published his *Lives of the Engineers* in 1857, as an example of 'self-help'. In the 1874 edition he commented on the 'enormous magnitude' of the railways.

In the year 1873, 401,465,086 passengers were carried by day tickets in Great Britain alone. But this was not all. For in that year 257,470 periodical tickets were issued by the different railways; and assuming half of them to be annual, one fourth half-yearly, and the remainder quarterly tickets, and that their holders made only five journeys each way weekly, this would give an additional number of 47,024,000 journeys, or a total of 448,489,086 passengers carried in Great Britain in one year. It is difficult to grasp the idea of the enormous number of persons represented by these figures. The mind is merely bewildered by them, and can form no adequate notion of their magnitude . . .

An Industrial Town and the Railways

The Bradford historian John James (1811–67) described the impact of the railways on one provincial town in his *Continuation and Additions to the History of Bradford* (1866).

In the railway mania of 1845 and 1846, Bradford largely participated. All classes of people, whether wealthy or poor, were infected with the morbid spirit of speculation. Inns and places of public resort were converted into share-broking establishments. The wildness of speculation in shares of railway lines in embryo,—schemes of the utmost extravagance,—exceeds all belief, and surpasses the most monstrous delusion the world ever witnessed. The mania was at its height in July, 1845. Great numbers of speculators were ruined in Bradford; well-to-do and prudent tradesmen became bankrupt or fled from their creditors; confidential servants embezzled large sums of money; and when the catastrophe arrived, a few had prospered on the bubble, but hundreds were crippled for years in their means. Eventually, however, Bradford indirectly gained by the spread of this speculative feeling. Many railway companies were started for supplying the town with railways; some of which proved abortive, but others carried out with success their plans.

The Railway Mania of 1845

Speculation in railway ventures was widespread among all classes. In

November 1845 Greville (*Journal of the Reign of Queen Victoria*, ii) noted the reactions of London society to railroad 'opportunities'.

It has been during the last two months that the rage for railroad speculation reached its height, was checked by a sudden panic in full career, and is now reviving again, though not by any means promising to recover its pristine vigour. I met one day in the middle of it the Governor of the Bank at Robarts', who told me that he never remembered in all his experience anything like the present speculation; that the operations of '25, which led to the great panic, were nothing to it, and that there could not fail to be a fearful reaction. The reaction came sooner than anybody expected, but though it has blown many of the bubbles into the air, it has not been as yet so complete and so ruinous as many of the wise men of the East still expect and predict. It is incredible how people have been tempted to speculate; half the fine ladies have been dabbling in stocks, and men the most unlikely have not been able to refrain from gambling in shares, even I myself (though in a very small degree), for the warning voice of the Governor of the Bank has never been out of my ears.

PART FOUR

Industrial Life

The wages of weavers at Glasgow are now reduced to one-fourth of what they were nineteen years ago, although the price of provisions and other necessaries has doubled in the mean time!

Louis Simond (1767–1831), *Journal of a Tour and Residence in Great Britain* (Edinburgh, 1815)

On every side, and far as the eye could see into the heavy distance, tall chimneys, crowding on each other, and presenting that endless repetition of the same dull, ugly, form, which is the horror of oppressive dreams, poured out their plague of smoke, obscured the light, and made foul the melancholy air.

Charles Dickens (1812–70), *The Old Curiosity Shop* (1841)

While the engine runs, the people must work—men, women, and children are yoked together with iron and steam. The animal machine . . . is chained fast to the iron machine, which knows no suffering and no weariness.

[Sir] James Kay [-Shuttleworth] (1804–77), *The Moral and Physical Condition of the Working Classes employed in the Cotton Manufacture in Manchester* (1832)

Factory labour, in many of its processes, requires little else but manual dexterity, and no physical strength; neither is there anything for the mind to do in it . . .

Peter Gaskell (1804–41), *Artisans and Machinery* (1836)

No one who will take the trouble to examine the state of the small courts and yards of the lower parts of this town can doubt that the dwellings of the numerous class which inhabits these places must be at the root of much of the excessive mortality. There are families living in cellars about as good as a gentleman's coal place, in which they eat, sleep, and wash.

James Braithwaite, *An Inquiry into the causes of the High Death Rate in Leeds* (Leeds, 1865)

The dust, the din, the work, the hissing and roaring of one person to another, the obscene language uttered, even by the youngest, and the imperious commands harshly given by those "dressed in a little brief authority", struck my young country heart with awe and astonishment.

[James Myles, 1819–51] *Chapters in the Life of a Dundee Factory Boy* (Dundee, 1850)

While in Liverpool one-fifth, and in Manchester and Salford, one-tenth, of the working classes were found to be living in cellars, in Hull there are only fifteen in every 10,000.

William Langton (1803–78), 'Summary of the Report of the Committee on the Condition of the Working Classes in Hull . . .', Manchester Statistical Society (1840–41)

The millions are a doomed class.

J. F. Bray (1809–95), *Labour's Wrongs and Labour's Remedies* (1839)

Here, brought into close neighbourhood, and estranged from the influence of superior example, [workers] are subject to temptations, hazards, and incitements far beyond those which approach the rural cottage . . .

Joseph Fletcher (1813–52), 'Moral and Educational Statistics of England and Wales', *Journal of the London Statistical Society* (1847)

There can be no doubt of the miserably depressed state of the frame-work-knitters. They appear to labour without energy, or hope, or heartiness . . .

Nottingham Review, 25 January 1850

I was twenty years among the hand-loom weavers, and ten years in a factory . . . and the longer and harder I have worked the poorer and poorer I have become every year, until, at last, I am nearly exhausted.

Richard Pilling (b. 1800), in *The Trial of Feargus O'Connor and 58 Others at Lancaster* (1843)

Manchester in 1795

The eighteenth-century growth of Manchester was described by the Warrington physician and topographer Dr. John Aikin (1747–1822), in his celebrated *Description of the Country from thirty to forty miles round Manchester* (1795).

When the Manchester trade began to extend, the chapmen used to keep gangs of pack-horses, and accompany them to the principal towns with goods in packs, which they opened and sold to shop-keepers, lodging what was unsold in small stores at the inns. The pack-horses brought back sheep's wool, which was bought on the journey, and sold to the makers of worsted yarn at Manchester, or to the clothiers of Rochdale, Saddleworth, and the West-Riding of Yorkshire. On the improvement of turnpike roads waggons were set up, and the pack-horses discontinued; and the chapmen only rode out for orders, carrying with them patterns in their bags. It was during the forty years from 1730 to 1770 that trade was greatly pushed by the practice of sending these riders all over the kingdom . . . As this was attended not only with more trouble, but with much more risk, some of the old traders withdrew from business, or confined themselves to as much as they could do on the old footing, which, by the competition of young adventurers, diminished yearly . . .

Within the last twenty or thirty years the vast increase of foreign trade has caused many of the Manchester manufacturers to travel abroad, and agents or partners to be fixed for a considerable time on the Continent, as well as foreigners to reside at Manchester. And the town has now in every respect assumed the style and manners of one of the commercial capitals of Europe.

Manchester in 1835

The French statesman and commentator Alexis de Tocqueville (1805–59) noted in his study *De La Démocratie en Amérique* (Paris, 1835) that in the United States 'the doctrine of enlightened self-interest . . . had been universally accepted.' Visits to Britain also troubled his Christian conscience. In July 1835 he was appalled by Manchester (*Journeys to England and Ireland*, ed. J. P. Mayer, 1958).

Thirty or forty factories rise on the tops of the hills . . . Their six stories tower up; their huge enclosures give notice from afar of the centralisation of industry. The wretched dwellings of the poor are scattered haphazard around them. Round them stretches land uncultivated but without the charm of rustic nature, and still without the amenities of a town . . . The roads which connect the still dis-jointed limbs of the great city, show, like the rest, every sign of hurried or unfinished work; the incidental activity of a population bent on gain, which seeks to amass gold so as to have everything else all at once, and, in the interval, mistrusts the niceties of life. Some of these roads are paved, but most of them are full of ruts and puddles into which foot or carriage wheel sinks deep. Heaps of dung, rubble from buildings, putrid, stagnant pools are found here and there among the houses and over the bumpy, pitted surfaces of the public places. No trace of surveyor's rod or spirit-level. Amid this noisome labyrinth, this great sombre stretch of brickwork, from time to time one is astonished by the sight of fine stone buildings with Corinthian columns. It might be a medieval town, with the marvels of the 19th century in the middle of it. But who could describe the interiors of these quarters set apart, homes of vice and poverty, which surround the huge palaces of industry and clasp them in their hideous folds? . . .

. . . Look up, and all around this place you will see the huge palaces of industry. You will hear the noise of furnaces, the whistle of steam. These vast structures keep air and light out of the human habitations which they dominate; they envelop them in perpetual fog; here is the slave, there is the master; there the wealth of some, here the poverty of most; there the organised effort of thousands to produce, to the profit of one man, what society has not yet learnt to give. Here the weakness of the individual seems more feeble and helpless even than in the middle of a wilderness; here the effects, there the causes.

A sort of black smoke covers the city. The sun seen through it is a disc without rays. Under this half daylight 300,000 human beings are ceaselessly at work. A thousand noises disturb this damp, dark labyrinth, but they are not all the ordinary sounds one hears in great cities . . .

From this foul drain the greatest stream of human industry flows out to fertilise the whole world. From this filthy sewer pure gold flows. Here humanity attains its most complete development and its most brutish; here civilisation works its miracles, and civilised man is turned back almost into a savage.

Manchester in 1844

The cotton metropolis of the nineteenth century was a place at once awesome and terrible to many observers. Engels, *op. cit.*, described the town in 1844, after twenty months' residence, as an office worker in the Manchester cotton firm of Ermen & Engels—in which his father was a partner. His work was to become a Marxist classic of anti-capitalist literature.

. . . Owing to the curious lay-out of the town it is quite possible for someone to live for years in Manchester and to travel daily to and from his work without ever seeing a working-class quarter or coming into contact with an artisan. He who visits Manchester simply on business or for pleasure need never see the slums, mainly because the working-class districts and the middle-class districts are quite distinct. This division is due partly to deliberate policy and partly to instinctive and tacit agreement between the two social groups. In those areas where the two social groups happen to come into contact with each other the middle classes sanctimoniously ignore the existence of their less fortunate neighbours. In the centre of Manchester there is a fairly large commercial district, which is about half a mile long and half a mile broad. This district is almost entirely given over to offices and warehouses . . . The lower floors of the buildings are occupied by shops of dazzling splendour . . . Around this commercial quarter there is a belt of built up areas on the average one and a half miles in width, which is occupied entirely by working-class dwellings . . . Beyond . . . lie the districts inhabited by the middle classes and the upper classes. The former are to be found in regularly laid out streets near the working-class districts—in Chorlton and in the remoter parts of Cheetham Hill. The villas of the upper classes are surrounded by gardens and lie in the higher and remoter parts of Chorlton and Ardwick or on the breezy heights of Cheetham Hill, Broughton and Pendleton. The upper classes enjoy healthy country air and live in luxurious and comfortable dwellings which are linked to the centre of Manchester by omnibuses which run every fifteen or thirty minutes . . .

. . . I will now give a description of the working-class districts of Manchester. The first of them is the Old Town . . . Here even the better streets . . . are narrow and tortuous. The houses are dirty, old and tumble-down . . . This is a remnant of the old Manchester of the days before the town became industrialised . . .

. . . Filth, heaps of refuse and ashes and dirty pools in the streets are common . . . There are large numbers of pigs, some of which are allowed to roam freely in the narrow streets, snuffing among the garbage heaps, while others are kept in little sties in the courts. In this area, as in most of the working-class districts of Manchester, pig breeders rent the courts and build the sties there. In nearly every court there are one or more little nooks in which pigs are kept. The inhabitants of the court throw all their garbage into these sties. This fattens the pigs, but also has the highly undesirable effect of impregnating the air—already stale because it is confined between four walls—with the disagreeable odour of decaying animal and vegetable matter . . .

. . . The New Town is composed of single rows of houses and groups of streets which might be small villages, lying on bare clayey soil which does not produce even a blade of grass. The houses—or rather the cottages—are in a disgraceful state because they are never repaired. They are filthy and beneath them are to be found damp, dirty cellar dwellings; the unpaved alleys lack any form of drainage. The district is infested with small herds of pigs . . . The lanes in this district are so filthy that it is only in very dry weather that one can reach it without sinking ankle-deep at every step . . .

. . . Little Ireland . . . lies in a fairly deep natural depression on a bend of the river [Medlock] and is completely surrounded by tall factories or high banks and embankments covered with buildings. Here lie two groups of about two hundred cottages, most of which are built on the back-to-back principle. Some four thousand people, mostly Irish, inhabit this slum. The cottages are very small, old and dirty, while the streets are uneven, partly unpaved, not properly drained and full of ruts. Heaps of refuse, offal and sickening filth are everywhere interspersed with pools of stagnant liquid. The atmosphere is polluted by the stench and is darkened by the thick smoke of a dozen factory chimneys. A horde of ragged women and children swarm about the streets and they are just as dirty as the pigs which wallow happily on the heaps of garbage and in the pools of filth. In short, this horrid little slum affords as hateful and repulsive a spectacle as the worst courts to be found on the banks of the Irk . . .

Huddersfield

Some celebrated reports on living and working conditions in the mid-century were published in supplements to the *Morning Chronicle* during the winter of 1849–50. The authors were Henry Mayhew (1812–87) (London), Alexander Mackay (1808–52) (country districts) and Angus Reach (1821–56) (manufacturing districts). In a report dated 3 December 1849 (published on 18 January 1850) Reach commented on some West Riding towns, including Huddersfield, a borough almost entirely owned by the Whig Sir John Ramsden, 5th Bt. (1831–1914).

The houses inhabited by the factory hands of Huddersfield consist in most cases of a large parlour-kitchen opening from the street, with a cellar beneath it, and either two small bedrooms or one large one above. In some instances a scullery is added to the main apartment. The general style of furniture is much the same as that which distinguishes the operative dwellings of the cotton districts. If there be any difference, I should say that that of Huddersfield seems the more plainly substantial of the two. The clock and the corner cupboards, and the shelves glittering with ranges of dishes and plates, are to be found as universally as in Manchester, and a plentiful supply of good water is in general conducted into every home.

Taking wages as the test of social condition, the operatives of Huddersfield may be considered as very fairly situated. Children below 13 years of age are seldom employed in the mills, and the average earnings of those over that age may be 5s. weekly. The earnings of the women may vary from 7s. or thereabouts—obtained by those who pick and boil—to 9s. or 10s., or thereabouts, obtained by those who weave. The average may be about 8s. 6d. The average wage of the women is raised by the number of their sex who work at the loom, as the average wage of men is depressed by the same cause. Slubbers, carders, spinners, dyers, fullers, raisers, and finishers may average about 18s. a week. Taking into account the number of adult males employed as weavers, both by power and hand, the general average sinks, and may be placed at from 14s. to 15s. per week. Admitting these estimates to be generally correct, the average wage earned by adults in Huddersfield may be placed at 11s. 6d. a week—an amount very similar to the general run of wages in the cotton districts, while the average earned by all sexes and ages may be estimated at something more than 9s. I have said that the Huddersfield cottage houses are generally constructed back and back, and that a common arrangement is their division into a cellar or store-place, a kitchen-parlour, and a large bedroom above it. The rents paid range from £7 to £8, or about 3s. per week.

The yarns given out by the mills to be spun and woven at the homes of the work people, are taken to the rural districts around, or to the remote suburbs of Huddersfield. At a little village called Paddock, about a mile from the town, a number of looms are generally going. Proceeding there, I entered upon a series of domiciliary visits. The general arrangements of the houses were similar. The looms invariably occupied the first floor. In some cases, one and two uncurtained beds, almost invariably left unmade, were placed in corners. In other instances, the sleeping arrangements were upon the ground floor, or within a third chamber roughly partitioned off from the loom apartment. In the first house I entered, one loom only was at work. The weaver was manufacturing a rough greyish cloth for a peculiar sort of great coat. It was a web by which he could earn 17s. a week. He had not always so good a job, and, with his wife to mind for him, he did not on the average earn so much as 10s. a week. There were four in the family—his wife, himself, and two children . . . I . . . found that the fare for the family consisted of two huge pig's pettitoes, with bread and potatoes . . .

In another house I found that only two people resided, a man and his wife . . . The man, who was busy, stopped his shuttle to speak to me. For the cloth which he was weaving he could have got, seven years ago, 10d. a yard; the price now paid was only 4½d. When he had pretty regular work, his average weekly earnings were about 10s. For this he frequently worked from six o'clock in the morning until eight o'clock at night. . . . The earnings of his wife amounted to about 3s. 6d. per week. Taking an average, he thought that their united earnings might be about 12s. 6d. or 13s. a week. This was when trade was tolerably good . . .

Dewsbury

Reach next visited Dewsbury, the centre of the 'shoddy' trade with its 'devil's dust' and the bronchial 'shoddy fever'. He thought the work 'the lowest and foulest which any phase of the factory system could show.'

There are some shoddy mills in the neighbourhood of Huddersfield; but the mean little town of Dewsbury may be taken as the metropolis of the manufacture . . . The first mill I visited was that belonging to the Messrs. Blakely, in the immediate outskirts of the town. This establishment is devoted solely to the sorting, preparing, and grinding of rags, which are worked up in the neighbouring factories. Great bales choke-full of filthy tatters lay scattered about the yard, and loaded waggons were fast arriving and adding to the heap. As for the mill, a glance at its exterior showed its character. It being a calm still day, the walls and part of the roof were covered with the thick clinging dust and fibre, which ascended in choky volumes from the open doors and glassless windows of the ground floor, and which also poured forth from a chimney constructed for the purpose, exactly like smoke . . .

We went first into the upper story [*sic*], where the rags are stored. A great wareroom was piled in many places from the floor to the ceiling with bales of woollen rags, torn strips and tatters of every colour peeping out from the bursting depositories. There is hardly a country in Europe which does not contribute its quota of material to the shoddy manufacturer . . . Denmark, I understand, is favourably looked upon by the tatter-merchants, being fertile in morsels of clothing, of fair quality. Of domestic rags, the Scotch bear off the palm; and possibly no one will be surprised to hear, that of all rags, Irish rags are the most worn, the filthiest, and generally the most unprofitable . . . The refuse of all, mixed with the stuff which even the shoddy-making devil rejects, is packed off to the agricultural districts for use as manure. I saw several unpleasant-looking lots which were destined to fertilise the hop-gardens of Kent.

Under the rag wareroom was the sorting and picking room. Here the bales are opened, and their contents piled in close poverty-smelling masses upon the floor. The operatives were entirely women . . . and the wages which they were paid for ten hours' [daily] work were 6s. per week . . . The atmosphere of the room was close and oppressive; and although I perceived no particularly offensive smell, we could not help being sensible of the presence of a choky, mildewy sort of odour—a hot, moist exhalation—arising from the sodden smouldering piles . . .

The devils were . . . upon the ground-floor. The choking dust burst out from door and window, and it was not until a minute or so that I could see the workmen, moving amid the clouds . . . The workmen were of course coated with the flying powder. They wore bandages over their mouths, so as to prevent as much as possible the inhalation of the dust . . . Not one of them, however, would admit that he found the trade injurious. No, the dust tickled them a little—that was all . . . I asked whether there was not a disorder known as "shoddy fever"? The reply was, that they were all more or less subject to it . . .

Leeds: Health and Morals

Of Leeds, the capital of the Yorkshire woollen industry, Sir George Head thought in 1835, that 'no manufacturing town in England' consumed more coal 'in proportion to its extent . . . The sun himself was obscured by smoke'. The first extract is from a report in *The Artizan*, October, 1843. The second is taken from [Sir] Edward Baines, *Social, Educational, And Religious State of The Manufacturing Districts* (1843). Baines (1800–90), the Liberal Congregationalist son and successor of the proprietor of the *Leeds Mercury*, was determined to defend his native town from attacks made by Lord Ashley and other Anglican Tories, in letters to Peel and Lord Wharncliffe.

(1) The higher or western districts are clean for so large a town, but the lower parts contiguous to the river [Aire] and its becks or rivulets are dirty, confined, and, in themselves, sufficient to shorten life, especially infant life; add to this the disgusting state of the lower parts of the town about Kirk-gate, March-lane, Cross-street, and Richmond-road, principally owing to a general want of paving and draining, irregularity of building, the abundance of courts and blind alleys, as well as the almost total absence of the commonest means of promoting cleanliness, and we have then quite sufficient data to account for the surplus mortality in these unhappy regions of filth and misery . . .

(2) When you find one in every ten of the population in Day Schools, and one in every $5\frac{2}{5}$ in Sunday Schools, and Churches

and Chapels that would hold nearly one-half of the entire population, I ask if this is a state of things to create a panic in Parliament; or to justify either the conclusions of the Children's Employment Commissioners, or the language of Lord Ashley, in speaking of these districts especially as a "great and terrible wilderness", peopled by "untutored savages"? . . .

. . . The prejudice against the Manufacturing Districts is of much older date than Lord Ashley's speech or the Report of the Children's Employment Commissioners. It has respect not merely to the alleged want of education and religious instruction, but to the social condition of the people and the nature and effects of their employments. This prejudice has been growing up ever since the first Committee on Factory Labour, eleven years since; and it has been industriously cultivated by many persons, and from various motives,—by Conservative politicians, because of the prevalence of Liberal opinions here,—by the Agricultural and Colonial interests, because here the monopolists were most actively assailed,—and by the High Church because in these districts the Dissenters outnumbered them . . .

. . . The factory system, so far from being injurious or oppressive to the workman, gives him the benefit of the most perfect and most expensive tools in the world—all the splendid inventions of Arkwright, Hargreaves, Crompton, Cartwright, Watt, and many others, combined and arranged in an admirable series, within one building; and it links with him, in an indissoluble band of interest, capitalists of the largest means and greatest skill and experience. The labour of the factory, instead of being severe, is light,—the heavy work being done by the steam-engine and the other machinery, and the duty of the workmen being chiefly to supply the material, to watch the movements of the machines, and to convey the article from one process to another. The hardest labour, perhaps, is in the woollen mills, which, however, contain the healthiest body of working men . . .

. . . Even the present Factory Bill has diminished by many thousands the children employed in factories, because it has been found troublesome to the employers to observe the regulations as to certificates and education, and therefore they have either employed older hands or machinery to do the work formerly done by children . . .

. . . I believe that the observance of the Lord's day is incomparably worse in the rural districts than in the manufacturing, especially in the practice of cricketing and other games on that day,—a practice too generally connived at by the unevangelical and fox-hunting clergy . . .

. . . The riots of "Swing" in Dorsetshire and throughout the South, and the insurrection in favour of the imposter Thom near Canterbury, ought to stop the mouths of Lord Ashley and the country gentlemen from inveighing against the Manufacturing Districts . . .

I might dwell upon the many institutions and associations for the diffusion of knowledge, and for the dispensing of every kind of good, which have arisen within the present or the last generation, and which flourish most in the manufacturing towns and villages; such as Mechanics' Institutes, Literary Societies, Circulating Libraries, Youths' Guardian Societies, Friendly Societies, Temperance Societies, Medical Charities, Clothing Societies, Benevolent and District Visiting Societies, etc.,—forty-nine fiftieths of which are of quite recent origin. The moral, intellectual, and physical good done by these associations is beyond calculation; and their existence is one of the most decisive proofs possible of the growth and commanding influence of true Christian principles in the communities where they have been formed.

Leeds: Town and Country

Baines was so incensed by the 1843 'Factory Education Bill' and its supporters' attacks on the manufacturing districts that he published a series of pamphlets against the (eventually unsuccessful) measure and in defence of the factory areas. The following extracts are taken from his pamphlet *The Manufacturing Districts Vindicated* (Leeds, 1843), an open letter to Lord Wharncliffe, dated 31 March 1843.

The danger of the present times is exceedingly aggravated by a combination of circumstances that appears fortuitous. Attempts have been made with great perseverance for some years past to *blacken the manufacturing districts in the eyes of Parliament and of the public*. Political conflicts to which I need not allude have furnished the motives to these attempts. Some men, influenced by undoubted humanity, such as LORD ASHLEY, have been instruments to the same end. Commissions of inquiry have been appointed to bring to light all the abuses and evils existing in the manufacturing and mining districts (*not* in the agricultural) and they have succeeded, as they would have done in any other part of the known world, in producing full budgets and painting very dark pictures. And, lastly, the sudden and momentary turnout of last August, though the most harmless movement on record, though provoked by severe distress, and though an experiment at the folly of which the workmen themselves laughed as soon as it was over, has been excessively magnified, so as to give the impression that the manufacturing districts are placed over a volcano ever ready to burst!

. . . My Lord, I engage to prove that the impression of alarm with respect to the state of the manufacturing districts, on which the authors of this Bill rely for success, is *absurdly false and injurious* . . .

LET it be observed, I do not charge Lord ASHLEY or the Children's Employment Commission with *intentional* misrepresentation. But I do say that the *impression* likely to be produced by his speeches and their Report is *one-sided*, *exaggerated*, and *erroneous* in the extreme . . .

. . . Of course we cannot expect that in this poor, provincial, manufacturing, dissenting town of Leeds, there should be any thing like the *same amount* of *education* or of *religion* as in the chosen abode of nearly all the Bishops and nearly all the Members of both Houses of Parliament. That would be extravagant. Let us expect nothing out of reason. Nevertheless, my Lord, I tell you, we have *more* of *both*! We have *more education*; we have *more religion*; and we have *less vice*!

. . . Now, my Lord, you can afford to abate a little of the pity you may have felt for poor Leeds. But, more, my Lord, much more than this—you will, I am sure, spare a little respect for that principle of *voluntary religious zeal* which has done *everything* in Leeds, and will moreover pause before you adopt a *compulsory* measure *which might cut the sinew of that voluntary zeal.*

WOULD your Lordship have the goodness just to put these facts before SIR ROBERT INGLIS, and to hold him fast by the button till you are sure he has heard of them? Would you ask him if he could give as good an account of Oxford? Would you also suggest to LORD ASHLEY and SIR JAMES GRAHAM to *look rather nearer home* . . .

I MUST not conclude without saying, that if LORD ASHLEY will appoint a Commission to inquire into the state of the *Agricultural* population, he will find a sphere for his benevolent anxiety possessing at least as many claims upon him as the manufacturing towns. I believe, on the authority of the "Report of the Constabulary Force Commissioners", that "the *majority* of the crimes attended with violence are now committed in the *rural* districts, although the population and property in towns have increased in a far more rapid proportion". I believe, on the evidence of the facts which induced your Lordship to propose the Bastardy clause of the New Poor Law, that the want of chastity in the rural districts is far more general than in the manufacturing districts. I believe, on the evidence of the wide-spread incendiarism and destruction of thrashing machines, that the lawlessness of the agricultural labourers, arising from their gross ignorance, is much more formidable than that of the manufacturing population. I believe, from such facts as the insurrection in favour of the imposter THOM in Kent, that the knowledge of religion is far less in the country than in towns. I am persuaded that there is no comparison between the manufacturing and agricultural labourers as to general intelligence, and habits of reading and thinking. It is beyond all question that the rate of wages is much higher in manufactures than in agriculture,—that the workmen employed in the former have better food, clothing, and houses, and greater comforts than those employed in the latter . . .

Birmingham: Evils and Cures

In 1784 the French traveller B. F. de St. Fond wrote that West Midland coal had created a 'miracle'—a town 'in the midst of a human desert' where 40,000 people 'lived in comfort and enjoyed all the conveniences of life'. Generally, small industrial units led to close relationships between masters and journeymen in Birmingham and to moderate political stances. But there was another side to the picture. The Rev. Thomas Nunns (d. 1854), a Lancashire man, Cambridge graduate and perpetual curate of S. Paul's, Burslem, in 1828–32 and of S. Bartholomew's, Birmingham, in 1833–43, wrote his *Letter to . . . Lord Ashley, on the Condition of the Working Classes in Birmingham* (Birmingham, 1842) as a concerned High Churchman. Later, as perpetual curate of S. Paul's, Leeds (1843–45) and vicar of Holy Trinity, Leeds (1845–54), he supported the Yorkshire factory reform campaign. Nunns' proposals are summarised in the second extract.

(1) ... I think it is obvious that improvement in general in the condition of the lower orders has been for these years an undertaking mainly of *private* benevolence; and that government and the public have been content to regard it in *that* light, rather than as a matter of public and national concern. While, doubtless, much good has been done in this way, the good required has not been done; efforts proportionate to the wants of the people have not been put forth ...

... TO BE an improvement, it must not be partial, but universal; not variable, but constant; not local, but general and national; not the work of individuals and societies, but of government and the nation ...

The first and worst, and most glaring evil, and the source of innumerable other evils under which the working classes here labour, and which tends to depress their condition and degrade their character, perhaps most, I conceive, is—

1. *The early age at which children, both boys and girls, are admitted to work in manufactories* ...
2. *The indiscriminate employment of boys and girls in the same workshop* ...
3. *The little regard paid by the masters to the moral and religious well-being, and the domestic comforts of their work-people* ...
4. *The utter ignorance of females arrived at womanhood, in all the departments of domestic economy* ...
5. *The low state of education generally, and its quality, compared with the population, its wants, and character* ...

... except in very few instances, never does the master manufacturer, in whose service the poor dying sufferer has lived and spent his best days, and on whom he has, therefore, the strongest claims, and by labouring for whose wealth his days are cut short, ever enter his dwelling; from him neither relief nor sympathy comes. "He is treated like a cast-off horse," to use the oft-quoted phrase of *Mr. McCulloch*, "that is past labour, to live or die as he may."

(2) I. TO KEEP YOUNG CHILDREN, BUT MOST ESPECIALLY FEMALES, OUT OF THE MANUFACTORIES ALTOGETHER.

I conceive it a perfect impossibility to effect any good, either religious, social, moral, or intellectual, among the lower orders, till something is done in this way ...

II. THAT EDUCATION MUST BE COMPULSORY ...

III. AN INCREASE OF SCHOOLS, AND AN IMPROVED SYSTEM OF EDUCATION . . .

I look upon—

IV. THE ESTABLISHED CHURCH, ADAPTED IN ITS APPLIANCES TO THE WANTS OF THE PEOPLE IN LARGE TOWNS—

as, after all, the grand instrument for effecting any real improvement in the character and condition of the lower orders . . . An immoral and irreligious people never can be a safe and contented people. A religious people cannot be any other.

Birmingham: Housing

Birmingham's homes mirrored the social mix of the town. Working-class accommodation was generally provided in little courts of tenements, with communal wash-houses, lavatories, ash pits and (often) pigsties. Visitors' and doctors' impressions seem to have been that Birmingham workers' little back-to-back tenements were better than most. Nevertheless, the 2,030 courts with 12,254 tenements noted by local medical practitioners in 1836 were often foul. The following description from *The Artizan* (October, 1843) was largely quoted by Engels.

Birmingham, the great seat of the toy and trinket trade, and competing with Sheffield in the hardware manufacture, is furnished by its position on a slope falling towards the Rea, with a very good natural drainage, which is much promoted by the porous nature of the sand and gravel, of which the adjacent high grounds are mainly composed. The principal streets, therefore, are well drained by covered sewers; but still in the older parts of the town there are many inferior streets and courts, which are dirty and neglected, filled with stagnant water and heaps of refuse. The courts of Birmingham are very numerous in every direction, exceeding 2,000 and comprising the residence of a large portion of the working-classes. They are for the most part narrow, filthy, ill-ventilated, and badly drained, containing from eight to twenty houses, each, the houses being usually three stories high, and often merely *single*, that is, built against some other tenement and the end of the courts being pretty constantly occupied by ashpits, etc., the filth of which would defy description. It is but just, however, to remark that the courts of more modern date are built in a more rational manner, and kept tolerably respectable; and the cottages, even in courts, are far less crowded than in Manchester and Liverpool, the result of which is, that the inhabitants, in epidemic seasons, have been much less visited by death than those of Wolverhampton, Dudley, and Bilston, at only a few miles distance. Cellar-residences also, are unknown in Birmingham, though some few are, very improperly, used as workshops. The low lodging-houses are pretty numerous (somewhat exceeding 400), chiefly in courts near the centre of the town; they are almost always loathsomely filthy and close, the resorts of beggars, trampers, thieves and prostitutes, who here, regardless alike of decency or comfort, eat, drink, smoke and sleep in an atmosphere unendurable by all except the degraded, besotted inmates.

Glasgow

Engels also quoted *The Artizan* on the greatest Scottish city. The salubrious little town noted by Defoe had greatly changed under the rule of the 'tobacco barons', cotton masters and chemical manufacturers. Indeed, in 1839, Assistant Commissioner J. C. Symons (1809–60) reported to the Handloom Weavers Commission that he 'did not believe until [he] visited the wynds of Glasgow, that so large an amount of filth, crime, misery, and disease existed on one spot in any civilized country'. The first extract is from *The Artizan* (October 1843) and the second from Edwin Chadwick's celebrated *Report on the Sanitary Condition of the Labouring Population of Gt. Britain* (1842). Dr. Neil Arnott (1788–1874), a Poor Law doctor, was Chadwick's friend and fellow-Benthamite and a housing expert. The visit to Glasgow was made in September 1840.

(1) Glasgow has its fine, airy, healthy quarters, that may vie with those of London and all wealthy cities; but it has others which, in abject wretchedness, exceed the lowest purlieus of St. Giles' or Whitechapel, the liberties of Dublin, or the wynds of Edinburgh. Such localities exist most abundantly in the heart of the city—south of the Trongate and west of the Saltmarket, as well as in the Calton, off the High-street, etc.—endless labyrinths of narrow lanes or wynds, into which almost at every step debouche courts or closes formed by old, ill-ventilated, towering houses crumbling to decay, destitute of water and crowded with inhabitants, comprising three or four families (perhaps twenty persons) on each flat, and sometimes each flat let out in lodgings that confine—we

dare not say accommodate—from fifteen to twenty persons in a single room. These districts are occupied by the poorest, most depraved, and most worthless portion of the population, and they may be considered as the fruitful source of those pestilential fevers which thence spread their destructive ravages over the whole of Glasgow.

(2) The most wretched of the stationary population of which I have been able to obtain any account, was that which I saw in company with *Dr. Arnott*, and others, in the wynds of Edinburgh and Glasgow.

I prefer citing his description of the residences we visited:

. . . 'In Glasgow, which I first visited, it was found that the great mass of the fever cases occurred in the low wynds and dirty narrow streets and courts, in which because lodging was there cheapest, the poorest and most destitute naturally had their abodes. From one such locality, between Argyll-street and the river, 754 of about 5,000 cases of fever which occurred in the previous year were carried to the hospitals . . .

'We entered a dirty low passage like a house door, which led from the street through the first house to a square court immediately behind, which court, with the exception of a narrow path around it leading to another long passage through a second house, was occupied entirely as a dung receptacle of the most disgusting kind. Beyond this court the second passage led to a second square court, occupied in the same way by its dunghill; and from this court there was yet a third passage leading to a third court, and third dungheap. There were no privies or drains there, and the dungheaps received all filth which the swarm of wretched inhabitants could give; and we learned that a considerable part of the rent of the houses was paid by the produce of the dungheaps. Thus, worse off than wild animals, many of which withdraw to a distance and conceal their ordure, the dwellers in these courts had converted their shame into a kind of money by which their lodging was to be paid. The interiors of these houses and their inmates corresponded with the exteriors. We saw half-dressed wretches crowding together to be warm; and in one bed, although in the middle of the day, several women were imprisoned under a blanket, because as many others who had on their backs all the articles of dress that belonged to the party were then out of doors in the streets . . .

'Who can wonder that pestilential disease should originate and spread in such situations? . . .'

. . . It might admit of dispute, but, on the whole, it appeared to us that both the structural arrangements and the condition of the population in Glasgow was the worst of any we had seen in any part of Great Britain.

Edinburgh

The Scottish capital was little better, in its slum areas, than Glasgow, the major Scottish industrial city. Reporting in 1840 on typhus epidemics (*Reports on the Sanitary Condition of the Labouring Population of Scotland*, 1842), Dr. Arnott was horrified by conditions in central Edinburgh. His account was reprinted by Chadwick.

'Edinburgh stands on a site beautifully varied by hill and hollow, and owing to this, unusual facilities are afforded for perfect drainage; but the old part of the town was built long before the importance of drainage was understood in Britain, and in the unchanged parts there is none but by the open channels in the streets, wynds, and closes or courts. To remedy the want of covered drains, there is in many neighbourhoods a very service of scavengers to remove everything which open drains cannot be allowed to carry but this does not prevent the air from being much more contaminated by the frequent stirring and sweeping of impurities than if the transport were effected under ground; and there are here and there enclosed spaces between houses too small to be used for any good purpose but not neglected for bad, and to which the scavengers have not access.

'Another defect in some parts of Edinburgh is the great size and height of the houses (some of them exceeding ten stories), with common stairs, sometimes as filthy as the streets or wynds to which they open. By this construction the chance of cleanliness is lessened, the labour of carrying up necessaries, and particularly water for the purposes of purifying is increased; and if any malaria or contagion exist in the house, the probability of its passing from dwelling to dwelling on the same stair is much greater than if there were no communication but through the open air . . .

'The facts here referred to go far to explain why fatal fever has been more common in Edinburgh than from other circumstances would have been anticipated.'

Bradford

Bradford grew rapidly from the eighteenth century, as the capital of the worsted industry. A local antiquary, John James (1811–67) described some typical improvements in his *History of Bradford* (1841). The town received its charter of incorporation in 1847.

The town had now risen to a size and population that required some municipal regulation for lighting and cleansing, and preventing nuisances and obstructions in the streets, and making provision for the effectual watching of the town. A bill was therefore brought into parliament in 1803, for accomplishing these purposes. The jurisdiction of the act extends over Bradford and part of the hamlet of Little-Horton. Fifty-eight persons were appointed commissioners, with power to appoint others—the qualification for office being an estate of £1,000, either real or personal. Very large powers are given to the commissioners, which if rigidly exercised, would be very obnoxious to the public; but hitherto they have been used with moderation and good judgment. I am unable to give even a summary of the multifarious sections of this long act. There is in it ample provision for preventing nuisances and obstructions in the streets, and for paving and improving lighting and watching them. There is in it one section which contains provisions which have not been enforced. In this section it is enacted that all persons resident within the township of Bradford and the hamlet of Little-Horton, making use in their buildings of fires casting up large quantities of smoke or flame, should construct the chimneys of such buildings of such a height as the commissioners may direct; for the purpose of preventing, as much as possible, the smoke and flame becoming a nuisance. And that the owner of every fire-engine or steam-engine within the above-named jurisdiction, should construct the fire-places and chimneys thereof in such a manner as most effectually to destroy and consume the smoke provided *they do not infringe on any patent*; and on their refusing to comply with these provisions, after notice from the commissioners, they are subject to a penalty.

The town had hitherto been lighted by oil lamps. In 1822 an act received the Royal assent for lighting Bradford and the neighbourhood with gas. The subscribers originally consisted of forty-one inhabitants of the place, who were incorporated under the title of the "Bradford Gas-Light Company", and empowered to raise a capital of £15,000, in £25 shares—no subscriber to hold more than forty shares. By this act it is rendered imperative upon the gas company to supply the public lamps of the town with gas, of such a quality as should at all times *afford a cheaper and better light* than could be obtained from oil . . .

Bradford and Halifax

The worsted manufacture was centred upon Bradford and Halifax, but (as Reach pointed out) the latter town also had a considerable carpet industry. In the *Morning Chronicle* (22 January 1850) Reach contrasted the two towns.

. . . [Bradford] is, perhaps, more quickly and keenly affected by the variations of trade than any other manufacturing depôt in England. The masters are generally reputed as bold speculators; and the millowner who ventures his money freely, hazards, of necessity, the wages of his people as well as his own profits. In Halifax, however, things are conducted more slowly and quietly. Compared with Bradford, the place has a touch of antiquity in its aspect and its tone. So far as appearance goes, no two towns can be more dissimilar. Halifax is an ancient borough, girdled by an *enceint* of mills and mill-hands' dwellings. Bradford seems spick and span new from the centre to the circumference. There are points in the town of Halifax, from which the gazer will be put in mind of the quaint cities of Normandy and Bavaria . . .

Mr. Smith, of Deanston, in a sanitary report made about 1837, describes Bradford as being the dirtiest town in England. Mr. Smith must have written ere he extended his researches to Halifax. At all events, Bradford is rapidly improving. The corporation is busy paving and draining; but that of Halifax has as yet been able to do nothing. I ought to add that both towns have received their municipal chapters within the last two years, and that Halifax is now, or has been until very lately, unprovided with any funds to carry on a sanitary campaign. The sooner, however, that it begins, the better. Few towns in England are better situated for being effectually drained. Mainly placed on the side of a steepish hill, with a rapid stream running at the bottom, Halifax ought to be a miracle of cleanliness, instead of as it is, a marvel of dirt . . .

. . . The streets of Halifax are disgracefully neglected. The remark applies especially to the courts and *cul-de-sacs* inhabited by the very poor—including, of course, the Irish—and locally termed "foulds". I inspected several very closely, and found them reeking with stench and the worst sort of abomination. The ash-pits and appurtenances were disgustingly choked, ordure and filthy stagnant slops lay freely and deeply scattered around, often at the very thresholds of swarming dwellings; and, among all this muck, uncared-for children sprawled by the score, and idle, slatternly women lounged by the half-dozen . . .

. . . In an architectural point of view, the best features of Bradford consist of numerous ranges of handsome warehouses. The streets have none of the old-fashioned picturesqueness of those of Halifax. The best of them are muddy, and not too often swept. Mills abound in great plenty, and their number is daily increasing, while the town itself extends in like proportion . . . Half a century ago it was a mere cluster of huts: now the district of which it is the heart contains upwards of 132,000 inhabitants. The value of life is about 1 in 40. Fortunes have been made in Bradford with a rapidity almost unequalled even in the manufacturing districts. In half a dozen years men have risen from the loom to possess mills and villas . . .

With the exception of a few of the main thoroughfares, . . . Bradford may be described as an accumulation of mean streets, steep lanes, and huge mills—intersected here and there by those odious patches of black, muddy, waste ground, rooted up by pigs, and strewn with oyster-shells, cabbage-stalks, and such garbage, which I have so often noticed as commonly existing in manufacturing towns . . . The two towns in England, indeed, which within the last half-century have sprung up most rapidly, form an odd pair. They are Brighton and Bradford.

New Lanark

In 1812, during a dispute with his partners, Robert Owen (1771–1858) issued his *Statement Regarding the New Lanark Establishment* from

Edinburgh, to justify his work as a social and industrial reformer. Owen was an eccentric, socialistic millowner at New Lanark.

About twenty-six years ago, the late Mr. DAVID DALE of Glasgow, whose benevolence and philanthropy are well known, commenced an extensive spinning establishment near the Falls of the Clyde, and he founded it on the combined principles of public and private advantage.

It was continued by him for upwards of thirteen years, when, having no sons to succeed him, and being far advanced in life, he sold it to some English merchants, and myself, who married his eldest daughter.

These gentlemen remained in partnership with me ten years, when some of them resold their interest in it to merchants resident in Glasgow, who still hold these shares. But from the first sale by Mr. Dale, until mid-summer last, the management of the establishment was under my direction. At the commencement of that period, I arranged the outline of a plan, on a principle on which I had previously acted in a different part of the kingdom for several years; which was intended to unite and bring into action all the local advantages of the situation; to produce the greatest ultimate profits to the proprietors, with the greatest comfort and improvement to the numerous population to whom it afforded employment; that the latter might be a model and example to the manufacturing community, which, without some essential change in the formation of their characters, threatened, and now still more threatens, to revolutionize and ruin the empire. The plan was founded on the simple and evident principle, that any characters, from the savage to the sage or intelligent benevolent man, might be formed, by applying the proper means, and that these means are to a great extent at the command and under the control of those who have influence in society; and, although mankind are generally unconscious of these important powers, there are few things admitting of any doubt, which are so easy as this, of full and complete demonstration. This system has been pursued at these works, without a single exception from the principle stated, for 13 years, and the result has been precisely that which was calculated. The population originally brought to the establishment was, with a few exceptions, a collection of the most ignorant and destitute from all parts of Scotland, possessing the usual characteristics of poverty and ignorance. They were generally indolent, and much addicted to theft, drunkenness, and falsehood, with all their concomitant vices, and strongly experiencing the misery which these ever produce. But by means so gradually introduced, as to be almost imperceptible to them, they have been surrounded with those circumstances which were calculated, first to check, and then to remove their inducements to retain these inclinations; and they are now become conspicuously honest, industrious, sober, and orderly; so that an idle individual, one in liquor, or a thief, is scarcely to be seen from the beginning to the end of the year; and they are become almost a new people, and quite ready to receive any fixed character which may be deemed the most advantageous for them to possess.

A Rural Lancashire Mill

At Turton near Bolton the Quaker Ashworth brothers—Edmund (1800–81) and Henry (1794–1880)—ran a celebrated rural mill community. Although bitter opponents of industrial legislation and supporters of the Poor Law, the Ashworths generally gained a good reputation, except among factory reformers. A typical liberal panegyric was published by William Cooke Taylor (1800–49), in his *Notes of a Tour in the Manufacturing Districts of Lancashire* (1842 edn.).

How a painter would have enjoyed the sight which broke upon my waking eyes this morning! To my right is one of the tributaries to the Irwell, winding through the depths of a richly wooded and precipitous valley, or rather ravine; the sun's rays, glinting from the waters, come like flashes through every opening in the foliage, . . . Beyond is the hill on which a great part of the busy town of Bolton is built. The intervening valley is studded with factories and bleach-works. Thank God, smoke is rising from the lofty chimneys of most of them! for I have not travelled thus far without learning, by many a painful illustration, that the absence of smoke from the factory-chimney indicates the quenching of the fire on many a domestic hearth, want of employment to many a willing labourer, and want of bread to many an honest family . . .

'Mick'

Victorian Britons had little esteem for the Irish. Drunken, superstitiously Papist, violent, shiftless and illiterate—such was the general picture of the Irish; and many workers resented Irish hostility to trade unionism and proclivities for strike-breaking and wage-undercutting. Angus Reach examined the Irish colony in Huddersfield (*Morning Chronicle*, 18 January 1850).

. . . Access to the [cellar] apartment—if it can be called one—had formerly been obtained by means of a flight of stairs from the ground-floor of the house above; but these had been blocked up, and as there was a small sunken area on the outside, an extra door, or rather hole, not four feet high, had been broken in the wall, and through this the inmates crawled backwards and forwards. This den—the place was about eight feet by six—was inhabited by a man, his wife, and several children. The man was a mason's labourer, and in constant work, earning 14s. per week. The woman did the house-work, as she said. Filthy plates, and tubs full of foul-smelling scum and slops lying everywhere about, testified how diligently she performed her duties, which were rendered more onerous by the children of a neighbour being committed to her care, while the mother was absent upon a country expedition, exchanging pots and pans against old iron, glass, bones, and rags. For taking charge of the children in question the women received from the mother four-pence a day. While we were talking, a stout-built fellow, the model of a stalwart navvy, lounged into the cellar, and seated himself on the window-sill. This man seemed a perfect specimen of good-natured laziness. He worked, he said, when he got a job. He could then make 15s. a week, but there wasn't much doing in his way at present. His wife was out gathering rags and bones. I asked him whether he could not get work at any of the factories? He burst into a loudish, good-natured laugh, as he replied, "Bedad, sir, and is it me fingers yer would like to see snipped off entirely by them blissed machinery? Sure I can handle a hoe or pick; but them mules and looms is a pig with another snout intirely."

. . . In one of the courts of one of the Irish quarters—a place, by the way, reeking with abominations, but which the authorities are energetically improving—I observed one house, poor indeed in appearance, but notably clean. On entering it I found that the inhabitants were English, the only English people in the court . . . The contrast between this poor family and their lazy Irish neighbours was very striking and very painful.

Trades Unionism

Trade unionism grew on the basis of the generally small, localised eighteenth-century trade clubs. By the 1830s ideas of national and general 'trades unionism', often with utopian and syndicalist undertones, were being spread by such men as Robert Owen (1771–1858), John Doherty (1798–1854), and James Morrison (d. 1835). In the first extract the boroughreeve and constables of Manchester report to the Home Office on Doherty's Grand General Union of Spinners (26 May 1830: H.O. Papers, 40-27 quoted in S. and B. Webb, *The History of Trade Unionism* (1894).) In the second Owen optimistically reports to Morrison (29 May 1833: Miss G. M. Phillips collection). The peak of the movement was reached with the Grand National Consolidated Trades Union of February 1834. It collapsed in August.

(1) The combination of workmen, long acknowledged a great evil, and one most difficult to counteract, has recently assumed so formidable and systematic a shape in this district that we feel it a duty to lay before you some of its most alarming features . . . A committee of delegates from the operative spinners of the three Kingdoms have established an annual assembly in the Isle of Man to direct the proceedings of the general body towards their employers, the orders for which they promulgate to their respective districts and sub-committees. To these orders the most implicit deference is shown; and a weekly levy or rent of one penny per head on each operative is cheerfully paid. This produces a large sum, and is a powerful engine, and principally to support those who have turned out against their employers, agreeable to the orders of the committee, at the rate of ten shillings per week for each person. The plan of a general turnout having been found to be impolitic, they have employed it in detail, against particular individuals or districts, who, attacked thus singly, are frequently compelled to submit to their terms rather than to the ruin which would ensue to many by allowing their machinery (in which their whole capital is invested) to stand idle.

(2) I rejoice in the energy and life of your proceedings, and let these be continued with judgment and our *speedy* success is certain . . .

Last night there was a second meeting for the sections of delegates of various trades—men of business who I now plainly see will carry on these measures into successful practice. I mentioned your proceedings in Birmingham. I read your letter, it was most useful. I hope to bring with me the commencement of the correspondence between the Working Classes of London and Birmingham . . . We must never allow the working men to despair again. They are beginning to know their power and strength, and all that is required is to give it a right direction.

The Amalgamated Engineers

In 1851 several groups of engineers combined to form the Amalgamated Society of Engineers, Machinists, Millwrights, Smiths and Pattern Makers, with William Allan (1813–74) as general secretary. The ASE became a 'new model' for unions of skilled, articulate and generally moderate craftsmen. The preface to its original rules explained its attitudes.

Our object is not to do anything illegally or indiscreetly, but on all occasions to perform the greatest amount of benefit for ourselves, without injury to others; and if we should be constrained to make restrictions against encroachments on our interests by those who may not have earned a right by a probationary servitude, we do so, knowing that such encroachments are productive of such awful consequences to a trade, that if they were persevered in unchecked they would result in reducing its condition to that of the ill-paid labourer without conferring a corresponding advantage on those who were admitted. It is our duty then to exercise the same control over that in which we have a vested interest, as the physician who holds his diploma, or the author who is protected by his copyright.

Hostility to Trade Unionism

Employers retorted to union militancy by legal actions, lockouts and the enforcement of the 'Document' renouncing union membership. In 1844 the Tory 3rd Marquess of Londonderry (1778–1854) broke a miners' strike in Durham by widespread evictions, the importation of labourers from his Irish estates and threats to Seaham shopkeepers against granting credit to the colliers. His statements were reprinted in the Chartist *Northern Star* (6, 27 July 1844). In the second extract the liberal writer and former cotton mill manager William Rathbone Greg (1809–81), Commissioner of Customs from 1856 and Comptroller of the Stationery Office from 1864, writes of the effects of unionism in the seventies (*The Nineteenth Century*, March 1879).

(1) Lord Londonderry again warns all the shopkeepers and tradesmen in his town of Seaham that if they still give credit to pitmen who hold off work, and continue in the Union, such men will be marked by his agents and overmen, and will never be employed in his collieries again, and the shopkeepers may be assured that they will never have any custom or dealings with them from Lord Londonderry's large concerns that he can in any manner prevent.

Lord Londonderry further informs the traders and shopkeepers that having by his measures increased very largely the last year's trade to Seaham, and if credit is so improperly and so fatally given to his unreasonable pitmen, thereby prolonging the injurious strike, it is his firm determination to carry back all the outlay of his concerns even to Newcastle.

Because it is neither fair, just, or equitable, that the resident traders in his own town should combine and assist the infatuated workmen and pitmen in prolonging their own miseries by continuing an insane strike, and an unjust and senseless warfare against their proprietors and masters.

(2) Distress among the working classes has been very general and very severe; and while much of this has been inevitable, and has been due to the disturbed and depressed state of trade throughout the world, it has been enormously aggravated and prolonged by their own mistaken and perverse proceedings. For a great deal of it they have themselves been directly and exclusively responsible. Work has been deplorably scarce, but they have made it, by their own voluntary action, far scarcer than it would otherwise have been. In many instances masters have been ruined and their works unavoidably closed and the men they employed have been thrown upon their own resources, and not infrequently reduced to destitution, by no fault of their own. But in many other instances the men have voluntarily thrown themselves out of work by refusing to accept it at the reduced rate of wages which was all their impoverished employers could afford to offer them. They deliberately *deprived themselves* of employment, and their consequent privations, however severe, were entirely gratuitous . . .

PART FIVE

Social Policy and Attitudes

That it is the duty of every man, according to his abilities and opportunities, to relieve his fellow creatures in distress, will no doubt be readily and generally admitted. It is the never-failing theme of the moralist and the Divine, and the politician is no less persuaded that the *Infant Poor* should be relieved from beggary and want, the *Sick Poor* restored to health, and that a bare subsistence for the *Aged Poor* is no more than the fair right of those, who have spent their best days, and exhausted their strength, in the service of the public.

Sir Frederic Morton Eden (1766–1809), *The State of the Poor* (1797)

The poor-laws of England were undoubtedly instituted for the most benevolent purpose, but there is great reason to think that they have not succeeded in their intention.

T. R. Malthus (1766–1834), *Essay on Population* (1798)

Indigence . . ., and not poverty, is the evil. It is that condition in society which implies want, misery and distress.

Patrick Colquhoun (1745–1820), *A Treatise on Indigence* (1806)

Every penny bestowed, that tends to render the condition of the pauper more eligible than that of the independent labourer, is a bounty on indolence and vice.

[Sir] Edwin Chadwick (1800–90) in *Report* of Royal Commission on Poor Laws (1834)

In some large factories, from one-fourth to one-fifth of the children were either cripples or otherwise deformed, or permanently injured by excessive toil, sometimes by brutal abuse.

Robert Dale Owen (1801–77), *Threading My Way* (1874)

Let the tyrants know that you have sworn, 'OUR CHILDREN SHALL BE FREE!'.

Richard Oastler (1798–1861), in *Leeds Intelligencer*, 20 Oct. 1831

. . . the health and morals of the people employed in cotton mills are at least equal to that of those engaged in other occupations . . ., the long hours of labour do *not* over-fatigue the children, or injure their health and constitutions, . . . the general charges of cruelty and ill-treatment . . . are entirely groundless; . . . the education of the factory children, as compared with others, is more carefully attended to . . .

Samuel (1804–75) and W. R. (1809–81) Greg, 'Condition of Manchester Cotton Operatives', Manchester Statistical Society (1833)

It has been said by officers enthusiastic in their profession that there are three causes which make a soldier enlist, viz. being out of work, in a state of intoxication, or, jilted by his sweetheart. Yet the incentives to enlistment, which we desire to multiply, can hardly be put by Englishmen of the nineteenth century in this form, viz. more poverty, more drink, more faithless sweethearts.

Florence Nightingale (1820–1910), *Notes on Matters Affecting the Health, Efficiency and Hospital Administration of the British Army* (1858)

Pure air, pure water, the inspection of unhealthy habitations, the adulteration of food, these and many kindred matters may be legitimately dealt with by the Legislature . . . After all, the first consideration of a minister should be the health of the people.

Benjamin Disraeli (1804–81), speech at Manchester, 3 April 1872

In a garret up three pairs of broken stairs was a common day school, with forty children in the compass of ten feet by nine. On a perch, forming a triangle with the corner of the room, sat a cock and two hens; under a stump bed, immediately beneath, was a dog kennel, in the occupation of three black terriers, whose barking, added to the noise of the children and the cackling of the fowls, on the approach of a stranger, were almost deafening.

Report on the state of education in Liverpool by the education committee of Manchester Statistical Society (1836)

The engine-man, the slubber, the burler, the overlooker, the wife of any of these, the small shopkeeper, or the next-door neighbour, with six or seven small children on the floor and in her lap, are by turns found 'teaching the young idea how to shoot'.

Factory Superintendent Robert Baker (1803–80), in *PP*. (1839) xlii, quoted in J. M. Ludlow, *Progress of the Working Class, 1832–1867* (1867)

How one longs for some outpouring of comfortable, unhesitating, old-fashioned, joyous bounty—not judicious administration of charity, but a good hearty swing of generosity—if only it might be innocently indulged in.

Caroline Stephen, in *The Nineteenth Century* (1879)

THE TREATMENT OF POVERTY

Gilbert's Act

The Elizabethan Poor Law of 1598 and 1601 long remained the basis of a system of relief administered by the parochial authorities. From 1662 it was supplemented by the Settlement Act, which permitted local overseers to return non-resident paupers to their own parishes. In 1782 Thomas Gilbert (1720–98) gained an Act allowing groups of parishes to join in unions and encouraging the provision of help for able-bodied unemployed outside the workhouse. The Act (22 Geo. III, c. 83) recited the list of complaints about the Poor Law.

Whereas, notwithstanding the many laws now in being for the relief and employment of the poor, and the great sums of money raised for those purposes, their sufferings and distresses are nevertheless very grievous; and, by the incapacity, negligence or misconduct of the overseers, the money raised for the relief of the poor is frequently misapplied, and sometimes expended in defraying the charges of litigations about settlements indiscreetly and unadvisedly carried on; and whereas by a clause in an Act passed in the ninth year of the reign of King George the First, intituled, 'An Act for the Amendment of the Laws relating to the Settlement, Employment and Relief of the Poor', power is given to the churchwardens and overseers in the manner therein mentioned to purchase or hire houses; and contract with any person for the lodging, keeping, maintaining and employing the poor, and taking the benefit of their work, labour, and service for their maintenance; and where any parish, town or township, should be found too small to unite two or more for those purposes, with the consent of the major part of the parishioners or inhabitants and the approbation of a justice of the peace; which provisions from want of proper regulations and management in the poor houses or work-houses that have been purchased or hired under the authority of the said Act, and for want of due inspection and control over the persons who have engaged in those contracts, have not had the desired effect, but the poor in many places, instead of finding protection and relief, have been much oppressed thereby . . .

A Warning on the Poor Laws

T. R. Malthus, always concerned about the 'danger' of over-population, regularly condemned the Poor Law for discouraging thrift and promoting early marriages. In his *Letter to Samuel Whitbread, Esq. M.P. on his Proposed Bill for the Amendment of the Poor Laws* (1807) Malthus explained his views.

The compulsory provision for the poor in this country has, you will allow, produced effects which follow almost necessarily from the principle of population. The mere pecuniary consideration of the rapid increase of the rates of late years, though a point on which much stress has been laid, is not that which I consider as of the greatest importance; but the cause of this rapid increase, the increasing proportion of the dependent poor, appears to me to be a subject so truly alarming, as in some degree to threaten the extinction of all honourable feeling and spirit among the lower ranks of society, and to degrade and depress the condition of a very large and most important part of the community.

Under this impression I ventured to propose a plan for the gradual abolition of a system, which it was acknowledged had produced effects very different from those which had been expected. And I still think that if we weigh on the one hand the great quantity of subjection and dependence which the poor laws create, together with the kind of relief which they afford, against the greater degree of freedom and the higher wages which would be the necessary consequence of their abolition, it will be difficult to believe that the mass of comfort and happiness would not be greater on the latter supposition, although the few that were then in distress would have no other resource than voluntary charity . . .

. . . The moral obligation of private, active, and discriminate charity I have endeavoured to enforce in the strongest language of which I was capable; and if I have denied the *natural right* of the poor to support, it is solely, to use the language of Sir F. M. Eden . . . because "it may be doubted whether any right, the gratification of which seems to be impracticable, can be said to exist." To those who do not admit this conclusion, the denial of such a right may appear to be unfavourable to the poor. But those who are convinced of its truth, may, with the most anxious desire of extending the comforts and elevating the condition of the lower classes of society, rationally express their apprehensions, that the attempt to sanction by law a right which in the nature of things cannot be adequately gratified, may terminate in disappointment, irritation, and aggravated poverty.

The Need for a Central Policy

Patrick Colquhoun's *Treatise on Indigence* (1806) was critical of the Poor Law's inability to differentiate between poverty ('a most necessary and indispensable ingredient in society') and indigence ('which implied want, misery and distress') and between the unfortunate and the idle. Colquhoun thought that the remedy lay in central control.

The great object is first to establish a foundation, a rallying point, a centre of action, a fixed responsible agency, a resource of talents, knowledge, application and industry, equal, if possible, to the difficult task of improving the condition of society in all those ramifications, where a gangrene either exists or is threatened.

1. By diminishing the number of the innocent indigent by judicious and timely props.
2. By restoring the culpable indigent to at least a useful condition in society, by a variety of combined regulations . . .

And thus, by an all pervading system of well regulated police, having its chief seat or central point in the metropolis, and from thence maintaining a close and connected chain of correspondence, by receiving information and communicating the same with regularity and promptitude to all parts of the Kingdom, by a permanent authority, competent . . . to report to his Majesty in Parliament such measures as shall in any degree be conducive to the great objects of the institution—The improvement of the condition of the labouring people—the increase of the productive labour of the country—the more effectual prevention of moral and criminal offences—to the lessening the demand for punishment—the diminution of the public burdens attached to pauper and criminal police, by turning the hearts and arresting the hands of evil-doers—by forewarning the unwary, and preserving in innocence the untainted.

Official Enquiry

The Royal Commission on the Poor Laws was set up in 1832, under C. J. Blomfield (1786–1857), the reforming Bishop of London. There were initially seven Commissioners and from 1833 nine. Twenty-six assistant commissioners collected evidence (eventually published in fifteen volumes). Their *Instructions* are quoted below.

The Central Commissioners are directed by His Majesty's Commission to make a diligent and full inquiry into the practical operation of the Laws for the relief of the Poor in England and Wales, and into the manner in which those laws are administered, and to report whether any, and what, alterations, amendments, or improvements may be beneficially made in the said laws, or in the manner of administering them; and how the same may be best carried into effect.

This extensive inquiry may be conveniently divided into four heads:—

I The form in which parochial relief is given.
II The persons to whom it is given.
III The persons by whom it is awarded.
IV The persons at whose expense it is given.

It is probable that this inquiry will suggest considerable alterations in the existing law; and it is also probable that those alterations may be facilitated by some further measures, such as—

V Affording facilities for emigration.
VI Facilitating the occupation and even the acquisition of land by labourers.
VII Removing the tax on servants, so far as it is found to interfere with their residence under their employer's roof.
VIII Improving the rural police.

Official Report

The Royal Commission's *Report* of 1834 was a seminal document, which formed the basis of the New Poor Law Act of the same year. It followed the ideas of the Oxford professor Nassau Senior (1790–1864) and the Benthamite secretary Edwin Chadwick (1800–90) and actually ignored much of the evidence on the operation of the old system.

The most pressing of the evils which we have described are those connected with the relief of the Able-bodied. They are the evils, therefore, for which we shall first propose remedies.

. . . We believe that, under strict regulations, adequately enforced, such relief may be afforded safely, and even beneficially.

In all extensive communities, circumstances will occur in which an individual, by the failure of his means of subsistence, will be exposed to the danger of perishing. To refuse aid, and at the same time to punish mendicity when it cannot be proved that the offender could have obtained subsistence by labour, is repugnant to the common sentiments of mankind; it is repugnant to them to punish even depredation, apparently committed as the only resource against want.

. . . But in no part of Europe except England has it been thought fit that the provision, whether compulsory or voluntary, should be applied to more than the relief of *indigence*, the state of a person unable to labour, or unable to obtain, in return for his labour, the means of subsistence. It has never been deemed expedient that the provision should extend to the relief of *poverty*; that is the state of one, who, in order to obtain a mere subsistence, is forced to have recourse to labour.

. . . It may be assumed, that in the administration of relief, the public is warranted in imposing such conditions on the individual relieved, as are conducive to the benefit either of the individual himself, or of the country at large, at whose expense he is to be relieved.

The first and most essential of all conditions, a principle which we find universally admitted, even by those whose practice is at variance with it, is, that his situation on the whole shall not be made really or apparently as eligible as the situation of the independent labourer of the lowest class . . . Every penny bestowed, that tends to render the position of the pauper more eligible than that of the independent labourer, is a bounty on indolence and vice. We have found, that as the poor's-rates are at present administered, they operate as bounties of this description, to the amount of several millions annually.

... The chief specific measures which we recommend ... are—

First, that except as to medical attendance, and subject to the exception respecting apprenticeship herein-after stated, all relief whatever to able-bodied persons or to their families, otherwise than in well-regulated workhouses (*i.e.* places where they may be set to work according to the spirit and intention of the 43rd. of Elizabeth) shall be declared unlawful, and shall cease, in manner and at periods hereafter specified; and that all relief afforded in respect of children under the age of 16 shall be considered as afforded to their parents.

... We recommend ... the appointment of a Central Board to control the administration of the Poor-Laws, with such Assistant Commissioners as may be found requisite; and that the Commissioners be empowered and directed to frame and enforce regulations for the government of workhouses, and as to the nature and amount of the relief to be given and the labour to be exacted in them, and that such regulations shall, as far as may be practicable, be uniform throughout the country.

Opposition to the New Poor Law

Hostility to the 1834 Act was initially slight, being confined to a few M.P.s and peers. Notable among M.P.s were the Radical journalist William Cobbett (1763–1835), here quoted (1) from *Hansard*, 3s. xxiv (1834) and (2) the owner of *The Times* John Walter (1776–1847), with his *Letter to the Electors of Berkshire on the New System for the Management of the Poor* (1834). In 1837 William Denison's introduction to his *Abstract of Evidence taken before the Committee ... to inquire into the Operation and Effect of the Poor Law Amendment Act* (3) and the Yorkshire Tory Richard Oastler's introduction (4) to his *Damnation! Eternal Damnation to the Fiend-Begotten, "Coarser Food" New Poor Law* attacked the operation of the Act. Another Tory, the Sheffield silversmith Samuel Roberts, wrote similarly (5) in *Lord Brougham and the New Poor Laws* (1838). By this time a considerable Northern agitation had briefly developed against the Act.

(1) If the poor man when in distress were thus deprived of his lawful means of relief, what principle in nature or justice was there to prevent his taking whatever he could lay his hands on to prevent himself from starving? Robbery and violence would then become a matter of dire necessity, the sacredness of property

would no longer be protected, and how would the House like the idea of that? They were now about to dissolve the bonds of society; they were going to break faith with the poor man; and then what claim could they pretend to have upon him in return? . . . Let the House read the Bible and this Bill at the same time, and then see if they could find it in their consciences to pass it.

(2) I think portions of the measure pregnant with evil: I think it a change in the British Constitution itself: I think it calculated to produce a revolution in the manners and habits of the British people; providing inadequately for its ostensible objects, and productive of consequences which cannot be looked at without dismay.

(3) It is distinctly proved that wherever the law has been brought into operation, it has pressed most grievously upon the able-bodied labourer with a family,—upon the able-bodied widow with a family; and has tended to produce a diminution in the amount doled out to the aged and infirm.

(4) I cannot *bless* that, which GOD and NATURE CURSE. The Bible being true, the Poor Law Amendment Act is false! The Bible containing the will of God,—this accursed Act of Parliament embodies the will of Lucifer. It is the Sceptre of Belial, establishing its sway in the Land of Bibles!! DAMNATION; ETERNAL DAMNATION to the accursed Fiend!!

(5) [The New Poor Law] is at variance with the laws of God, the constitution of these Realms, the liberty of Englishmen, the rights and very existence of the poor, and the repression of profligacy and vice, while it has a tendency to promote child murder, with many other evil consequences.

The Law at Work

From 1834 the three Central Commissioners—the 'Bashaws of Somerset House'—and their secretary, Chadwick, tried to enforce a national system upon local Union guardians. Their stern order prohibiting outdoor relief from December 1844 re-aroused opposition, despite exceptions for emergencies, sickness, burials, widowhood and soldiers' dependents.

Every able-bodied person, male or female, requiring relief from any Parish within any of the said Unions, shall be relieved wholly in the Workhouse of the Union, together with such of the family of every such able-bodied person as may be resident with him or her, and may not be in employment, and together with the wife of every such able-bodied male person, if he be a married man, and if she be resident with him; . . .

The End of the Commission

A constant succession of complaints was made against the Commission, culminating in the scandal of the Andover workhouse in 1845. Meanwhile, Chadwick argued with his masters. And in the Commons such Radicals as Thomas Wakley (1795–1862) and 'Oastlerite' Tories like Busfeild Ferrand maintained regular attacks. During the June 1847 debates on Sir George Grey's proposal to replace the Commission with a Poor Law Board more closely supervised by Ministers, Ferrand delivered a typically strong speech, reported in *The Standard* of 26 June.

. . . Millions in this country panted for an opportunity of revenging themselves upon their oppressors and the oppressors of their aged parents and relatives.

. . . He said it was the height of cruelty to break up for ever the home of a workman who might be compelled to apply at a workhouse for relief. He solemnly believed that that treatment, if persevered in, would speedily produce a revolution in this country . . .

It was said that he used violent language; but if he did so, let it be remembered that the treatment which he denounced was most barbarous, and that the disease which he sought to cure demanded a violent remedy. He was attached to the institutions of his country, and had been a Tory throughout his life, as well as a loyalist; but he would never be a party to oppressing the poor and then expecting them to be loyal. If he were a poor man he would rebel against such treatment. If he saw his wife and children torn from him and his furniture sold when he had committed no crime, he should care very little what became of the rich; any change he should regard as a change for the better, and he would pray for a revolution. The poor had been treated in this manner for 30 years, and they had borne that treatment with a humility, which was truly wonderful. They were dying of starvation in Yorkshire and Lancashire . . . Year after year the evil was becoming worse and worse; year by year the poor were subjected to tyranny and oppression. But, let them mark his words, the time would come when they would rebel against such treatment . . .

The Board at Work

The Board ran the Poor Law from 1847 until it was taken over by the Local Government Board in 1871. It was not notably less bleak than its predecessor, and the Outdoor Relief Regulation Order of August 1852 (printed in the Board's *Fifth Annual Report*) soon had to be modified after widespread protests.

Article 1. Whenever the Guardians shall allow relief to any indigent poor person, out of the Workhouse, *one third* at least of such relief allowed to any person who shall be indigent and helpless from age, sickness, accident, or bodily or mental infirmity, or who shall be a widow having a child or children dependent on her incapable of working, and *one half* at least of the relief allowed to any able-bodied person, other than such widow as aforesaid, shall be given in articles of food or fuel, or in other articles of absolute necessity.
Article 2. In any case in which the Guardians allow relief for a longer period than one week to an indigent poor person, without requiring that such person shall be received into the workhouse, such relief shall be given or administered weekly.

Scottish Problems

The Scottish Poor Law 'for punishment of the strong and idle beggars, and relief of the poor and impotent' was basically established by James VI's Acts of 1579 and 1597, under which kirk sessions were empowered to punish idlers and help the needy. It was a largely voluntary system: poor rate assessments were rarely made until the nineteenth century. In 1856 Sir George Nicholls (1781–1865), a former mariner, engineer and banker, English overseer and (in 1834–47) a Poor Law Commissioner, published his *History of the Scotch Poor Law*, as a companion volume to his *History of the English Poor Law* (1854). The following extracts from the former book illustrate Scottish problems in the 1830s and following the Scottish Poor Law Act of 1845 (which still left the system largely voluntary).

The chief characteristic of Scottish Poor Law administration, as contrasted with that of England, is the pertinacity with which all claim to relief on behalf of the able-bodied poor has been resisted. The General Assembly in their Report of 1839, however, admit "that the situation of people destitute of employment was not to be overlooked, and that many cases might occur in which men of this class ought to obtain temporary relief in times of occasional sickness or unusual calamity, although not as a matter of right" . . .

The allowances to the parochial poor, are in the Report of 1839 said to be in all cases remarkably moderate. The principle on which the amount is fixed, is—"that except in very rare instances of total and absolute destitution, the aliment to be provided by the parish is not such as would render the pauper independent of other sources . . ." . . . A small sum in aid of their resources will, it is said, afford the relief that is necessary, and anything in addition would be adverse to the true interests of the parish, and the moral habits of the people . . .

The rigid economy observed in everything connected with the relief of the poor in Scotland, was no doubt a means of preventing many of the evils which occurred in England from practices directly the reverse. But either extreme is to be deprecated . . .

The Continuing Problem

Despite all its deterrents, the New Poor Law—to many Victorians' apparent surprise—did nothing to cure poverty. In a report on the agricultural districts, Alexander Mackay commented on the problem of keeping warm encountered by many rural folk (*Morning Chronicle*, 18 January 1850) in some western counties.

When they have to buy their turf, or when there is neither furze or turf, and they must look for their fuel to coal or wood, the greatest privations are suffered as the consequence of their very scanty supply. When they buy their wood, they buy it in faggots—a faggot being frequently little better than a bundle of green twigs. Even this they are not always able to purchase; when, unless they are permitted to take wood, which is very rarely indeed the case, they have to look to theft alone for their supply of fuel . . . throughout the greater part of Somerset, and, I may say, the whole of Bucks, Berks, and Oxford—where they have nothing but wood or coal to burn, one universal system of pilfering prevails in respect to fuel. Both as regards themselves and others, this is a perilous alternative to which the poor are driven by the sad necessities of their position. Without expending any of their means in the purchase of fuel, they manage, in most cases, to eke out but a mere existence, generally on an almost exclusively vegetable diet. To buy as much coal, wood, or turf as would serve them, not only for culinary purposes, but also to warm, during the cheerless months of winter, their damp, cold, and desolate homes, would, in very many instances, make greater inroads than they could bear into their means of procuring more edibles. The consequence is, that such fuel as they cannot buy or get in charity they are driven to steal. The evil of this is manifest, for it is generally through the instrumentality of the children that the wants of the household are thus supplied. Petty theft is thus the first positive vice with which they are brought in contact, and in the practice of which they are almost daily instructed. What is the consequence? The child who becomes an adept in stealing wood is soon qualified for robbing a hen-roost. From that, again, to stealing a sheep there is but another step; and, in the words of a clergyman with whom I was conversing on this subject, "when a man goes out to steal a sheep, he is ready for anything." Is it any wonder, seeing how many children are thus perniciously instructed, that so large a proportion of those who figure in the statistics of crime are juvenile delinquents? . . .

Let me say, in summing up the whole, that a pervading moral apathy is the general characteristic of the peasantry, when positive crime is absent—an apathy which leads, in too many cases, to an utter indifference to the distinction between right and wrong.

In connection with this subject, it is extremely discouraging to find how little good is effected by the education received in the workhouse. It is painful to find how few of the children who are turned out from some of the workhouses come to any good. This shows two things: first, how difficult it is to eradicate the pernicious influences of an essentially vicious domestic education; and secondly, how little proper training accompanies the mere act of teaching in the workhouse. In many instances have cases been pointed out to me of boys entering the gaol soon after leaving the house, and of girls returning pregnant to it a year or two after they had left it.

To many who have not been prepared for such revelations, the foregoing may appear to be one sweeping calumny against the agricultural labourer. But it is not hastily that I have prepared this indictment . . .

Distress in Manchester

Hippolyte Taine (1828–93), a French philosopher and author, visited Britain from 1861 and published his *Notes on England* in 1871. The English version, translated by W. F. Rae, was issued in 1874. Taine was much impressed by the operations of a Manchester workhouse, but noted the reluctance of the poor to enter it.

. . . The building is spacious, perfectly clean, well kept; it has large courts, gardens are attached to it, looks upon fields and stately trees; it has a chapel, and rooms of which the ceilings are twenty feet high. It is evident that the founders and managers had made it a matter of conscience to produce a work which should be beautiful, correct, and useful . . . Everything has been considered and arranged to maintain a pleasing effect. One room is set apart for the lunatics, another for the female idiots . . . In another room the children are taught their lessons, one of the elder children acting as monitor. The kitchen is monumental . . . We were astounded; this was a palace compared with the kennels in which the poor dwell. One of us seriously asked our friend to reserve a place for him here during his old age. Recollect that a Manchester or Liverpool labourer can scarcely procure meat once a week by working ten hours a day! Here an able-bodied pauper works about six hours, has newspapers, the Bible, and some good books and reviews to read, lives in a wholesome air, and enjoys the sight of trees. Nevertheless there is not an able-bodied inmate of this workhouse at this moment; it is almost empty, and will not be filled till the winter . . . Today at a street corner I saw an old woman grubbing with her skinny hands in a heap of rubbish, and pulling out scraps of vegetables; probably she would not give up her drop of spirits. But what of the others? I am informed that they prefer their home and their freedom at any price, that they cannot bear being shut up and subjected to discipline. They prefer to be free and to starve . . . The workhouse is regarded as a prison; the poor consider it a point of honour not to go there . . .

FACTORY REFORM

Early Revelations

Child labour was traditional and widely-accepted, but when adopted by the factory master instead of the home-working parent, it led to obvious abuses. One pioneer commentator was Aikin, *op. cit.* In the following passages on Eccles, Royton and Dukinfield he noted the effects of child labour in the cotton spinning mills in the closing years of the eighteenth century.

The invention and improvements of machines to shorten labour, has had a surprising influence to extend our trade, and also to call in hands from all parts, especially children for the cotton mills. It is the wise plan of Providence, that in this life there shall be no good without its attendant inconvenience. There are many which are obvious in these cotton mills, and similar factories, which counteract that increase of population usually consequent on the improved facility of labour. In these, children of very tender age are employed; many of them collected from the workhouses in London and Westminster, and transported in crowds, as apprentices to masters many hundred miles distant, where they serve unknown, unprotected, and forgotten by those to whose care nature or the laws had consigned them. These children are usually too long confined to work in close rooms, often during the whole night: the air they breathe from the oil, &c, employed in the machinery, and other circumstances, is injurious; little regard is paid to their cleanliness, and frequent changes from a warm and dense to a cold and thin atmosphere, are predisposing causes to sickness and disability, and particularly to the epidemic fever which so generally is to be met with in these factories. It is also much to be questioned, if society does not receive detriment from the manner in which children are thus employed during their early years. They are not generally strong to labour, or capable of pursuing any other branch of business, when the term of their apprenticeship expires. The females are wholly uninstructed in sewing, knitting, and other domestic affairs, requisite to make them notable and frugal wives and mothers. This is a very great misfortune to them and the public, as is sadly proved by a comparison of the families of labourers in husbandry, and those of manufactures in general. In the former we meet with neatness, cleanliness, and comfort; in the latter with filth, rags, and poverty; although their wages may be nearly double to those of the husbandman. It must be added, that the want of early religious instruction and example, and the numerous and indiscriminate association in these buildings, are very unfavourable to their future conduct in life. To mention these grievances, is to point out their remedies; and in many factories they have been adopted with true benevolence and much success. But in all cases "The public have a right to see that its members are not wantonly injured, or carelessly lost".

...[At Royton] The manufactures employ all the people, except some colliers, shop-keepers, and husbandmen. The gains are from 2d. per day by young children, to 3s. 6d. and 4s. by grown people. Women will sometimes earn 16 and 17s. per week by spinning with a jenny.

...The cotton trade introduced here [in Dukinfield], while it affords employment to all ages, has debilitated the constitutions and retarded the growth of many, and made an alarming increase in the mortality. The effect is greatly to be attributed to the pernicious custom, so properly reprobated by Dr. Percival and other physicians, of making the children in the mills work by night and day, one set getting out of bed when another goes into the same, thus never allowing the rooms to be well ventilated.

The Demand for Reform

In 1802 Sir Robert Peel, 1st Bt. (1750–1830), a Tory cotton master, secured his 'Health and Morals of Apprentices Act', restricting pauper children to 12 hours' daily work. But the increased use of steam power led to a wider employment of unrestricted 'free' children. In January 1815 Robert Owen (1771–1858), the eccentric socialist pioneer who, with his partners, had bought the great New Lanark cotton mills from his father-in-law, David Dale (1739–1806) in 1799, urged Glasgow masters to support further legislation. They refused, and so he issued (1) his 'Observations on the Cotton Trade' (*Glasgow Chronicle*, Feb. 1815) and (2) *Observations on the Effect of the Manufacturing System*

(1815). Both papers were subsequently reprinted in his *Life of Robert Owen* (1858) vol. i.a.

(1) It is only since the introduction of the cotton trade that children at an age before they had acquired strength of body or mental instruction have been forced into cotton-mills—those receptacles, in too many instances, for living human skeletons, almost disrobed of intellect, where, as the business is often now conducted, they linger out a few years of miserable existence, acquiring every bad habit, which they disseminate throughout society. It is only since the introduction of this trade, that children, and even grown people, were required to labour more than twelve hours in the day, including the time allotted for meals. It is only since the introduction of this trade, that the sole recreation of the labourer is to be found in the pot-house or gin-shop. It is only since the introduction of this baneful trade, that poverty, crime, and misery, have made rapid and fearful strides throughout the community.

. . . Deeply as I am interested in the cotton manufacture, highly as I value the extended political power of my country, yet, knowing as I do, from long experience both here and in England, the miseries which this trade, as it is now conducted, inflicts on those to whom it gives employment, I do not hesitate to say,—perish the cotton trade, perish even the political superiority of our country, (if it depends on the cotton trade,) rather than they shall be upheld by the sacrifice of everything valuable in life by those who are the means of supporting them.

The measure which appears to me alone calculated to remove the evils which I have stated, is to endeavour to procure an Act of Parliament—

First.—To prevent children from being employed in cotton or other mills of machinery, until they are twelve years old. (At present they are put in at seven years old, and upwards,—sometimes even at six.)

Secondly.—That the hours of work in mills of machinery, including one hour and a-half for meals and recreation, shall not exceed twelve per day. (In most mills, the time of working, for children, as well as adults, is fourteen hours per day; and in many cases they are dismissed during that period for only one hour, usually from twelve till one o'clock.)

And lastly, that, after a period to be fixed, no child shall be received in a mill of machinery until he shall have been taught to read, to write a legible hand, and to understand the first four rules of arithmetic; and girls also taught to sew their common garments of clothing. (At admission they are now often, most frequently indeed, destitute of all useful instruction.)

(2) The general diffusion of manufactures throughout a country generates a new character in its inhabitants; and as this character is formed upon a principle quite unfavourable to individual or general happiness, it will produce the most lamentable and permanent evils, unless its tendency be counteracted by legislative interference and direction.

The manufacturing system has already so far extended its influence over the British empire, as to effect an essential change in the general character of the mass of the people. This alteration is still in rapid progress; and ere long, the comparatively happy simplicity of the agricultural peasant will be wholly lost amongst us. It is even now scarcely to be found without a mixture of those habits which are the offspring of trade, manufactures, and commerce.

... Not more than thirty years since, the poorest parents thought the age of fourteen sufficiently early for their children to commence regular labour: and they judged well; for by that period of their lives they had acquired by play and exercise in the open air, the foundation of a sound robust constitution; and if they were not all initiated in book learning, they had been taught the far more useful knowledge of domestic life, which could not but be familiar to them at the age of fourteen, and which, as they grew up and became heads of families, was of more value to them (as it taught them economy in the expenditure of their earnings) than one half of their wages under the present circumstances.

Yorkshire Slavery

Owen's campaign petered out with Peel's Act of 1819, which restricted children aged 9–16 in the cotton mills to a twelve hours day. Thereafter, little occurred in the factory reform campaign until a Yorkshire Tory land agent, Richard Oastler (1789–1861), published his celebrated letter on 'Yorkshire Slavery' in the *Leeds Mercury* of 16 October 1830.

Let truth speak out, appalling as the statement may appear. The fact is true. Thousands of our fellow-creatures, both male and female, the miserable inhabitants of a Yorkshire town, (Yorkshire now represented in Parliament by the giant of anti-slavery principles) are this very moment existing in a state of slavery, *more horrid* than are the victims of that hellish system '*colonial slavery*'. These innocent creatures drawl out, unpitied, their short but miserable existence, in a place famed for its profession of religious zeal, whose inhabitants are ever foremost in *professing* 'temperence' and 'reformation', and are striving to outrun their neighbours in missionary exertions, and would fain send the Bible to the farthest corner of the globe—aye, in the very place where the anti-slavery fever rages most furiously, her *apparent charity* is not more admired on earth, than her *real cruelty* is abhorred in Heaven. The very streets which receive the droppings of an 'Anti-Slavery Society' are every morning wet by the tears of innocent victims at the accursed shrine of avarice, who are *compelled* (not by the cart-whip of the negro slave-driver) but by the dread of the equally appalling thong or strap of the over-looker, to hasten, half-dressed, *but not half-fed*, to those magazines of British infantile slavery—*the worsted mills in the town and neighbourhood of Bradford!!!*

Official Enquiry

Oastler's call was taken up by a network of Short-Time Committees in northern England and Scotland, and in 1832 his Tory friend Michael Sadler (1780–1835) proposed a Ten Hours Bill. Legislation was postponed, however, until after the *Report* of the Royal Commission on the Employment of Children in Factories (1833), from which the crucial lines are selected.

From the whole of the evidence laid before us, we find—
1st—That the children employed in all the principal branches of manufacture throughout the Kingdom work the same number of hours as the adults.
2nd—That the effects of labour during such hours are, in a great number of cases,
Permanent deterioration of the physical condition;
The production of disease often wholly irremediable; and

The partial or entire exclusion (by reason of excessive fatigue) from the means of obtaining adequate education and acquiring useful habits, or of profiting by those means when afforded.

3rd—That at the age when the children suffer these injuries from the labour they undergo, they are not free agents, but are let out to hire, the wages they earn being received and appropriated by their parents and guardians.

We are therefore of opinion that a case is made out for the interference of the Legislature in behalf of the children employed in factories.

Black and White Slavery

The 1833 Factory Act limited children of 9–13 to 8 hours labour (with two hours' education) and young persons of 13–18 to 12 hours. Oastler and his allies hopelessly continued their 'Ten Hours' campaign. The new Parliamentary leader from 1833 was Lord Ashley (1801–85), later 7th Earl of Shaftesbury. But the most bitter struggle was waged in the North, with mounting abuse. Oastler's *Slavery in Yorkshire. Monstrous Barbarity!!!* (Bradford, 1835), with its attack on the Leeds Liberal M.P. and editor, Edward Baines (1774–1848) is typical.

[Baines is] the champion of a set of interested mill-owners, tyrannical overlookers, and drunken parents, who, AT YOUR RECOMMENDATION, have been holding "hole and corner" meetings, and signing "hole and corner" petitions to parliament, and trying to induce British senators to permit these monsters to work poor little British children, just four hours in every day longer than they will allow full grown BLACK "apprentices" to be worked! Yes, sir, no sooner does one of those "hole and corner" petitions find its way into the House of Commons than a MR. BAINES jumps up, to give it HIS most "cordial support".

. . . Now, sir, this is the unholy position which you have taken as a British Senator, as the representative of the ten pounders of Leeds; you know that the petitions in favour of Mr. Sadler's and Lord Ashley's Factory Bill are from PUBLIC meetings, composed of thousands upon thousands of individuals—of ministers of religion belonging to all denominations—doctors—lawyers—bankers—merchants—manufacturers—shopkeepers and operatives—and that your "pet" petitions—your "hole and corner" petitions—your petitions in favour of child murder are, as they ought to be, the progeny of a set of monsters, from a gang of interested overseers, a banditti of drunken parents. And allow me to say, sir, they have met with a most proper guardian, and a proper champion, in yourself.

But, Mr. Baines, are you the same man who bore your name some years ago? He was Editor of the Leeds Mercury, and used to weep such big round tears, for sufferings which he never saw! He could not rest in bed for noises which he heard of clanking chains —and cracking whips—and shrieking slaves! He heard them, though the sound passed the Atlantic, e'er it reached his ears! . . .

. . . Now then tell me, Baines, right honestly, tell me like a man, speak out for once, and say why did you laud and praise these men for warring against slavery in foreign parts, and now denounce them because they hurt this more accursed slavery at home?

. . . True, sir, the horrors of black slavery were bad enough—its history was indeed a bloody one—but, Mr. Baines, *that* monster spared the little ones! It did not work even the male *adult* slaves, with such cruel rigour, as the white slave monster works his *youthful* victims, the little free-born English slaves!

. . . the perpetrators of such crimes as *these* are the only men whose evidence *you eulogize* in a *British House of Commons*—now if it be possible for a man *who forsook his own first-born* to blush, then blush and hide thyself.

Opposition

Further progress in factory reform was not made until Sir James Graham (1792–1861) passed his Act of 1844, which restricted women to 12 hours' labour, provided for the fencing of machinery and reduced children's work to 6½ hours. One reason for Parliamentary hostility to 'interfering' legislation was undoubtedly the spate of 'expert' volumes advocating *laisser-faire* attitudes. Edward Tufnell (1806–86), a Whig lawyer and Assistant Commissioner for both the Poor Law and Factory Commissions, expressed many doubts in his report in 1833 (*Parliamentary Papers* (1834) xix).

No good can come of any Bill, unless all occupations which are harder than factory occupations are included in the Bill; that is, the Bill must have effect in every private house in the kingdom, and then as many of the children would earn nothing and many of the families can only live by the assistance of their children's earnings, such families must go to the parish or perish immediately. If, on the other hand, the Bill is not observed, it inevitably gives rise to falsehood and perjury . . .

The true interest of humanity, of justice and of morality require that not only no new factory bill should be passed, but that every former one be instantly repealed. If the parents are inhuman enough to overwork their children, Parliament cannot remedy the evil by setting up as a universal guardian of the offspring of the poor. The cause of the grievance obviously lies in the bad moral character of the parents, and on raising that character, which factory bills more effectually debase, depends the only chance of cure.

An Academic View

Dr. Andrew Ure (1778–1857), Professor of Chemistry and Natural Philosophy at Anderson's College, Glasgow, in 1804–30, and later a London chemist and industrial writer, was a major apologist of the factory system. Ure's tour of the cotton districts in 1833 convinced him that factories had made Britain 'the arbiter of many nations and the benefactor of the globe itself'. Furthermore, they brought important benefits to British workers—a point which (thought the liberal Ure) was not appreciated by envious landed opponents of *nouveaux-riches* manufacturers. Ure stressed this view in his *Philosophy of Manufactures* (1835).

The blessings which physico-mechanical science has bestowed on society, and the means it has still in store for ameliorating the lot of mankind, has been too little dwelt upon; while, on the other hand, it has been accused of lending itself to the rich capitalists as an instrument for harassing the poor, and of exacting from the operative an accelerated rate of work. It has been said, for example, that the steam-engine now drives the power-looms with such velocity as to urge on their attendant weavers at the same rapid pace; but that the hand-weaver, not being subjected to this restless agent, can throw his shuttle and move his treadles at his convenience. There is, however, the difference in the two cases, that in the factory, every member of the loom is so adjusted, that the driving force leaves the attendant nearly nothing at all to do, certainly no muscular fatigue to sustain, while it procures for him good, unfailing wages, besides a healthy workshop *gratis*; whereas the non-factory weaver, having everything to execute by muscular exertion, finds the labour irksome, makes in consequence innumerable short pauses, separately of little account, but great when added together; earns therefore proportionately low wages, while he loses his health by poor diet and the dampness of his hovel . . .

. . . In my recent tour, continued during several months, through the manufacturing districts, I have seen tens of thousands of old, young, and middle-aged of both sexes, many of them too feeble to get their daily bread by any of the former modes of industry, earning abundant food, raiment, and domestic accommodation, without perspiring at a single pore, screened meanwhile from the summer's sun and the winter's frost, in apartments more airy and salubrious than those of the metropolis in which our legislative and fashionable aristocracies assemble. In those spacious halls the benignant power of steam summons around him his myriads of willing menials, and assigns to each the regulated task, substituting for painful muscular effort on their part, the energies of his own gigantic arm, and demanding in return only attention and dexterity to correct such little aberrations as casually occur in his workmanship . . . Under its auspices, and in obedience to Arkwright's polity, magnificent edifices, surpassing far in number, value, usefulness, and ingenuity of construction, the boasted monuments of Asiatic, Egyptian, and Roman despotism, have, within the short period of fifty years, risen up in this kingdom, to show to what extent capital, industry, and science may augment the resources of a state, while they meliorate the condition of its citizens. Such is the factory system, replete with prodigies in mechanics and political economy, which promises in its future growth to become the great minister of civilization to the terraqueous globe, enabling this country, as its heart, to diffuse along with its commerce the life-blood of science and religion to myriads of people still lying "in the region and shadow of death".

Industrial Leadership

Ure became a pioneer industrial 'consultant' and an 'expert' on factory siting and construction. He was generally pleased by the reception of his first volume—though angered by the surprising hostility of the

Whig *Edinburgh Review*. In 1836 he published his 2-volume *Cotton Manufacture of Great Britain*, tracing the history of and describing the current state of 'the most important and intricate branch of manufactures'. He carefully dedicated the work to the Whig Lord Lansdowne. In the following passage he describes a nineteenth-century view of the origins of British industrial pre-eminence. The list became fairly standard in many histories.

Great Britain . . . has enjoyed admirable opportunities for cultivating productive industry and traffic on the greatest scale; perfect security from external invasion and from internal misrule, during more than a century; free intercourse between its several provinces at home facilitated by fine roads and canals; and with its colonies abroad and other distant nations by myriads of merchants' ships sailing every sea under the protection of a triumphant navy. Thus the productions of every clime were abundantly supplied either to gratify taste and encourage consumption, or to furnish raw materials to the mechanical and chemical arts. Nor ought we to place in the back ground of the picture its inexhaustible mines of the useful metals, most advantageously worked by its fire instinct steam-engines, and cheaply smelted by its boundless stores of pit-coal. But, certainly, nothing has so directly contributed to the pre-eminence of Great Britain in manufactures as her race of laborious, skilful and inventive artisans, cherished as they have been by the institutions of a free country, which opened to the possessors of talents and knowledge, in however humble a station, the amplest career of honour and fortune to stimulate effort and dignify success. The reformation of religion, in spreading knowledge through the middle and lower classes of society, has distinguished the Protestant population even in Catholic countries for their superior skill in the useful arts; a fact illustrated in a remarkable manner at the revocation of the edict of Nantes, when Protestantism, being banished from France, drew away manufactures in its train, and enriched all those neighbouring states which gave the conscientious exiles shelter and protection. The number of holidays in Catholic countries has always proved a great obstacle to factory labour, which more than any other form of industry cannot brook interruption or suspension without serious injury to the machines, and to the equality of the workmanship.

In many districts of England a most laudable zeal to encourage the arts prevailed at an early period of their growth . . .

An Economist's View

Nassau Senior (1790–1864), Professor of Political Economy at Oxford in 1825–30 and 1847–52, was a prominent defender of liberal economic theory over both the factory and Poor Law agitations. He became Master in Chancery in 1836 and published his *Letters on the Factory Act* in 1837. Senior considered that a ten hour day 'would be attended by the most fatal consequences', opposed any further legislation and advocated amendments to the 1833 Act. His crucial arguments are given below.

I have always been struck by the difference between the hours of work usual over the whole world in cotton factories and in other employments; and did not, until now, perceive the reasons. It seems to arise from two causes: first, the great proportion of fixed to circulating capital, which makes long hours of work desirable; and, secondly, the extraordinary lightness of the labour, if labour it can be called, which renders them practicable . . .

Under the present law, no mill in which persons under eighteen years of age are employed (and, therefore, scarcely any mill at all) can be worked more than eleven and a half hours a-day, that is, twelve hours for five days in the week and nine on Saturday.

Now, the following analysis will show that in a mill so worked, the whole net profit is derived *from the last hour*. I will suppose a manufacturer to invest £100,000: £80,000 in his mill and machinery, and £20,000 in raw material and wages. The annual return of that mill, supposing the capital to be turned once a-year and gross profits to be fifteen per cent., ought to be goods worth £115,000, produced by the constant conversion and reconversion of the £20,000 circulating capital, from money into goods and from goods into money, in periods of rather more than two months. Of this £115,000 each of the twenty-three half hours of work produces 5-115ths, or one twenty-third. Of these 23-23rds (constituting the whole £115,000) twenty, that is to say, £100,000 out of the £115,000, simply replace the capital—or one twenty-third (or £5,000 out of the £115,000), makes up for the deterioration of the mill and machinery. The remaining 2-23rds, that is the last two of the twenty-three half hours of every day, produce the net profit of ten per cent . . .

The exceeding easiness of cotton-factory labour renders long hours of work *practicable*. With the exception of the mule spinners, . . . the work is merely that of watching the machinery, and piecing the threads that break . . .

. . . Any plan, therefore, which should reduce the present comparatively short hours, must either destroy profit, or reduce wages to the Irish standard, or raise the price of the commodity, by an amount which is not easy for me to estimate . . .

I have no doubt, therefore, that a ten hours' bill would be utterly ruinous. And I do not believe that any restriction whatever, of the present hours of work, could be safely made.

. . . The manufacturer is tired of regulations—what he asks is tranquillity—*implora pace* . . .

The factory work-people in the country districts are the plumpest, best clothed, and healthiest looking persons of the labouring class that I have ever seen . . .

. . . The difference in appearance when you come to the Manchester operatives is striking; they are sallow and thinner . . .

. . . To enforce ventilation and drainage, and give means and motives to education, seems to me all that can be done by positive enactment.

An Industrialist's View

Robert Hyde Greg (1795–1875), a member of the great manufacturing family of Styal in Cheshire, was Liberal M.P. for Manchester in 1839–41. He was appalled by the use made by reformers of a paper by his brother William (1809–81), *Enquiry into the State of the Manufacturing System* (1831), which he described as 'little more than a college thesis'. His own defence of the masters and attack on reformers was published in 1837, under the title *The Factory Question*. Greg was basically concerned to attack the evidence published by Sadler's Committee in 1832 and the pamphlet *Curse of the Factory System* (1836), published by the Todmorden Radical millowner and M.P. John Fielden (1784–1849)—who, in 1847, finally carried the Ten Hours Bill through the Commons.

These facts, resting as they do upon general and unquestionable data, show how much the public mind has been abused, respecting the extent and amount of the evils resulting from Factory employment. The *evils*, such as they have been, *have no necessary connection with factory labour*, and the circumstance that we are anxious, most emphatically, to press upon our reader's attention, is, that *they did not arise under the present law, but when there was no law, and when children might enter the mills at any age, and work any number of hours, and when, in fact, they did work 72 hours, in the best regulated mills.*

What evil can possibly be apprehended now, under a law scrupulously enforced . . .?

. . . Our only advantages consist in cheap machinery and low rate of interest. By restricting our mills to 69 hours a week, we have given up these advantages; by restricting them to 58, we not only annihilate them, but *hand them over to the enemy* . . .

. . . In case of a 'Ten Hours Bill' being passed, the actual migration of English mill-owners, machinery, and capital will hasten the period, *already approaching with certainty*, when the markets of Europe and America will be closed, and when our customers will become our rivals.

A Visitor's View

Sir George Head (1782–1855) was an Army officer who visited the factory districts in 1835. He first published his *Home Tour through the Manufacturing Districts of England* in 1836.

With respect to the general state of the workmen, and especially the children in the factories, I certainly gained, by personal inspection, a happy release from opinions previously entertained; neither could I acknowledge those resemblances, probably the work of interested artists, by whom such touching portraits of misery and overfatigue had been from time to time embellished; I saw around me wherever I moved, on every side, a crowd of apparently happy beings, working in lofty well-ventilated buildings, with whom a comparison could no more in fairness be drawn with the solitary weaver plying his shuttle from morning to night in his close dusty den, than is the bustle and occupation of life with soul-destroying solitude.

PUBLIC HEALTH

Industrial Health

Among supporters of factory legislation were many Northern medical practitioners, who were horrified by the ill-health of industrial workers. A Leeds Tory surgeon, Charles Turner Thackrah (1795–1833), published the final version of his study of *The Effects of Arts, Trades, and*

Professions, and of Civic States and Habits of Living, on Health and Longevity in 1832.

. . . Masters however enlightened and humane, are seldom aware, never fully aware, of the injury to health and life which mills occasion. Acquainted far less with physiology, than with political economy, their better feelings will be overcome by the opportunity of increasing profit . . . The sound of the steam-engine anticipates often the cock-crowing of the morning. While the engine works, the people must work. Men, women, and children, are thus yoke-fellows with iron and steam; the animal machine—fragile at best; subject to a thousand sources of suffering, and doomed by nature, in its best state to a short-lived existence, changing every moment, and hastening to decay—is matched with an iron machine insensible to suffering and fatigue: all this moreover, in an atmosphere of flax-dust, for 12 or 13 hours a day, and for six days in a week . . .

. . . I stood in Oxford-row, Manchester, and observed the streams of operatives as they left the mills, at 12 o'clock . . . Here I saw, or thought I saw, a degenerate race,—human beings stunted, enfeebled, and depraved,—men and women that were not to be aged,—children that were not to be healthy adults. It was a mournful spectacle . . . I feel convinced that independently of moral and domestic vices, the long confinement in mills, the want of rest, and shameful reduction of the intervals for meals, and especially the premature working of children, greatly reduce health and vigour, and account for the wretched appearance of the operatives . . .

Sanitary Reform

Chadwick's great *Report* on sanitary conditions in 1842, with its horrifying details of urban squalor and filth, was a seminal work which led to wider interest in public health. Chadwick summarised his conclusions in presenting the work to the House of Lords in July, 1842.

First, as to the extent and operation of the evils which are the subject of the inquiry:—

That the various forms of epidemic, endemic, and other disease caused, or aggravated, or propagated chiefly amongst the labouring classes by atmospheric impurities produced by decomposing animal and vegetable substances, by damp and filth, and close and overcrowded dwellings prevail amongst the population in every part of the kingdom, whether dwelling in separate houses, in rural villages, in small towns, in the larger towns—as they have been found to prevail in the lowest districts of the metropolis.

That such disease, wherever its attacks are frequent, is always found in connexion with the physical circumstances above specified, and that where those circumstances are removed by drainage, proper cleansing, better ventilation, and other means of diminishing atmospheric impurity, the frequency and intensity of such disease is abated; and where the removal of the noxious agencies appears to be complete, such disease almost entirely disappears.

That high prosperity in respect to employment and wages, and various and abundant food, have afforded to the labouring classes no exemptions from attacks of epidemic disease, which have been as frequent and as fatal in periods of commercial and manufacturing prosperity as in any others.

That the formation of all habits of cleanliness is obstructed by defective supplies of water.

That the annual loss of life from filth and bad ventilation are greater than the loss from death or wounds in any wars in which the country has been engaged in modern times . . .

Secondly, As to the means by which the present sanitary condition of the labouring classes may be improved:—

The primary and most important measures, and at the same time the most practicable, and within the recognized province of public administration, are drainage, the removal of all refuse of habitations, streets, and roads, and the improvement of the supplies of water.

That the chief obstacles to the immediate removal of decomposing refuse of towns and habitations have been the expense and annoyance of the hand labour and cartage requisite for the purpose.

That this expense may be reduced to one-twentieth or to one-thirtieth, or rendered inconsiderable, by the use of water and self-acting means of removal by improved and cheaper sewers and drains.

That refuse when thus held in suspension in water may be most cheaply and innoxiously conveyed to any distance out of towns, and also in the best form for productive use, and that the loss and injury by the pollution of natural streams may be avoided.

That for all these purposes, as well as for domestic use, better supplies of water are absolutely necessary . . .

And that the removal of noxious physical circumstances, and the promotion of civic, household, and personal cleanliness, are necessary to the improvement of the moral condition of the population; for that sound morality and refinement in manners and health are not long found co-existent with filthy habits amongst any class of the community . . .

The Board of Health

The Public Health Act of 1848 did not incorporate all of Chadwick's ideas, but it marked an important change in Government attitudes. A network of local health boards was established (either by local petition or compulsorily where the death rate rose over 23 per 1,000), together with a central board composed of Chadwick, Lord Ashley and Dr. Southwood Smith. In 1854, when the board was dismantled and its work passed to John Simon's medical committee of the Privy Council, it surveyed its six years of work (P.P. 1854, xxxv). The Act did not apply in Scotland, to Chadwick's regret.

We have now to state 284 towns have memorialized and petitioned in form for the application of the Act. Of these, up to the 31st December 1853, the requisite forms and proceedings prescribed by the Act, have been complied with in 182, including nine in which the Act has been incorporated with local Acts, comprising altogether a total population, according to the census of 1851, of upwards of two millions.

Within the last three months we have had petitions for the application of the Act from upwards of twenty towns.

Though in many of the 182 towns, the application of the Act has been comparatively recent, yet, in one hundred and twenty-six cases, surveys with a view of carrying the Act into operation have been completed or are in progress.

In seventy, plans of new works founded on the surveys have been laid out.

. . . The demands on their time and energy which, for the saving of life, we were obliged to make on boards of guardians during the prevalence of cholera, excited in numerous instances loud complaints. We have already stated the general and favourable change which has taken place in the opinion of boards of guardians and other local authorities with reference to our proceedings on that occasion.

EDUCATION

The Sunday School

Samuel Bamford (1788–1872), a Lancashire radical, described working-class life in his *Passages in the Life of a Radical* (1844), giving a picture of the weaving communities. His education included a period at a Methodist Sunday school, one of the numerous institutions which followed the success of Robert Raikes (1735–1811) at Gloucester.

At this time the Methodists of Middleton kept a Sunday school in their chapel at Bottom of Barrowfields, and this school we young folks all attended. I was probably a far better speller and reader than any teacher in the place, and I had not gone there long when I was set to writing. I soon mastered the rudimental lines, and quitting "pot-hooks and ladles," as they were called, I commenced writing "large-hand". For the real old Arminian Methodists, the immediate descendants of the Wesleys, the Nelsons, and the Taylors, thought it no desecration of the Sabbath to enable the rising generation on that day to write the Word of God as well as to read it. Had the views and very commendable practice of these old fathers been continued in Sunday schools generally, the reproach would not have been cast upon our labouring population, as it was on the publication of the census of 1841, that a greater proportion of the working classes of Lancashire were unable to write their names than were to be found in several counties less favoured by means of instruction. The modern Methodists may boast of this feat as their especial work. The Church party never undertook to instruct in writing on Sundays; the old Arminian Wesleyans did undertake it, and succeeded wonderfully, but the Conferential Methodists put a stop to it; other religious bodies, if I am not mistaken, did the same, and in 1841 it was a matter of surprise to many that our working population was behind that of other counties in the capability of writing names. Let the honour of this stoppage be assumed by those who have earned it, by the "ministers of religion", so called, generally, and by those of the Conferential Methodists especially.

Every Sunday morning at half-past eight o'clock was this old Methodists school open for the instruction of whatever child crossed its threshold . . .

Home Influence

In 1847 James Kay-Shuttleworth (1804–77) commented in a report for the Committee of the Council for Education that Sunday schools had 'prepared public opinion for the more general efforts to form voluntary associations for the promotion of elementary education by means of the days schools'. Certainly Andrew Bell's Anglican 'National Society for the Education of the Poor in the Principles of the Established Church' (founded in 1811) provided the bulk of early nineteenth-century elementary education. Joseph Lancaster's nonconformist schools, run from 1814 by the British and Foreign School Society, gave a much smaller service. From 1833 both societies received small but growing State grants. On 12 May 1834 the poet Robert Southey (1774–1843) wrote in typical style to Lord Ashley. The letter was published in Sir Edwin Hodder, *The Life and Work of the 7th Earl of Shaftesbury, KG* (1886).

. . . The Factory Question is overlaid at present by the Unions; but when the excitement which their menacing attitude has caused throughout the manufacturing districts subsides, the cry against that evil will again be heard. Unhappily some of the best intended efforts for mitigating the wretched consequences of this system have a sure tendency to deprave still further the very persons for whose relief they are designed. I allude to Infant, and even to Sunday Schools. Teach a mother to teach her children what all mothers used to teach theirs fifty years ago, and the instruction is given in love and received in love, and is wholesome for the whole family. The duty is undertaken *for her* now—nay, it is even *taken from* her, for the sake of making display, and the Sunday is made for the children the longest school-day in the week!

As for Infant Schools, they are only good when they are remedies for an enormous evil: when you rescue infants from the filth and pollution of the streets. But when infants are sent to them to be *out of the mother's way*, the mother goes out to day-labour, and the husband gets his meals at the beershop, and there is an end of all domestic affection. I have much to say upon these subjects. The better parts of the old English character will never be restored unless we can bring back something like the old habits of domestic teaching, for the rudiments of religion—for all that is necessary to be believed—and of domestic industry . . .

The Need for Moral Education

The 1833 Factory Bill had provided two hours' compulsory education for textile factory children, but (as the Inspectors revealed) the factory schools were generally of poor calibre. On 28 February 1843 Lord Ashley spoke on the need for improved moral teaching in the industrial districts. He published this Commons speech as a pamphlet, *Moral and Religious Education of the Working Classes* (1843).

I will next take the town of Leeds; and there it will be seen that the police details would be very similar in character, though differing in number, to those of Manchester and Birmingham—the report of the state of Leeds for 1838, is to this effect:—

"It appears that the early periods of life furnish the greatest portion of criminals. Children of seven, eight, and nine years of age are not infrequently brought before magistrates; a very large portion under 14 years. The parents are, it is to be feared in many instances, the direct cause of their crime."

"The spirit of lawless insubordination (says Mr. Symons the sub-commissioner) which prevails at Leeds among the children is very manifest: it is matter for painful apprehension." James Child, an inspector of police, states that which is well worthy of the attention of the House: he says there is "a great deal of drunkenness, especially among the young people. I have seen children very little higher than the table at these shops. There are some beer-shops where there are rooms upstairs, and the boys and girls, old people, and married of both sexes, go up two by two, as they can agree, to have connection . . . I am sure that sexual connection begins between boys and girls at 14 and 15 years old." John Stubbs, of the police force, confirms the above testimony. "We have," he says, "a deal of girls on the town under 15, and boys, who live by thieving. There are half a dozen beer shops where none but young ones go at all. They support these houses."

. . . A partial remedy for these evils will be found in the moral and religious culture of the infant mind; but this is not all: we must look further, and do more, if we desire to place the working-classes in such a condition that, the lessons they have learned as children, they may have freedom to practise as adults . . .

I speak not now of laws and regulations to abridge, but to enlarge his freedom; not to limit his rights, but to multiply his opportunities of enjoying them; laws and regulations which shall give him what all confess to be his due; which shall relieve him from the danger of temptations he would willingly avoid, and under which he cannot but fall; and which shall place him, in many aspects of health, happiness, and possibilities of virtue, in that position of independence and security, from which, under the present state of things, he is too often excluded.

. . . Will any man after this tell me that it is to any purpose to take children for the purposes of education during two hours a day, and then turn them back for twenty-two to such scenes of vice, and filth, and misery? . . .

. . . When disaffection stalks abroad, we are alarmed, and cry out that we are fallen upon evil times, and so we are; but it is not because poverty is always seditious, but because wealth is too frequently oppressive.

. . . We owe to the poor of our land a weighty debt. We call them improvident and immoral, and so many of them are; but that improvidence and that immorality are the results, in a great measure, of our neglect, and, in not a little, of our example. We owe them, too, the debt of kinder knowledge, and more frequent intercourse . . .

Dissenting Views

Ashley's speech was followed by Graham's 'Factory Education Bill', proposing a 6½-hours' working day for child textile workers, with 3 hours' daily education in Anglican-dominated schools. Dissenting fury knew no bounds, and even the Methodists now joined the attack on the Church, largely because of fears of 'Puseyite' influence. In the first quotation an anonymous (and deceased) observer of French schools gives *Reasons against Government Interference in Education* (1843). The second extract is from an anonymous Southwark Sunday school teacher's *Strictures on the Educational Clauses of the Altered Factories Bill* (1843), the third from the lawyer J. C. Evans's pamphlet *Letter to Sir James Graham* (1843), the fourth from the pamphlet *No modifications; A Letter . . . to . . . Lord John Russell* (1843) by Dr. F. A. Cox (1783–1853), a celebrated preacher, the fifth from *Factories' Education*

Bill. A Speech delivered by Dr. Andrew Reed (1787–1862) to the 'British' Society's annual meeting on 8 May 1843, and the sixth from Spencer Murch's *Ten Objections against the Factories Education Bill* (1843). Such dissenters' attitudes varied and were even contradictory.

(1) That there is a party in Britain disposed to give up the direction and superintendence of Education to the Government . . .

That Education has most prospered in those countries where it has remained a family and local concern . . .

That a great many inconveniences and even dangers are ever attendant on Government interference in such matters . . . It is impossible for government to establish State education in Britain without committing something worse than highway robbery . . . State education is a hindrance to the discovery of truth.

That whatever be the form of Government, Educational Liberty should be maintained intact . . .

That the natural support of Education is the Fees which the Learner pays the Teacher for his labours . . . Holding, as I do, the good old Scottish doctrine, that any succour, except to the helpless poor, is in the end productive of evil, instead of good, even to the poor themselves, I am of course opposed to the endowment of seminaries of learning; and I am of opinion that, with the exception of the really necessitous, people should just pay for their education as they do for anything else; and that the income of every teacher should just depend on his own exertions and capacity.

(2) Sir James Graham's Bill, as I shall endeavour to shew, *takes its rise on false assumptions,—adopts unjust and injurious means,—and aims a destructive blow at civil and religious liberty* . . .

It adds to children's labour, by compelling them to go prescribed distances, and to spend a stipulated number of hours in the routine of school duty, to an excessive degree, which, in many instances, will aggravate rather than improve their present condition.

. . . We regard TOLERANCE AS SOPHISTICATED INTOLERANCE! and take the little they would give us as only the earnest of how much they would withhold, but for "the pressure from without" . . .

. . . Lord Ashley must be called in to engage the sympathies of the House and of the country, and whilst all are thus thrown off their guard, this obnoxious, sinister, destructive measure is interwoven from the beginning to the end of his proposals.

(3) . . . Your Bill ought to be at once rejected, by every friend of civil and religious liberty . . . I know that you take Lord Sidmouth for your model . . . [Dissenters] discover the Jesuit lurking behind every clause; and we are thus led to believe, that, if not actually drawn up, as some have supposed, in the College of Jesuits at Rome, it has at least been revised, though not improved, by the College of Jesuits at Oxford.

. . . Under this Act, if it should become the law, a parent cannot even give his child a *half holiday*, though that child may have been working *standing* for *six hours and a half*!

. . . We have endured the existence of the Established Church and church-rates, and many other grievances, because we are men of peace; and hope that, by the spread of Christian truth and equity, all these hindrances to the cause of Christ may be quietly removed . . .

(4) Why should dissenting parents be placed in the situation of *protesters* with regard to their principles?

. . . Besides, why is a child's employment in a factory to be suspended on his receiving a particular mode of religious education? I ask respectfully, Ought people to be compelled to be religious or to lose their bread?

. . . Toleration itself is but essential despotism—the worse for being religious.

(5) A profession of liberality which has nothing of reality in it . . . I denounce all compulsion in the matter of education . . . The child is not allowed to pay: there is some virtue in paying.

We are connected, in a certain interesting relation, with the Sovereign of [Prussia]. He is the recognised god-father of the Prince of this realm; I trust he may look well to his religious charge, and see rather that he incline to Lutheranism than that his *will be forced* to Puseyism.

. . . So many of [the Church's] sons are blotting the name of Protestant from their brow as a disgrace, and disturbing the settlement of the very throne, by denominating the Reformation a robbery, and the Revolution rebellion! Just now . . . they are labouring to elevate tradition above the Scriptures—the sacraments above the Gospel—the Church above Christ—and the priest above all!

. . . The poor [should] possess their rights—their undoubted rights—the first of all civil rights, next to the safety of the person—that of selling their labour in the dearest markets and buying the fruits of the earth for their families in the cheapest markets.

We ask, then, that we shall be free; in labour, free; in trade, free; in action, free; in thought, free; in speech, free; in religion, free—perfectly free.

(6) Petition, and petition still,
For 'tis in fact a Tory* Bill . . .
Yours is the treat to pay, and boast;
Theirs to possess, and rule the roast . . .
Resist, in every form and state
This Pusey scheme to educate . . .
. . . all should tell the State
She has no right to educate.

* Tory, means a savage, a robber; is derived from the Irish word *toree*, which signifies "Give me your money".

Anglican Views

Despite nonconformist attacks on Graham's Bill as an Anglican plot, many Anglicans remained lukewarm, fearing State intervention. A typical spokesman was the Rev. George Sandys, who published *A Letter to the Rt. Hon. Sir James R. G. Graham* in 1843. The bitterly disappointed Ashley now looked for increased educational work by the Church. The second extract is from his journal for 16 June 1843 (Hodder, *op. cit.*).

(1) The Church lays exclusive claim to its own internal regulations; it jealously protests against Erastian interference, it cannot fulfil its sacred functions if it be crippled and fettered; experience tells us that the civil power *has* controlled it already, and, concurrently, the popular voice *has expressed* dissatisfaction with what it has learned to entitle "*the State Church*" and has been loud in its approval of self-governing and self-regulating bodies . . .

. . . Sir, the affectation of a zeal for the preservation of religious liberty of conscience, is in this case a transparent subterfuge, it is equivalent to saying, "let our poor be dissenters,—let them be infidels,—let them be atheists,—let them be anything so that they be not Churchmen . . .

. . . The Church first displayed the will to educate, when the people were not ripe for education, now they are ripe for it *give her the means.*

(2) Graham withdrew, last night, the Education Clauses of the Factory Bill. The Government are right, it could not have been carried in the House except by forced and small majorities; it could not have been reduced to practice in the country, without fierce and everlasting collisions—as harmony was the object, so harmony must have been the means. The fierceness and strength of opposition, however, were not the sole reasons of withdrawal; at least in my mind, the apathy of our own friends, lay and clerical, was a death-blow to any hope of immediate or final success. No one liked the scheme, though many acquiesced in it; all desired that it should not pass, because one part thought it would do real harm, and the other believed it would do no good. One result has issued to my conviction, and I dare say to that of many others. "Combined Education" must never again be attempted—it is an impossibility, and worthless if possible—the plan is hopeless, the attempt full of hazard. So I will never vote for combined education —let us have our own schools, our Catechism, our Liturgy, our Articles, our Homilies, our faith, our own teaching of God's Word.

Hostility to Compulsion

State aid to the voluntary educational societies continued to grow, but sectarian divisions and 'voluntaryist' theory alike restrained further State action. In 1861 the Commission on the State of Popular Education in England, under the 5th Duke of Newcastle (1811–64), reported against compulsory education on the Prussian model (P.P. 1861, xxi). Only in 1870 did the Education Act provide for a national English system of elementary education through a network of schoolboards to supplement voluntary work; attendance was made compulsory in 1880 and fees were abolished in 1891.

. . . Any universal compulsory system appears to us neither attainable nor desirable. In Prussia, indeed, and in many parts of Germany, the attendance can scarcely be termed compulsory. Though the attendance is required by law, it is a law which entirely expresses the convictions and wishes of the people. Such a state of feeling renders the working of a system of compulsion, among a people living under a strict government, comparatively easy. Our own condition, it need scarcely be stated is in many respects essentially different. But we also found that the results of this system, as seen in Prussia, do not appear to be so much superior to those which have been already attained amongst ourselves by voluntary efforts, as to make us desire an alteration which would be opposed to the feelings, and, in some respects, to the principles of this country. An attempt to replace an independent system of education by a compulsory system, managed by the Government, would be met by objections, both religious and political, of a far graver character in this country than any with which it has had to contend in Prussia; and we have seen that, even in Prussia, it gives rise to difficulties which are not insignificant . . .

Secondary Education

The Victorian 'secondary' schools ranged from ancient foundations like Eton and Winchester and numerous provincial grammar schools to new middle-class institutions. In 1864 the Public Schools Commission, under the 4th Earl of Clarendon (1800–70) reported on the major public schools, and in the same year the Schools Inquiry Commission was set up, under the 1st Lord Taunton (1799–1869), with a wider remit. Taunton's *Report* (P.P. 1867–8, xxviii) demonstrated the class divisions inherent in Victorian secondary education.

Private schools again find it difficult, in some cases impossible, to resist the class-feeling which compels the exclusion of boys of a lower rank than the rest. In this way, if a private school be the only provision for education within reach, gross injustice is sometimes done. A boy of superior talents is not allowed, even if he is able to pay the school fees, to enter a school attended by children, above him in the social scale. The parents threaten to withdraw their children, unless the social distinction is rigidly maintained, and the private school master is often powerless to resist the threat. Thus parents in a lower rank who may perhaps be sensible of the advantages of education, and may be willing to undergo great privations for the sake of giving these advantages to their children, are discouraged by meeting with a barrier which they cannot pass.

Universities

Until the nineteenth century England had two ancient Anglican universities at Cambridge and Oxford, while Scotland had medieval foundations at S. Andrews, Aberdeen and Glasgow and an early seventeenth-century university at Edinburgh. The cheaper Scottish universities developed medical and scientific studies; but Oxford and Cambridge, where autonomous colleges were for long more powerful and wealthy than the central authorities and where ancient and sometimes restrictive ordinances applied, found it difficult to move with the times: reform came only with the Acts of 1854, 1856 and 1871 and through vigorous internal campaigns. Despite all difficulties, however, the universities regularly gave opportunities to 'lads o' pairts'. And universities expanded with the foundation of the Welsh Anglican college at Lampeter (1822), Anglican Durham University (1832), non-denominational London University (1836) [amalgamating the Benthamite University College of 1828 and Anglican King's College of 1829] and the undenominational Owen's College at Manchester (1851). In the following extracts unreformed Oxford is attacked by (1) the bitterly hostile *Edinburgh Review* (xiv, 1809) and by (2) de Tocqueville, *op. cit.* (in August 1833)—in both cases unfairly. The third extract is taken from *The Idea of a University* (1852) by John Henry Newman (1801–90), Anglican priest, Roman Catholic cardinal and rector of Dublin Roman Catholic University in the 'fifties. The final quotation is from Sir Henry Roscoe (1833–1915), Professor of Chemistry at Owen's College from 1857, reminiscing about early days to Charles Rowley (*Fifty Years of Work without Wages*, 1912).

(1) . . . Though this learned body have occasionally availed themselves of the sagacity and erudition of Rhunken, Wyttenbach, Heyne, and other *foreign* professors, they have of late added nothing of their own, except what they derived from the superior skill of British manufacturers, and the superior wealth of their establishment, namely, whiter paper, blacker ink, and neater types . . .

(2) One's first feeling on visiting Oxford is of unforced admiration for the men of old who founded such immense establishments to aid the development of the human spirit, and for the political institutions of the people who have preserved them intact through the ages. But when one examines these things closely and gets below the surface of this imposing show, admiration almost vanishes and one sees a host of abuses which are not at first sight obvious.

... The principal study ... is that of Latin and Greek, as in the Middle Ages. I should see no harm in that if the studies of the nineteenth century had been added to those of the fourteenth. But that is only done very incompletely ...

... University education is not in the least free of charge.

... All of them have *six* months of vacations.

Oxford at the present time is menaced with reform. Thus all the secondary abuses upon which the aristocracy leans, are falling. After its fall will England be happier? I think so. As great? I doubt it.

(3) ... I suppose as follows: When a multitude of young men, keen, open-hearted, sympathetic, and observant, as young men are, come together and freely mix with each other, they are sure to learn from one another, even if there be no one to teach them; the conversation of all is a series of lectures to each, and they gain for themselves new ideas and views, fresh matter of thought, and distinct principles for judging and acting, day by day ...

... Thus it is that, independent of direct instruction on the part of superiors, there is a sort of self-education in the academic institutions of Protestant England; a characteristic tone of thought, a recognized standard of judgement is found in them, which, as developed in the individual who is submitted to it, becomes a twofold source of strength to him, both from the distinct stamp it impresses on his mind, and from the bond of union which it creates between him and others,—effects which are shared by the authorities of the place, for they themselves have been educated in it, and at all times are exposed to the influence of its ethical atmosphere. Here then is a real teaching, whatever be its standards and principles, true or false; and it at least tends towards cultivation of the intellect; it at least recognizes that knowledge is something more than a sort of passive reception of scraps and details; it is a something, and it does a something, which never will issue from the most strenuous efforts of a set of teachers, with no mutual sympathies and no inter-communion, of a set of examiners with no opinions which they dare profess, and with no common principles, who are teaching or questioning a set of youths who do not know them, and do not know each other, on a large number of subjects, different in kind, and connected by no wide philosophy, three times a week, or three times a year, or once in three years, in chill lecture-rooms or on a pompous anniversary.

(4) Coming from Heidelberg University, I saw that the only chance of making a successful college in Manchester was to give importance to scientific studies, and in this [Principal J. G.] Greenwood fully agreed. So after a few years of active work in chemistry I induced the trustees to appoint a Professor of Physics —and Clifton came and was a tower of strength. From 1857 onwards things looked up. Our students increased in number, original scientific work began, students were gradually inoculated with the spirit of research, and the College became known as a place where a manufacturer could send his son to learn something that would prove useful to him. Our men took high honours in chemistry year after year in the University of London, so that the name of Owens became a household word to people interested in scientific education throughout the land. There was certainly 'go' and fervour about the dwellers in those old premises in Quay Street. All the 'old men' of the years 1857–67 look back with feelings of fond regard to the shabby rooms, crowded laboratory, and squalid surroundings of those times . . .

LIFE IN THE MINES

'Sad Evils'

At Ashley's prompting, in August 1840 a 'Children's Employment Commission' was set up, to investigate a wide range of child labour. Its first *Report* (P.P. 1842, xv–xvii) in May 1842 was an horrific document, describing the conditions under which women and children worked in the mines, generally in those owned by smaller proprietors. The illustrations depicting semi-naked men, women and children toiling in conditions of danger and indecency disgusted a generation. On 7 June 1842 Ashley proposed a Bill to regulate female and child labour in the collieries. His two-hour speech, reprinted in *Speeches of the Earl of Shaftesbury*, (1868) was very successful, giving him 'hopes for the Empire, hopes for its permanence, hopes for its services in the purposes of the Messiah'.

. . . Now, it appears that the practice prevails to a lamentable extent of making young persons and children of a tender age draw loads by means of the girdle and chain. This practice prevails generally in Shropshire, in Derbyshire, in the West Riding of Yorkshire, in Lancashire, in Cheshire, in the east of Scotland, in

North and South Wales, and in South Gloucestershire. The child, it appears, has a girdle bound round its waist, to which is attached a chain, which passes under the legs, and is attached to the cart. The child is obliged to pass on all fours, and the chain passes under what, therefore, in that posture, might be called the hind legs; and thus they oftentimes more contracted. This kind of labour they have to continue during several hours, in a temperature described as perfectly intolerable. By the testimony of the people themselves it appears that the labour is exceedingly severe; that the girdle blisters their sides and causes great pain . . . In the West Riding, it appears, girls are almost universally employed as trappers and hurriers, in common with boys. The girls are of all ages, from 7 to 21. They commonly work quite naked down to the waist, and are dressed—as far as they are dressed at all—in a loose pair of trousers. These are seldom whole on either sex. In many of the collieries the adult colliers, whom these girls serve, work perfectly naked . . .

. . . Nothing can be more graphic, nothing more touching, than the evidence of many of these poor girls themselves. Insulted, oppressed, and even corrupted, they exhibit, not unfrequently, a simplicity and a kindness that render tenfold more heart-rending the folly and cruelty of [the] system . . .

Surely, it is evident that to remove, or even to mitigate, these sad evils, will require the vigorous and immediate interposition of the legislature. That interposition is demanded by public reason, by public virtue, by the public honour, by the public character, and, I rejoice to add, by the public sympathy . . .

Morals and the Pits

Ashley's Mines Bill of 1842, passed after some controversy in August, prohibited women, girls and boys under the age of 10 from working underground, provided for some safety measures and led to the appointment of H. S. Tremenheere (1804–93) as the first Mines Inspector. The speedy enactment of reform was aided by a moved public opinion, as evinced in the *Quarterly Review*, lxx (1842), the Tory journal.

The legislature of past years has undoubtedly been to blame in taking no cognizance of such a state of things as is now exhibited.

But are they blameless who employ these men, and reap the benefit of labours which have induced a premature old age in their service? Have they, with so much in their power, fulfilled their duties—have they considered how to strengthen the connection of the master and the hireling by other ties than those of gain? Has our Church, clerical and lay, been diligent in civilising these rough natures? Have proprietors, enriched by the development of minerals, enabled the Church to increase her functionaries in proportion to the growth of new populations? These are questions which must be asked, and answered, before the burden of change is laid on a few, which should be borne by many. We feel that this benefit must be conferred by all; and the power of the state must be propped by the self-denial of the owner—and the mild, untiring energies of the Church must be aided by the kindly influences of neighbourhood—before it can be hoped that such a race as the miners can be brought to abandon their rooted prejudices and brutal indulgences. Living in the midst of dangers—and on that account supplied with higher wages, and with much leisure to spend them—they unite in their character all that could flow from sources which render man at once reckless and self-indulgent—a hideous combination, when unleavened by religion and the daily influences of society—little likely to be removed by Acts of Parliament alone . . .

Aristocrats and the Pits

In general, it appears that conditions in collieries belonging to such noblemen as the 5th Duke of Buccleuch (1806–84), 4th Earl of Dartmouth (1784–1853), 1st Earl of Dudley (1817–85), 2nd Earl of Durham (1828–79), 3rd Earl Fitzwilliam (1786–1857), 3rd Marquess of Londonderry (1778–1853), 1st Earl of Lonsdale (1757–1844), 4th Duke of Portland (1768–1854) and 2nd Duke of Sutherland (1786–1861) were much better than in smaller ventures. In 1843 Thomas Tancred, reporting on South Staffordshire for the First Report of the Midland Mining Commission (P.P. 1843, xiii), stressed this point of view: rural paternalism seemed to continue in mines managed by at least some of the greater estates.

It appears a legitimate deduction from what has been already stated that the rank and wealth of the employers of mining labour has an important influence upon the welfare of the workmen. We have seen that some of the best managed concerns are those of the trustees of Lord Ward, of the British Iron Company, of Mr. Foster of Shutt End, of the lessees of the Earl of Dartmouth, of the Duke of Sutherland, &c. In these no truck prevails, the Sabbath is not desecrated by working the furnaces during that day. Butties are either dispensed with altogether, or placed under strict regulations. It is not unreasonable to imagine *à priori*, that men of rank and capital will not condescend to adopt the shifts and expedients to which an inferior class of proprietors are as it were driven to resort. Besides, the former may be generally presumed to have enjoyed a better education, and also to be more amenable to public opinion. Hence mining districts may be expected to vary in regard to the general and customary treatment of the workmen, according as the proprietors are generally and on an average of greater or less rank and wealth. We have seen that the butty system and the truck system are merely methods of supplying a lack of adequate capital on the part of the mine-owner, and whatever exceptions there may be, I think it will be found that the general customs prevailing in the treatment of workpeople in any district will be established and regulated by the sense of the majority of the great proprietors, and will be more or less liberal and considerate according to the scale on which the mining operations are conducted.

This view is much confirmed by a comparison of the general customs with regard to the payment and treatment of workmen prevailing in South Staffordshire, and in the Northumberland and Durham coal fields respectively. In the former district the immediate employers of labour, *i.e.*, the lessees of Royalties, and many of the owners of mineral property also, are men whose fathers, if not themselves, have risen to their present situation from the ranks—speculators who have become wealthy *per saltum*, with the rapid progress of manufacturing prosperity.

On the other hand, if we inquire into the general character for wealth and rank of the employers of mining labour on the Tyne and Wear, we shall find them to be the nobility and gentry and landed proprietors of those counties, as is the case also in Cornwall; the moral effects of which upon the mining population is proved to be strikingly beneficial, by the Report of Seymour Tremenheere, Esq., Government Inspector of Schools . . .

POPULATION

The Mid-Century Census

Despite a torrent of Malthusian propaganda, Britain's population rose rapidly (probably because of both declining adult death rates and infant mortality rates). And this increased population (assessed by a census in each decade from 1801) was subjected to ever-closer investigation by Government and other statisticians. In 1851, when the population of Great Britain had reached 17,927,609, the *Census of Great Britain*, i, reported on the cardinal features of half a century's population changes.

The most important result which the inquiry establishes, is the addition in half a century, of *ten millions* of people to the British population. The increase of population in the half of this century nearly equals the increase in all preceding ages . . . Contemporaneously with the increase of the population at home, emigration has proceeded since 1750 to such an extent, as to people large states in America, and to give permanent possessors and cultivators to the land of large colonies in all the temperate regions of the world; . . . The current of the Celtic migration is now diverted from these shores; and chiefly flows in the direction of the United States of America, where the wanderers find friends and kindred . . .

It is one of the obvious physical effects of the increase of population, that the proportion of land to each person diminishes; and the decrease is such, that within the last fifty years, the number of acres to *each person* living, has fallen from 5·4 to 2·7 acres in Great Britain; from *four* acres to *two* acres in England and Wales . . .

At the same time, too, that the populations of the towns and of the country, have become so equally balanced in number—*ten millions* against *ten millions*—the union between them has become, by the circumstance which has led to the increase of the towns, more intimate than it was before; for they are now connected together by innumerable relationships, as well as by the associations of trade . . .

PART SIX

Religion

Let us, as ministers of the gospel of peace, co-operate in our proper stations with our superiors, in promoting harmony and good order in society, in preserving a due respect to the authority, and a proper confidence in the ability and integrity of those who are set over us.

Richard Watson (1737–1816), *Christianity Consistent with Every Social Duty* (Cambridge, 1769)

It would be consistent with right that the churches be sold, and the money arising therefrom be invested as a fund for the education of children of poor parents of every profession, and, if more than sufficient for this purpose, that the surplus be appropriated to the support of the aged poor.

Tom Paine (1737–1809), *Letter to Camille Jordan* (1797)

I wish to see the established church of England great and powerful; I wish to see her foundations laid low and deep, that she may crush the giant powers of rebellious darkness; I would have her head raised up to the Heaven to which she conducts us. I would have her open wide her hospitable gates by a noble and liberal comprehension. But I would have no breaches in her wall.

Edmund Burke (1729–97), *Speech for the Relief of Protestant Dissenters* (1773)

Besieged as the Church of England is on all sides, her defenders would do well to capitulate, whilst honourable terms may be had, and not to wait from indolence or obstinacy or false pride until the Establishment is stormed by popular indignation which is fast gathering around the dilapidated edifice.

Christian Reformer (1833)

Poverty is often both honourable and comfortable; but indigence can only be pitiable, and is usually contemptible. Poverty is not only the natural lot of many, in a well-constituted society, but is necessary, that a society may be well constituted. Indigence, on the contrary, is seldom the natural lot of any, but is commonly the state into which intemperance and want of prudent foresight push poverty: the punishment which the moral government of God inflicts in this world upon thoughtlessness and guilty extravagance.

J. B. Sumner (1780–1862), *A Treatise on the Records of The Creation* (1816)

Society has been regarded as a mere collection of individuals looking each after his own interests, and the business of government has been limited to that of a mere police whose sole use is to prevent these individuals from robbing or knocking each other down.

Thomas Arnold (1795–1842), *Principles of Church Reform* (1833)

If the purifying spirit of the Gospel be not breathed upon the corrupt and fermenting mass, a contest will and must come—God only knows how soon—a contest of classes.

Henry Phillpotts (1778–1869), *A Charge Delivered to the Clergy of the Diocese of Exeter* (1845)

Though the clergy should never so lower down their high calling as to become political rather than spiritual men, yet . . . it appertains to their office, as instructors and guides of thought and opinion, that they should closely watch all measures which tend to promote the general welfare, and above all, the morals of the people.

Samuel Wilberforce (1805–73), *A Charge Delivered to the Clergy of the Diocese of Oxford* (1848)

'Tracts on Christian Socialism' is, it seems to me, the only title which will define our object, and will commit us at once to the conflict we must engage in sooner or later with the unsocial Christians and the unchristian Socialists.

F. D. Maurice (1805–72), in Frederick Maurice, *The Life of Frederick Denison Maurice* (1885)

The unbelief of the lower classes in the present day, is not merely the unbelief of vicious practice. Their principles are undermined: which renders the evil more serious, and the remedy more difficult.

J. B. Sumner, *A Charge delivered to the Clergy of the Diocese of Chester* (1832)

Evangelical Faith

William Wilberforce (1759–1833) issued his *Practical View of the Prevailing Religious Conceptions of Professed Christians in the Higher and Middle Classes in this Country contrasted with Real Christianity* in 1797. A Pittite 'Tory' M.P., Wilberforce experienced a conversion to Evangelicalism in 1785. He led the campaign against negro slavery in the colonies from his native Yorkshire, and became a prominent member of the 'Clapham Sect' of Evangelical leaders. His message was that Christians should act on their beliefs more completely.

Doubtless there have been too many, who, to their eternal ruin, have abused the doctrine of Salvation by Grace; and have vainly trusted in Christ for pardon and acceptance, when by their vicious lives they have plainly proved the groundlessness of their pretensions. The tree is to be known by its fruits: and there is too much reason to fear that there is no principle of faith when it does not decidedly evince itself by the fruits of holiness. Dreadful indeed will be the doom, above that of all others, of those loose professors of Christianity, to whom at the last day our blessed Saviour will address those words, 'I never knew you; depart from me, all ye that work iniquity'. But the danger of error on this side ought not to render us insensible to the opposite error: an error against which in these days it seems particularly necessary to guard. It is far from the intention of the writer of this work to enter into the niceties of controversy. But surely without danger of being thought to violate this design, he may be permitted to contend, that they who in the main believe the doctrines of the Church of England, are bound to allow, that our dependence on our blessed Saviour, as alone the meritorious cause of our acceptance with God, and as the means of all its blessed fruits and glorious consequences, must be not merely formal and nominal, but real and substantial; not vague, qualified and partial, but direct, cordial and entire. 'Repentance towards God, and faith towards our Lord Jesus Christ,' was the sum of the apostolical instructions. It is not an occasional invocation of the name of Christ, or a transient recognition of his authority, that fills up the measure of the terms, *believing in Jesus*. This we shall find no easy task: and, if we trust that we do believe, we should all perhaps do well to cry out in the words of an imploring suppliant (he supplicated not in vain) 'Lord, help thou our unbelief.' We must be deeply conscious of our guilt and misery, heartily repenting of our sins, and firmly resolving to foresake them: and thus penitently 'fleeing for refuge to the hope set before us', we must found altogether on the merit of the crucified Redeemer our hopes of escape from their deserved punishment, and of deliverance from their enslaving power. This must be our first, our last, our only plea. We are to surrender ourselves up to him to 'be washed in his blood', to be sanctified by his Spirit, resolving to receive him for our Lord and Master, to learn in his School, to obey all his commandments.

Evangelical Practice

Hannah More (1745–1833), a friend of Wilberforce, became a prolific Evangelical pamphleteer and a prominent philanthropist. From 1789 she established a number of schools (combining religious and industrial education), friendly societies and women's clubs in her native West Country. A Gloucestershire woman, she settled at Cheddar in Somerset and described her work there in a letter to Wilberforce in 1791. It was published by William Roberts in his *Memoirs of the Life and Correspondence of Mrs. Hannah More* in 1834.

. . . We found more than two thousand people in the parish, almost all very poor; no gentry, a dozen wealthy farmers, hard, brutal, and ignorant. We visited them all, picking up at one house, (like fortune-tellers) the name and character of the next. We told them we intended to set up a school for their poor. They did not like it. We assured them we did not desire a shilling from them, but wished for their concurrence, as we knew they could influence their workmen. One of the farmers seemed pleased and civil; he was rich, but covetous, a hard drinker, and his wife a woman of loose morals, but good natural sense; she became our friend, sooner than some of the decent and formal, and let us a house, the only one in the parish, at £7 per annum, with a good garden. Adjoining to it was a large ox-house; this we roofed and floored; and by putting in a couple of windows, it made a good school-room. While this was doing, we went to every house in the place, and found every house a scene of the greatest ignorance and vice. We saw but one Bible in all the parish, and that was used to prop a flower-pot. No clergymen had resided in it for forty years. One rode over, three miles from Wells, to preach once on a Sunday, but no weekly duty was done, or sick persons visited; and children were often buried without any funeral service. Eight people in the morning, and twenty in the afternoon, was a good congregation. We spent our whole time in getting at the characters of all the people, the employment, wages, and number of every family; and this we have done in nine parishes. On a fixed day, of which we gave notice in the church, all the women, with all their children above six years old, met us. We took an exact list from their account, and engaged one hundred and twenty to attend on the following Sunday. A great many refused to send their children, unless we should pay them for it! and not a few refused, because they were not sure of my intentions, being apprehensive that at the end of seven years, if they attended so long, I should acquire a power over them, and send them beyond sea. I must have heard this myself in order to have believed that so much ignorance existed out of Africa . . .

We now began to distribute Bibles, Prayer Books, and other good books, but never at random, and only to those who had given some evidence of their loving and deserving them. They are always made the reward of superior learning, or some other merit, as we can have no other proof that they will be read. Those who manifest the greater diligence, get the books of most importance . . .

Finding the wants and distresses of these poor people uncommonly great, (for their wages are but 1s. per day), and fearing to abuse the bounty of my friends, by too indiscriminate liberality, it occurred to me that I could make what I had to bestow go much further by instituting clubs, or societies for the women, as is done for men in other places . . .

We have an anniversary feast of tea, and I get some of the clergy, and a few of the better sort of people to come to it. We wait on the women, who sit and enjoy their dignity. The Journal and state of affairs is read after church; and we collect all the facts we can as to the conduct of the villagers; whether the church has been more attended, fewer or more frauds, less or more swearing, scolding, or sabbath-breaking. All this is produced for or against them, in battle array, in a little sort of sermon made up of praise, censure, and exhortation, as they may be found to have merited . . .

We are now in our sixth year at Cheddar, and two hundred children and above two hundred old people constantly attend. God has blessed the work beyond all my hopes. The farmer's wife, (our landlady) is become one of the most eminent Christians I know;

and though we had last year the great misfortune to lose our elder mistress, her truly Christian death was made the means of confirming many in piety . . .

Catholic Faith

The Rev. John Keble (1792–1866), the saintly Professor of Poetry at Oxford, produced his book *The Christian Year. Thoughts in Verse for the Sundays and Holydays throughout the Year* in 1827. 'Next to a sound rule of faith,' he explained, 'there is nothing of so much consequence as a sober standard of feeling in matters of practical religion: and it is the peculiar happiness of the Church of England to possess, in her authorized formularies, an ample and secure provision for both.' Fearing that such virtues might be lost, he attempted to bring his readers' 'own thoughts and feelings into more entire unison with those recommended and exemplified in the Prayer Book.' The extract is from Keble's lines on 'King Charles the Martyr', whose quasi-judicial murder on 30 January 1649 was widely commemorated

True son of our dear Mother, early taught
With her to worship and for her to die,
Nursed in her aisles to more than kingly thought,
Oft in her solemn hours we dream thee nigh.

For thou didst love to trace her daily lore,
And where we look for comfort or for calm,
Over the self-same lines to bend, and pour
Thy heart with hers in some victorious psalm.

And well did she thy loyal love repay;
When all forsook, her Angels still were nigh,
Chain'd and bereft, and on thy funeral way,
Straight to the Cross she turn'd thy dying eye.

And yearly now, before the Martyr's King,
For thee she offers her maternal tears,
Calls us, like thee, to His dear feet to cling,
And bury in His wounds our earthly fears.

The Angels hear, and there is mirth in Heaven,
Fit prelude of the joy, when spirits won
Like thee to patient Faith, shall rise forgiven,
And at their Saviour's knees thy bright example own.

The Tractarians

In 1833 Keble bravely condemned what he considered to be current Erastianism over the State's reduction of Church of Ireland bishoprics, in his celebrated 'Assize Sermon' at Oxford. His lead was followed by a group of younger dons, intent on restoring the importance of the Sacraments in Anglican tradition and looking back to the High Anglicanism of Archbishop Laud and King Charles I. From 1833 the group expressed its traditionalist, Catholic views in a series of *Tracts for the Times*. *Tracts* I (1833) and XC (1841) were particularly important statements of Anglican Catholicism. Both were written by the brilliant John Henry Newman (1801–90), who, after long torment, joined the Roman Catholic Church in 1845, eventually becoming a cardinal. The two *Tracts* are quoted below. In the first Newman stressed the importance of the Apostolic Succession; in the second he enraged Protestants by giving a Catholic interpretation of the 39 Articles.

(1) I am but one of yourselves,—a Presbyter; and therefore I conceal my name, lest I should take too much on myself by speaking in my own person. Yet speak I must; for the times are very evil, yet no one speaks against them . . .

Consider a moment. Is it fair, is it dutiful, to suffer our Bishops to stand the brunt of the battle without doing our part to support them? . . .

To them then we willingly and affectionately relinquish their high privileges and honours; we encroach not upon the rights of the successors of the Apostles; we touch not their sword and crosier. Yet surely we may be their shield-bearers in the battle without offence, and by our voice and deeds be to them what Luke and Timothy were to St. Paul.

Now then let me come at once to the subject which leads me to address you. Should the Government and Country so far forget their God as to cast off the Church, to deprive it of its temporal honours and substance, *on what* will you rest the claim of respect and attention which you make upon your flocks? Hitherto you have been upheld by your birth, your education, your wealth, your connections; should these secular advances cease, on what must Christ's Ministers depend? Is not this a serious practical question? We know how miserable is the state of religious bodies not supported by the State. Look at the Dissenters on all sides of you, and you will see at once that their Ministers, depending simply upon the people, become the *creatures* of the people. Are you content that this should be your case? Alas! can a greater evil befall Christians than for their teachers to be guided by them, instead of guiding? How can we 'hold fast the form of sound words', and 'keep that which is committed to our trust,' if our influence is to depend simply on our popularity? Is it not our very office to *oppose* the world? can we then allow ourselves to *court* it? to preach smooth things and prophesy deceits? to make the way of life easy to the rich and indolent, and to bribe the humbler classes by excitements and strong intoxicating doctrine? Surely it must not be so;—and the question recurs, on *what* are we to rest our authority when the State deserts us?

Christ has not left His Church without claim of its own upon the attention of men. Surely not. Hard Master He cannot be, to bid us oppose the world, yet give us no credentials for so doing. There are some who rest their divine mission on their own unsupported assertion; others, who rest it upon their popularity; others, on their success; and others, who rest it upon their temporal distinctions. This last case has, perhaps, been too much our own; I fear we have neglected the real ground on which our authority is built,—OUR APOSTOLICAL DESCENT.

We have been born, not of blood, nor of the will of the flesh, nor of the will of man, but of God. The Lord Jesus Christ gave His Spirit to His Apostles; they in turn laid their hands on those who should succeed them; and these again on others; and so the sacred gift has been handed down to our present Bishops, who have appointed us as their assistants, and in some sense representatives.

Now every one of us believes this. I know that some will at first deny they do; still they do believe it. Only, it is not sufficiently practically impressed on their minds. They *do* believe it; for it is the doctrine of the Ordination Service, which they have recognised as truth in the most solemn season of their lives . . .

. . . I know the grace of ordination is contained in the laying on of hands, not in any form of words;—yet in our own case (as has ever been usual in the Church) words of blessing have accompanied the act. Thus we have confessed before God our belief that through the Bishop who ordained us, we received the Holy Ghost, the power to bind and to loose, to administer the Sacraments and to preach . . . It is plain then that [the Bishop] but *transmits*; and that the Christian Ministry is a *succession*. And if we trace back the power of ordination from hand to hand, of course we shall come to the Apostles at last. We know we do, as a plain historical fact: and therefore all we, who have been ordained Clergy, in the very form of our ordination acknowledged the doctrine of the Apostolical Succession.

(2) One remark may be made in conclusion. It may be objected that the tenor of the above explanations is anti-Protestant, whereas it is notorious that the Articles were drawn up by Protestants, and intended for the establishment of Protestantism; accordingly, that it is an evasion of their meaning to give them any other than a Protestant drift, possible as it may be to do so grammatically, or in each separate part.

But the answer is simple:

1. In the first place, it is a *duty* which we owe both to the Catholic Church and to our own, to take our reformed confessions in the most Catholic sense they will admit; we have no duties towards their framers. (Nor do we receive the Articles from the original framers, but from several successive convocations after their times; in the last instance, from that of 1662).

2. In giving the Articles a Catholic interpretation, we bring them into harmony with the Book of Common Prayer, an object of the most serious moment to those who have given their assent to both formularies . . .

4. It may be remarked, moreover, that such an interpretation is in accordance with the well-known general leaning of Melancthon, from whose writings our Articles are principally drawn, and whose Catholic tendencies gained for him that same reproach of popery which has ever been so freely bestowed upon members of our own reformed Church . . .

7. Lastly, their framers constructed them in such a way as best to comprehend those who did not go so far in Protestantism as themselves. Anglo-Catholics then are but the successors and representatives of those moderate reformers; and their case has been directly anticipated in the wording of the Articles. It follows that they are not perverting, they are using them, for an express purpose for which among others their authors framed them. The interpretation they take was intended to be admissible; though not that which their authors took themselves. Had it not been provided for, possibly the Articles never would have been accepted by our Church at all. If, then, the framers have gained their side of the

compact in effecting the reception of the Articles, let Catholics have theirs too in retaining their own Catholic interpretation of them.

The Parish Priest

Dr. Walter Farquhar Hook (1798–1875) was a remarkable Vicar of Leeds from 1837 to 1859, when he became Dean of Chichester. He radically reformed Church life in a vast industrial parish, introducing 'High Church' practices into the hitherto 'evangelical' community and demonstrating the Church's concern for the working classes. His first reactions to Leeds are described in the following extracts from letters, published by his son-in-law, W. R. W. Stephens, *The Life and Letters of Walter Farquhar Hook* (1879 edn.), to (1) Georgiana Hook (5 July 1837), (2) the Rev. J. W. Clarke (7 July 1837), (3) the Rev. Samuel Wilberforce (July 1837) and (4) W. P. Wood (July 1837).

(1) . . . To Yorkshire manners I am becoming a little reconciled. I am beginning with the greatest delicacy to hint to the people that this is not quite public property. Hitherto everybody seems to have thought himself justified in entering it, and in criticising all that the Vicar had been doing; while sturdy beggars, men out of work, meet me at every turn, and almost demand relief. I am now in full work; the poor curates, sexton, clerk, &c. are surprised: they evidently thought that I should let them go on in their own slovenly way, while I should be employed in some grand undertakings, such as building new churches and schools; whereas the learned doctor (they doctor me here, 'Yes, Doctor, No, Doctor,' at almost every second word), says, 'fair and softly', one thing at a time. They heard nothing of me the first week. I first set my study in order, and next the parish church must be put in order; so as to show how things shall and must be done, I am taking all the full curate's duty; I have this day offered the prayers three times, besides burying, baptising, and churching. The stated services in this church are prayers three times a day; and instead of seeking for a congregation, the curates, sexton, clerk, &c. have endeavoured to prevent one being formed, and then used that as an excuse for having no service. I have ordered the sexton whenever there is no congregation, to go into the street and to give two old women sixpence a-piece to come in and form one; so that no sham excuse can be tolerated. The curates have now but little to do, though I

make them attend; for when I ordered the funerals to be properly performed, they have urged that is was impossible, so with baptisms &c.; and, therefore, in order to refute them, I have taken the duty myself, just to prove that 'what is impossible can sometimes come to pass.' The black looks with which I am regarded, notwithstanding the soft words used, are rather amusing; but the services of the Church *shall* be performed as they ought to be, before anything else is done. I am also busily employed with an architect, devising some plan to make decent my nasty, dirty, ugly old church. I am determined to get that into something like order, if possible. The difficulties are tremendous, but I am in good heart.

(2) My system is, not to care for the trouble of the clergy, but to consult the convenience of the public, and to enamour them of our services by having them solemnly and devoutly performed . . . If you and I show that we attach importance to the solemn performance of even the slightest duty connected with our dear Master's service; that we consider even the office of a doorkeeper in His house an office of honour; that, convinced of His presence, we are as devout in offering the prayers when only two or three are present, as when there are two or three hundred; we shall find His blessing attending us, and we shall be the means of converting others. I confess I attach the very greatest importance to the solemn performance of the occasional duties . . . It might be well also to read over the Oxford Tracts; not that I care whether you agree with them or not, but because the people here are all reading them, and it would be expedient to know something of them, and because, however you may differ on particular points, you cannot but be delighted with the fine, noble, and truly Christian spirit with which they are written.

(3) There are altogether twenty-two clergymen in this parish, who are somewhat under my jurisdiction, and I propose giving them a breakfast once a month at my house, where we shall form a kind of club. There are three 'Evangelicals' of the old school, about four or five high Establishment men, beginning to understand a little about the Church, and the rest are 'orthodox-men' of the old school; all steady, quiet, but (except the four or five I have alluded to) illiterate men. These are my materials: my wish is to infuse into them a Church spirit . . . I do not find my position here an

easy one. The Town you know, and therefore I need not tell you that it is more smoky than any town in England; the vicarage is, I am thankful to say, a comfortable, airy house, or I should fear for the health of my children. We meet with much civility and kindness from the people; but the lower orders are disagreeably uncouth in their manners. The church is the most horrid hole you ever saw; dirty, and so arranged that it is impossible to perform the Communion service in the chancel; and moreover it is situated in the very worst part of the town, the very sink of iniquity, the abode of Irish papists . . . As to Church feeling, to Catholicism, the thing is utterly unknown to clergy and laity. The *de facto* established religion is Methodism, and the best of our church-people, I mean the most pious, talk the language of Methodism; the traditional religion is Methodism . . .

You see that I have no easy course before me; but I shall hope that God has called me to this post to be the instrument of a great change, and I shall expect the prayers of all true friends of Catholicism . . .

(4) I do not oppose Dissenters by disputations and wrangling, but I seek to exhibit to the world the Church in her beauty; let the services of the Church be properly performed, and right-minded people will soon learn to love her . . . The real fact is, that the established religion in Leeds is Methodism, and it is Methodism that all the most pious among the Churchmen unconsciously talk. If you ask a poor person the ground of his hope, he will immediately say that he feels that he is saved, however great a sinner he may be; so that you see I have much to contend with.

Church and State

In his essays *On the Constitution of Church and State* (1820) Samuel Taylor Coleridge (1772–1834), the Devonshire-born 'Lakeland poet', developed the themes of man's need for spirituality, the ethical basis of Christianity, the notion of an organic rather than individualistic society and a belief in the divine nature of the Church. Coleridge was undoubtedly important, as Tory, Churchman and moralist, after dropping his Cambridge undergraduate radicalism, Unitarianism and rationalism. But his message about the revealed nature of Christianity was undoubtedly obscured by his interest in various Continental philosophies —and, perhaps, by his addiction to opium.

... I can have no difficulty in setting forth the right idea of a national Church as in the language of Queen Elizabeth the third great venerable estate of the realm; the first being the estate of the landowners or possessors of fixed property, consisting of the two classes of the Barons and the Franklins; and the second comprising the merchants, the manufacturers, free artizans, and the distributive class. To comprehend, therefore, the true character of the third estate, in which the reserved Nationality was vested, we must first ascertain the end or national purpose, for which such reservation was made.

Now, as in the first estate the permanency of the nation was provided for; and in the second estate its progressiveness and personal freedom; while in the king the cohesion by interdependence, and the unity of the country, were established; there remains for the third estate only that interest which is the ground, the necessary antecedent condition, of both the former. These depend on a continuing and progressive civilization. But civilization is itself but a mixed good, if not far more a corrupting influence, the hectic of disease, not the bloom of health, and a nation so distinguished more fitly to be called a varnished than a polished people, where this civilization is not grounded in cultivation, in the harmonious development of those qualities and faculties that characterize our humanity. We must be men in order to be citizens.

... The object of the two former estates of the realm, which conjointly form the State, was to reconcile the interests of permanence with that of progression—law with liberty. The object of the national Church, the third remaining estate of the realm, was to secure and improve that civilization, without which the nation could be neither permanent nor progressive.

Church and Society

George Stringer Bull (1799–1864) had served in the Royal Navy and as a missionary in Africa before becoming perpetual curate of Bierley, Bradford, in 1826. From 1831 he was a prominent speaker and pamphleteer for Richard Oastler's factory reform agitation. In 1833 he protested against the Factory Commissioners' arrival in Bradford, believing that they would support the textile employers. Bull, who moved to Birmingham in 1840, was a pioneer of the Church of England's concern for industrial life and labour.

PROTEST OF THE REV. G. S. BULL

Addressed to the Commissioners for Factory Enquiry.

I protest as a Christian Man, and as a Minister of the Church of England.

The God whom I desire to serve is "no respecter of persons," and has told you as well as me by the mouth of Solomon, "*it is not good to have respect of persons in judgement*". Now it was palpably "respect of persons", of Rich Capitalists and their influence in Parliament which induced the ministry to set up a Royal Commission, sanctioned by an insignificant majority of one or two in the House of Commons, to adopt a method for the trial of the cause of the rich, diametrically opposite in Constitution and character to that, which they—yes the self same parties adopted for the trial of the cause of the Poor.

I Protest as a Christian Man:—

Because that Divine Redeemer and Lawgiver, who rebuked even his own disciples, when they would have kept the children from him—who pronounced twelve hours occupation to be a day's work for men—would never have suffered any Rich Capitalist of that day to have asserted his *right* because he was rich, to work children longer than their parents, depriving them of health, moral improvement and youthful recreation. No, Sirs, had such a right been asserted by the chiefest of all the Pharisees, neither his sleek, sanctimonious visage—his many prayers—his ostentatious alms-deeds, his broad phylacteries, nor his hoard of Gold would have obtained for him a "Commission" to redeem his respectability—to receive his evidence *in secret*, or to delay for an hour the release of those helpless ones whom the Saviour owned and blessed as a peculiarly beloved portion of his kingdom below.

As a Minister of the Church of England, I conceive it my duty to maintain the cause of the oppressed and the poor, and I regard this favourite system of *Commissions*, now so generally adopted, as so many parts of a Dexterous Conspiracy, which certain Political Philosophers are under plotting, the effect of which is, to establish the domination of wealth, and the degradation of industrious poverty. I feel, too, that the interests of Christianity itself are betrayed, into the hands of unreasonable and wicked men, by the Judas-like conduct of many of its professors, whose capital is embarked in the Factory System, whose lips salute our altars with apparent devotion—who raise their hands in her sanctuary as if to adore, but who make them fall with tyrannous weight upon the children of the needy. Whether such bitter foes of the true Religion of Christ are shrouded in a Priestly Mantle, or dwell in those Mansions and are surrounded by those parks and lawns which the over laboured infant has enabled them to procure, my Ministerial duty to my Country is the same; and whether I regard its general prosperity, its social happiness or its religious advantage, I am bound to rebuke and oppose them.

I believe, the oppression of the Rich—of those especially who hypocritically assume a Christian profession, has done more to injure Christianity than all that Voltaire or Paine ever produced.

Dissenting Attacks

By the early nineteenth century dissenters ranged from Roman Catholics to the various Baptist, Congregationalist (Independent), Quaker, Unitarian and (though, not yet entirely separated from the Church) Methodist denominations. Divided by a multitude of theological arguments, they could unite for such ventures as the repeal of the Test and Corporation Acts in 1828, the defeat of the Anglican-planned Factory Education Bill of 1843 and the propagation of a 'voluntaryist', anti-Establishment propaganda. In the following extracts (1) the celebrated Baptist Robert Hall describes his view of religious freedom [from Olinthus Gregory (ed.) *Works of Robert Hall*, iii (1831)]; (2) the Liberal Congregationalist M.P. George Hadfield (1787–1879) lists dissenting demands (*Baptist Magazine*, 3s. xxv, Dec. 1833); (3) an anonymous writer [*An Analytical Digest of the Education Clauses of the Factories Bill* (1843)] and (4) the Congregationist Edward Baines [*Letter to . . . Lord Wharncliffe . . . on Sir James Graham's Bill* . . . (1843) and (5) *The Manufacturing Districts Vindicated* (Leeds, 1843)] further reveal the bitterness of opposition to the 1843 Bill.

(1) The religious opinions of Dissenters are so various that there is perhaps no point in which they are agreed except in asserting the rights of conscience against all human authority. From the time of Elizabeth, under whom they began to make their appearance, their views of religious liberty have gradually extended . . . Their total separation from the Church did not take place for more than a century after; till, despairing of seeing it erected on a comprehensive plan, and being moreover persecuted for their difference of opinion, they were compelled at last reluctantly to withdraw.

Having thus been directed by a train of events into the right path, they pushed their principles to their legitimate consequences, and began to discern the impropriety of all religious establishments whatever; a sentiment in which they are now nearly united.

(2) We are required to submit to the domination of a corrupt state church; to be governed by bishops; to see 3,500,000£ at the least (but more likely 5,000,000£) annually expended in the maintenance of a clergy, of whom a vast majority do not preach the gospel; to see the cure of souls bought and sold in the open market; to have the Universities closed against us, and all the iniquities of those degraded places continued; to be taxed, tithed, and rated to the support of a system which we abjure; to be compelled to submit to objectionable rites and ceremonies at marriage, baptism, and burial:—in one word, to be left out of the social compact, and degraded . . . The real points at issue between the government and us are very few, and may soon be stated. They are chiefly as follow, viz:—

1st A total disconnexion between church and state, leaving the details consequent thereupon to be dealt with by parliament.

2nd The repeal of the Act of Charles II, which enables bishops to sit in the House of Lords.

3rd The repeal of all laws which grant compulsory powers to raise money for the support of any church whatever.

4th The reformation of the universities, the repeal of all religious tests, and a grant of equal rights in them.

5th A reformation of the laws relating to marriage and registration with equal rights in places of public burial.

(3) . . . It is a tyrannical stretch of power to compel parents to send their children to any school at all, much more to do so without leaving them any choice as to the school, and, most of all, to compel attendance and exact the payment of a school-fee.

. . . This measure would probably be made an instrument for the dissemination of the principles commonly called Puseyism; not merely because those principles are entertained, and more or less openly avowed, by the great majority of the Established Clergy, but because it is actually proposed that the usual fasts and festivals of the Church, (which have long fallen into utter desuetude in the Church itself) shall henceforth be religiously observed; and also because a privilege is accorded to Roman Catholics, which is denied to every other denomination of Dissenters.

(4) . . . This is the deep scheme for *getting the education of the whole people into the hands of the Church* . . .

That the mighty and fatal corruption which has been growing up within the last few years in the Church, and which is rapidly bringing back the Clergy of the Establishment to the doctrines, the rites, and the spirit of Popery, would make the attempt to place Clergymen over the schools incomparably more hateful and revolting than it would have been before that great corruption took its rise . . . In Leeds, for example, there are schools of both kinds, supported by Evangelical Clergymen, whose dread and abhorrence of the modern Semi-Popery is as deep as that of the modern Dissenters, but who must see that the new system would gradually bring all their schools under the control of our Puseyite Vicar . . .

THIS BILL, my Lord, is *a Declaration of War against all the Dissenters in the kingdom* . . . True, [the dissenters] look not to Acts of Parliament as their Charter, or to tyrannical and voluptuous monarchs as their founders. True, they cannot boast of "a Popish Liturgy, an Arminian Clergy, and Calvinistic Articles." True, they have not a mighty golden link of temporal interest, to hold together in false union parties wide as the poles asunder in religious opinion . . . It may be genteel to sneer at the Dissenters. It may be dignified to despise them. But I declare, my Lord, I do not think it would be safe to trample upon them.

(5) MY LORD,—If ever there was one occasion on which the Dissenters and Methodists throughout the Kingdom felt as one man, and on which their feelings of indignation, spring out of the deep conviction of their judgement, were strong and unconquerable, it was when they discovered the true character of SIR JAMES GRAHAM's Bill for establishing a *Compulsory Church* Education at the public expense . . . The cause of religious Liberty is now, and will long continue to be, in the most serious danger. There is at the bottom of this attack a spirit of High Church bigotry, forested by clergymen whose ambition is as intense and insatiable as it is deep and crafty; and from the spirit—patient, vigilant, adroit, and trained in the very school of the Jesuits—we have everything to fear . . .

The 'Menace' of Rome

The election of Daniel O'Connell at the County Clare by-election of 1828 effectively sealed the fate of the laws against Roman Catholics holding public office, and Emancipation was enacted in 1829. O'Connell had suggested this result in his manifesto of June 1828 (here quoted from R. Huish, *Memoirs of Daniel O'Connell*, 1836). The second extract, from *Letters addressed to the Rev. W. F. Hook* (1840), represents the growing amount of Roman Catholic propaganda after 1829. The author, 'Verax, a Catholic Layman,' protested rather too much. Bishop Wiseman's 'papal aggression' of 1850 led to wide over-reaction in England against the establishment of a Roman Catholic territorial hierarchy. In the third extract the Whiggish diarist Charles Greville condemns in his diary for 21 November 1850 "the 'No Popery' hubbub" following Lord John Russell's letter to the Bishop of Durham (C. C. F. Greville, *A Journal of the Reign of Queen Victoria* (1885) iii).

(1) You will be told I am not qualified to be elected: the assertion, my friends, is untrue. I am qualified to be elected, and to be your representative. It is true that as a Catholic, I cannot, and of course never will, take the oaths at present prescribed to members of Parliament; but the authority which created these oaths (the Parliament), can abrogate them: and I entertain a confident hope that, if you elect me, the most bigotted of our enemies will see the necessity of removing from the chosen representative of the people, an obstacle which would prevent him from doing his duty to his King and to his country.

The oath at present required by the law is, 'that the sacrifice of the mass, and the invocation of the blessed Virgin Mary, and other saints, as now practised in the church of Rome, are impious and adulterous.' Of course, I will never stain my soul with such an oath: I leave that to my honourable opponent, Mr. Vesey Fitzgerald; he has often taken that horrible oath; he is ready to take it again, and asks your votes to enable him so to swear. I would rather be torn limb from limb than take it. Electors of the county of Clare! choose between me, who abominates that oath, and Mr. Vesey Fitzgerald, who has sworn it full twenty times! Return me to Parliament, and it is probable that such a blasphemous oath will be abolished for ever. As your representative, I will try the question in Parliament with the friends of Mr. Vesey Fitzgerald.—They may send me to prison.—I am ready to go there to promote the cause of the Catholics, and of universal liberty. The discussion which the attempt to exclude your representative from the House of Commons must excite, will create a sensation all over Europe, and produce such a burst of contemptuous indignation against British bigotry, in every enlightened country in the world . . .

(2) Let protestants ponder well on these words of the prophet Miche, "All the nations of the earth shall run there to find their salvation." Protestants can infallibly find out which is the true church by the marks which the holy scripture gives us, in order to distinguish her from all heretical churches,—and these marks may be reduced to four, which are contained in the Nicene creed . . . Unam, sanctam, Catholicam, et Apostolicam Ecclesiam, and which teach that the church is one holy catholic and apostolic.

How can protestants (in accusing us of acting contrary to the custom of the primitive church, in performing our service in the Latin language, little understood by the generality of the people), presume to bring such a charge against the Catholic Church, when they themselves stand convicted before the bow of public opinion of using other languages in their public services, than that which the primitive church always had used throughout the whole of the churches, particularly in Europe,—the Latin language. It is the protestant church, and not the Catholic, therefore, which acts contrary to the usage of the primitive church; and for this reason, the catholic church ever preserves the Latin language for her service, in which the primitive church always celebrated the holy mysteries. Whereas the protestant churches, disregarding antiquity, perform their public services in the vulgar languages.

Would to heaven that protestants would be prevailed upon to think and examine for themselves, and not to be, as the learned protestant divine Thorndyke says, "led by the nose" by interested declaimers, who, if they have an appearance of outward respectability, derive that respectability from the very men whom they are base enough to traduce and nickname. Yes, did every protestant but act on the golden principle of doing unto others, as he would be done by, and to examine into the truths or falsehoods of the statements concerning us, when made from the pulpit or from the press,—then catholics would not be much longer condemned to hear such vile expressions; but we feel them not as grievances; we have been well trained by three centuries of opprobrium, to smile at such practises, and cheerfully do we commiserate those who employ them.

(3) The Protestant agitation has been going on at a prodigious pace, and the whole country is up: meetings everywhere, addresses to Bishops and their replies, addresses to the Queen; speeches, letters, articles, all pouring forth from the press day after day with a vehemence and a universality such as I never saw before. The Dissenters have I think generally kept aloof and shown no disposition to take an active part. A more disgusting and humiliating manifestation has never been exhibited; it is founded on prejudice and gross ignorance. As usual the most empty make the greatest noise, and the declaimers vie with each other in coarseness, violence, and stupidity. Nevertheless, the hubbub is not the less mischievous for being so senseless and ridiculous. The religious passions and animosities that have been excited will not speedily die away, nor will the Roman Catholics forget the insults that have been heaped on their religion, nor the Vatican all the vulgar abuse that has been lavished on the Pope. In the midst of all this Wiseman has put forth a very able manifesto, in which he proves unanswerably that what has been done is perfectly legal, and a matter of ecclesiastical discipline, with which we have no concern whatever. He lashes John Russell with great severity, and endeavours to enlist the sympathies of the Dissenters by contrasting the splendour and wealth of the Anglican clergy with the contented poverty of the Romanists, and thus appeals to all the advocates of the voluntary system. His paper is uncommonly well done, and must produce a considerable effect, though of course none capable of quieting the storm that is now raging. Wiseman does not evince any intention of receding in the slightest degree, but on the contrary there appears to lurk throughout his paper a consciousness of an impregnable position, round which the tempest of public rage and fury may blow ever so violently without producing the slightest effect.

. . . There is great difference of opinion whether this agitation will prove favourable or the reverse to the Roman Catholic religion in England, that is, to its extension. The Roman Catholics themselves evidently think we have by our violence been playing their game and that it will promote their proselytising views. Time alone can show how this will be . . .

November 26th— . . . The Protestant movement goes on with unabated fury, and the quantity of nonsense that has been talked and written, and the amount of ignorance and intolerance displayed, exceed all belief, and only show of what sort of metal the mass of society is composed. Of all that has been written and spoken there has been nothing tolerable but the Bishop of Oxford's speech, which was very clever; the letter of Page Wood in the 'Times' in answer to Wiseman; and everything without exception which has emanated from the Archbishop of Canterbury. He has displayed a very proper and becoming spirit with great dignity, moderation, and good sense. All the rest is a mass of impotent fury and revolting vulgarity and impertinence, without genius or argument or end and object—mere abuse in the coarsest and stupidest shape. It is not a little remarkable what a strong anti-Papist Clarendon is. He writes to me in that sense, but not so vehemently as he does to others; and I see how his mind is inflamed, which is odd in so practical a man. But this is obviously the result of the bitter hostility he has had to encounter in Ireland from the Roman Catholic clergy, notwithstanding the efforts he made to conciliate them.

Doubts and Difficulties

The Church faced increasing trouble, not so much from the attacks of rival denominations as from internal rows and the impact of new scientific writing. Whig Erastianism continued, and not only Tractarians were offended when Melbourne appointed Dr. Renn Dickson Hampden (1793–1868), a Broad Churchman, Regius Professor of Divinity at Oxford; the University opposed the nomination on theological grounds. When Lord John Russell nominated him as Bishop of Hereford in 1847 the row was even stormier. The first two extracts (from Henry Christmas (1811–68), *A Concise History of the Hampden Controversy* (1848)) illustrate the rival attitudes of prominent ecclesiastics and of Russell (replying to John Merewether, Dean of Hereford, who refused to support the nomination). The third and fourth, by the agnostic Thomas Henry Huxley (1825–95) and the Anglican Rowland Williams (1817–70), represent new departures. Charles Darwin's study of *The Origin of Species* (1859) took a generation by storm by expounding evolutionary theory. Huxley defended Darwin against 'Soapy Sam' Wilberforce at the British Association meeting of 1860 and re-published his *Westminster Review* notice of 1860 in *Lay Sermons, Addresses and Reviews* (1860), to which one contributor was Dr. Williams, Vice Principal of Lampeter. Williams introduced German Biblical criticism to Anglicans—and was prosecuted for heresy. The extract is taken from his essay on 'Bunsen's Biblical Researches'. The fifth quotation is from

'The Interpretation of Scripture', in the same volume, by Professor Benjamin Jowett (1817–93), later the redoubtable Master of Balliol College Oxford.

(1) MY LORD,—We, the undersigned Bishops of the Church of England, feel it duty to represent to your lordship, as head of her Majesty's Government, the apprehension and alarm which have been excited in the minds of the clergy by the rumoured nomination to the See of Hereford of Dr. Hampden, in the soundness of whose doctrine the University of Oxford has affirmed, by a solemn decree, its want of confidence.

We are persuaded that your lordship does not know how deep and general a feeling prevails on this subject, and we consider ourselves to be acting only in the discharge of our bounden duty both to the Crown and to the Church, when we respectfully but earnestly express to your lordship our conviction, that if this appointment be completed, there is the greatest danger both of the interruption of the peace of the Church, and of the disturbance of the confidence which it is most desirable that the clergy and laity of the Church should feel in every exercise of the Royal Supremacy, especially as regards that very delicate and important particular, the nomination to vacant Sees.

We have the honour to be, my lord,

Your lordship's obedient faithful servants,

C. J. LONDON	J. H. GLOUCESTER AND BRISTOL
C. WINTON	H. EXETER
J. LINCOLN	E. SARUM
CHR. BANGOR	A. T. CHICHESTER
HUGH. CARLISLE	J. ELY
G. ROCHESTER	SAML. OXON
	RICH. BATH AND WELLS.

(2) Woburn Abbey, Dec. 25

SIR,—I have had the honour to receive your letter of the 22nd instant, in which you intimate to me your intention of violating the law.

I have the honour to be your obedient servant

J. RUSSELL.

(3) The Darwinian hypothesis has the merit of being eminently simple and comprehensible in principle, and its essential positions

may be stated in a very few words: all species have been produced by the development of varieties from common stocks by the conversion of these first into permanent races and then into new species, by the process of *natural selection*, which process is essentially identical with that artificial selection by which man has originated the races of domestic animals—the *struggle for existence* taking the place of man, and exerting, in the case of natural selection, that selective action which he performs in artificial selection.

The evidence brought forward by Mr. Darwin in support of his hypothesis is of three kinds. First, he endeavours to prove that species may be originated by selection; secondly, he attempts to show that natural causes are competent to exert selection; and thirdly, he tries to prove that the most remarkable and apparently anomalous phenomena exhibited by the distribution, development, and mutual relations of species, can be shown to be deducible from the general doctrine of their origin, which he propounds, combined with the known facts of geological change; and that, even if all these phenomena are not at present explicable by it, none are necessarily inconsistent with it.

There cannot be a doubt that the method of inquiry which Mr. Darwin has adopted is not only rigorously in accordance with the canons of scientific logic, but that it is the only adequate method . . .

. . . Inductively, Mr. Darwin endeavours to prove that species arise in a given way. Deductively, he desires to show that, if they arise in that way, the facts of distribution, development, classification, &c., may be accounted for, *i.e.* may be deduced from their mode of origin, combined with admitted changes in physical geography and climate, during an indefinite period. And this explanation, or coincidence of observed with deduced facts, is, so far as it extends, a verification of the Darwinian view.

(4) When geologists began to ask whether changes in the earth's structure might be explained by causes still in operation, they did not disprove the possibility of great convulsions but they lessened the necessity for imagining them. So, if a theologian has his eyes opened to the Divine energy as continuous and omnipresent, he lessens the sharp contrast of epochs in Revelation, but need not assume that the stream has never varied in its flow. Devotion raises time present into the sacredness of the past; while Criticism reduces the strangeness of the past into harmony with the present.

Faith and Prayer (and great marvels answering to them) do not pass away: but, prolonging their range as a whole, we make their parts less exceptional . . .

Bunsen's enduring glory is neither to have paltered with his conscience nor shrunk from the difficulties of the problem; but to have brought a vast erudition, in the light of a Christian conscience, to unroll tangled records, tracing frankly the Spirit of God elsewhere, but honouring chiefly the traditions of His Hebrew sanctuary . . .

The traditions of Babylon, Sidon, Assyria, and Iran, are brought by our author to illustrate and confirm, though to modify our interpretation of, Genesis. It is strange how nearly those ancient cosmogonies approach what may be termed the philosophy of Moses, while they fall short in what Longinus called his 'worthy conception of the divinity'. Our deluge takes its place among geological phenomena, no longer a disturbance of law from which science shrinks, but a prolonged play of the forces of fire and water, rendering the primaeval regions of North Asia uninhabitable, and urging the nations to new abodes. We learn approximately its antiquity, and infer limitation in its range, from finding it recorded in the traditions of Iran and Palestine (or of Japhet and Shem), but unknown to the Egyptians and Mongolians, who left earlier the cradle of mankind. In the half ideal half traditional notices of the beginnings of our race, compiled in Genesis, we are bid notice the combination of documents, and the recurrence of barely consistent genealogies . . .

. . . A recurrence to first principles, even of Revelation, may, to minds prudent or timid, seem a process of more danger than advantage; and it is possible to defend our traditional theology, if stated reasonably, and with allowance for the accidents of its growth. But what is not possible, with honesty, is to uphold a fabric of mingled faith and speculation, and in the same breath to violate the instinct which believed, and blindfold the mind which reasoned. It would be strange if God's work were preserved, by disparaging the instruments which His wisdom chose for it.

(5) . . . That objections to some received views should be valid, and yet that they should always be held up as the objections of infidels, is a mischief to the Christian cause. It is a mischief that critical observations which any intelligent man can make for himself, should be ascribed to atheism or unbelief. It would be a

strange and almost incredible thing that the Gospel, which at first made war only on the vices of mankind, should now be opposed to one of the highest and rarest of human virtues—the love of truth. And that in the present day the great object of Christianity should be, not to change the lives of men, but to prevent them from changing their opinions; that would be a singular inversion of the purposes for which Christ came into the world. The Christian religion is in a false position when all the tendencies of knowledge are opposed to it. Such position cannot be long maintained, or can only end in the withdrawal of the educated classes from the influences of religion. It is a grave consideration whether we ourselves may not be in an earlier stage of the same religious dissolution, which seems to have gone further in Italy and France . . .

. . . When interpreted like any other book, by the same rules of evidence and the same canons of criticism, the Bible will still remain unlike any other book; its beauty will be freshly seen, as of a picture which is restored after many ages to its original state; it will create a new interest and make for itself a new kind of authority by the life which is in it. It will be a spirit and not a letter; as it was in the beginning, having an influence like that of the spoken word, or the book newly found.

The Claims of the Church of Scotland

The growing resentment among evangelicals in the Church of Scotland against an Act of 1712 providing for lay patronage of ministers reached a peak over the Auchterarder case in 1834, when Lord Kinnoul's nominee was rejected by the congregation and the presbytery. The General Assembly passed the 'Veto Act', but was overruled by the Court of Session and House of Lords. As relations between Church and State deteriorated, in 1842 the Assembly issued its 'Claim, Declaration and Protest' against Erastianism (here quoted from W. Hanna, *Life and Writings of Thomas Chalmers*, Edinburgh, 1849–52). In 1843 Dr. Chalmers (1780–1847) finally led a major secession to found the Free Church of Scotland.

Whereas it is an essential doctrine of this Church, and a fundamental principle in its constitution, as set forth in the Confession of Faith thereof, in accordance with the Word and law of the most holy God, that "there is no other Head of the Church but the Lord Jesus Christ," (ch. xxv. sec. 6); and that, while "God, the supreme Lord and King of all the world, hath ordained civil magistrates to be under him over all the people, for his own glory, and to the public good, and to this end, hath armed them with the power of the sword," (ch. xxiii. sec. 1); and while "it is the duty of the people to pray for the magistrates, to honour their persons, to pay them tribute and other dues, to obey their lawful commands, and to be subject to their authority for conscience' sake," "from which ecclesiastical persons are not exempted," (ch. xxiii. sec. 4); and while the magistrate hath authority, and it is his duty, in the exercise of that power which alone is committed to him, namely, "the power of the sword," or civil rule, as distinct from the "power of the keys", or spiritual authority, expressly denied to him, to take order for the preservation of purity, peace and unity in the Church, yet "the Lord Jesus, as King and Head of his Church, hath therein appointed a government in the hand of Church officers distinct from the civil magistrate," (ch. xxx. sec. 1); which government is ministerial, not lordly, and to be exercised in consonance with the laws of Christ, and with the liberties of his people . . .

Therefore the General Assembly, while, as above set forth, they fully recognise the absolute jurisdiction of the Civil Courts in relation to all matters whatsoever of a civil nature, and especially in relation to all the temporalities conferred by the State on the Church, and the civil consequences attached by law to the decisions, in matters spiritual, of the Church Courts,—DO, in name, and on behalf of this Church, and of the nation and people of Scotland, and under the sanction of the several statutes and the Treaty of Union herein before recited, CLAIM as of RIGHT, That she shall freely possess and enjoy her liberties, government, discipline, rights, and privileges, according to law, especially for the defence of the spiritual liberties of her people, and that she shall be protected therein from the foresaid unconstitutional and illegal encroachments of the said Court of Session, and her people secured in their Christian and constitutional rights and liberties . . .

And they protest, that all and whatsoever Acts of the Parliament of Great Britain, passed without the consent of this Church and nation, in alteration or derogation to the foresaid government, discipline, rights, and privileges of this Church . . . as also, all and whatever sentences of Courts in contravention of the same government, discipline, right, and privileges, are, and shall be, in themselves void and null, and of no legal force and effect . . .

The Religious Census, 1851

On 30 March 1851 the Census Commissioners attempted to discover how many of the population of 17,927,609 English people had attended some religious service. Inefficient and inaccurate though the census was, it horrified contemporaries by its figures on non-attendance; however, its figures of attendances are an impressive reminder of the influence of Victorian belief. The figures were printed in P.P. (1852–3) lxxxix.

The great facts which appear to me to have been elicited by this inquiry are,—that, even taking the accommodation provided by all the sects, including the most extravagant, unitedly, there are 1,644,734 inhabitants of England who, if all who might attend religious services were willing to attend, would not be able, on account of insufficient room, to join in public worship: that this deficiency prevails almost exclusively in *towns*, especially *large* towns: that, if these 1,644,734 persons are to be deprived of all excuse for non-attendance, there must be at least as many additional sittings furnished, equal to about 2,000 churches and chapels, and a certain number more if any of the present provision be regarded as of doubtful value; and that even such additional accommodation will fall short of the requirement if the edifices are so often as at present, closed. Further, it appears that as many as 5,288,294 persons able to attend, are every Sunday absent from religious services, for all of whom there is accommodation for at least one service: that neglect like this, in spite of opportunities for worship, indicates the insufficiency of any mere addition to the number of religious *buildings*: that the greatest difficulty is to fill the churches when provided; and that this can only be accomplished by a great addition to the number of efficient, earnest, religious *teachers*.